D0423030

Revaluing French
Feminism

Revaluing French Feminism

CRITICAL ESSAYS ON DIFFERENCE, AGENCY, AND CULTURE

EDITED BY
Nancy Fraser
AND
Sandra Lee Bartky

INDIANA UNIVERSITY PRESS
Bloomington and Indianapolis

Judith Butler's essay, "The Body Politics of Julia Kristeva," also appears as a chapter in her book, *Gender Trouble* (Routledge 1990).

© 1992 by Hypatia, Inc.
All rights reserved

No part of this book may be reproduced or utilized in any form or by any means, electronic or mechanical, including photocopying and recording, or by any information storage and retrieval system, without permission in writing from the publisher. The Association of American University Presses' Resolution on Permissions constitutes the only exception to this prohibition.

The paper used in this publication meets the minimum requirements of American National Standard for Information Sciences—Permanence of Paper for Printed Library Materials, ANSI Z39.48-1984.

Manufactured in the United States of America

Library of Congress Cataloging-in-Publication Data

Revaluing French feminism : critical essays on difference, agency, and
    culture / edited by Nancy Fraser and Sandra Lee Bartky.
        p.   cm.
    Includes bibliographical references and index.
    ISBN 0-253-32436-X (cloth). — ISBN 0-253-20682-0 (paper)
    1. Feminist theory.   2. Feminist criticism—France.   I. Bartky,
Sandra Lee.
HQ1190.R48   1992
305.42'01—dc20   91-8415

1 2 3 4 5 96 95 94 93 92

Contents

Introduction:
Revaluing French Feminism

NANCY FRASER

Ten years have now passed since the publication of Elaine Marks's and Isabelle de Courtivron's *New French Feminisms* (1980). This was the book that first introduced writers like Hélène Cixous, Catherine Clément, Christine Delphy, Claudine Hermann, Luce Irigaray, Julia Kristeva, and Monique Wittig to an Anglophone feminist reading public. Or rather, since some of these writers had already been translated here and there, it was the book that first constructed "French feminism" as a distinctive cultural object for English-speaking readers.[1]

A distinctive object and an alluring one. The textual collage fashioned by Marks and de Courtivron beckoned us to enter a heady, new discursive world, a world studded with exotic terms like "phallocentrism" and "jouissance" and trumpeting new modes of subversion like "writing the body." Ten years ago, this often seemed an upside-down world in which for some writers "equality" and even "feminism" itself were dirty words, while "difference" and "femininity" were badges of honor.

One need only recall those early bewildered reactions to see how far we have come in the intervening decade. Today, many of the characteristic terms and themes of "the new French feminisms" are commonplace in Anglophone feminist writing. More profoundly, some problematics—that of "difference," for example—have been transplanted here virtually whole. Finally, "French feminism" has become the subject of a veritable outpouring of books and journal articles. These include translations from the French, of course, but also a large body of indigenous English writing, which consists not only of commentaries and theoretical polemics, but also of appropriations, transformations, and concrete applications in cultural studies.

To be sure, the reception of "French feminism" here has been partial and selective. It has focused almost exclusively on one or two strands—the deconstructive and psychoanalytic—of a much larger, more variegated field. The result is a curious synecdochic reduction: despite the relatively catholic selection proffered ten years ago by Marks and de Courtivron,[2] for many English-speaking readers today "French feminism" simply *is* Irigaray, Kristeva, and Cixous.[3] In addition, the influence of these writers remains centered in the academy, where they have been championed by a network of feminist scholars based primarily in literature and film. Indeed, the writing of deconstructive and psychoanalytic French feminists, with its technical character and unfamiliar vocabulary, has sometimes served here as a discourse of professional legitimation, provoking complaints about esotericism.

Nevertheless, despite the limited range of authors read here and the academic base of their primary readership, the impact of French feminism in the United States has been substantial. Thanks to "bridge" media like *Sojourner*, *Off Our Backs*, and *The Women's Review of Books*, some of the signature conceptions of deconstructive and psychoanalytic French feminist theories have reached a broader, extra-academic public. These conceptions seem to resonate—however imperfectly—with widespread indigenous concerns rooted in the current dilemmas of our own feminist politics. Conversely, as French feminist terms and expressions have achieved wider currency here, they have acquired a degree of formative power to reshape some Anglophone feminist agendas. In sum, elements of those discourses that go under the name "French feminism" have influenced feminist culture in the United States and may be helping to reconfigure it.

The prospect of such an important cultural reconfiguration merits some critical reflection. What have English-speaking feminists gained, and what have we lost, through our encounter with the "new French feminisms"? What new capabilities—both intellectual and political—has the reception of these paradigms yielded us? And what countervailing disabilities? Finally, what outstanding unresolved problems has the assimilation of these discourses helped construct for us, and what prospects for resolving them does it promise? With ten years of the "new French feminisms" in the United States now behind us, it is time to take the measure of their impact.

The essays collected here represent one attempt at such an accounting. In order to appreciate what is distinctive about their approach, it helps to recall the social context in which the new French feminist theories emerged. These theories were generated in the Paris of the 1970s. For what was then an emerging new women's movement, it was a time of exuberance and revolutionary élan, still deeply marked by the spirit of 1968. It was axiomatic that existing social relations and institutions were wholly repressive and that no mere reforms could put things right. On the contrary, the realization of the feminist vision would require the creation of an entirely new form of life—new social relations among new social subjects. Furthermore, the route to radical change of this magnitude could only be via direct action; it would be necessary to bypass altogether the deadening routines of institutions and the complicities of politics as usual.[4]

The French feminisms we debate today were spawned in this *gauchiste* milieu. The spirit of that milieu marks their basic theoretical postulates to this day, despite subsequent elaboration and revision. For example, most deconstructive and psychoanalytic French feminists posit the existence of a repressive "phallocentric symbolic order" that underlies—and constrains—every aspect of our lives. Some of them conclude that our task is to destroy that order and to install in its place an entirely new, feminine "imaginary." A number of these feminists privilege symbolic, vanguardist forms of practice, such as avant-garde writing, and are uninterested in or dismissive of mundane institutional reforms. In sum, these paradigms codify the self-understanding of a radical countercultural movement at a very specific historical moment—when the spirit was revolutionary and the radicalism hyperbolic.

That spirit is not unknown to U.S. feminists of a certain age, but it is not particularly salient here today. On the contrary, the context in which we have received and sought to use new French feminist theories stands in marked contrast to the context of their production. The difference is due chiefly to the time lag in reception. During the decade or so it took to convey and absorb French feminist writings here, massive political changes occurred in both societies, most notably the collapse of the New Left and the rise of a conservative backlash. In France, the resurgence of "neo-liberalism" was preceded by, and tempered by, the ascension to power in 1981 of a (nominally) Socialist government. In the United States, in contrast, the eighties were the Reagan years, a time in which a triumphant neoconservatism managed to discredit even the mildest liberalism, to stall reform efforts, and to reverse some of the civil rights gains of the sixties.

Yet, oddly, despite the unfavorable broader Zeitgeist, this has not been a wholly dark period for feminist movements. During the decade separating the French origins of deconstructive and psychoanalytic feminism from their Anglophone reception, a fairly small, culturally radical, student-dominated, sociologically and ethnically homogeneous women's liberation movement has metamorphosed into something more complex. Feminist movements today are larger and considerably more heterogeneous than before. Moreover, they are engaged in a more varied array of practices. Certainly, the movement in the United States today encompasses a continuum of struggles in which demands for social and legal reforms are inextricable from symbolic struggles over social identities and cultural meanings.

One important feature of this new phase of struggle is that feminists no longer stand at arm's length from institutions. Rather, we occupy a variety of institutional sites, apparently dug in for "the long march." For example, feminists can be found today not only in separatist communities but also in trade unions and neighborhood groups, political parties and art world institutions, professional organizations and ethnic associations, allied social movements and government agencies. Moreover, we now struggle in and against such institutions under a variety of self-descriptions. We position ourselves as "women," to be sure, but also as workers, as parents, as lesbians, as producers and consumers of culture, as people of color, and as inhabitants of a threatened biosphere.[5]

In the wake of developments like these, some new French feminist assumptions seem to warrant renewed scrutiny. For example, does it make sense now, when feminist interpretations challenge misogynist interpretations in a variety of cultural spheres, to posit a monolithic, pervasive, phallocentric symbolic order? Likewise, how apropos today is a model of change that requires a total break with existing meanings and the creation ex nihilo of new ones? Moreover, at a time when feminist practice encompasses efforts to transform existing institutions as well as efforts to build alternative counterinstitutions, and when efforts of both sorts often combine synergistically, do we still find it meaningful to insist on the opposition between reform and revolution? Likewise, in a period in which we increasingly understand the collective force of our heterogeneous practices as the building of a counterhegemony, do we still think it useful to oppose symbolic struggles to social struggles, and to privilege the first over the second? Finally, at a time when feminist movements encompass sociologically heterogeneous groups of women with diverse interests and identities, is it appropriate to describe the goal of our identity politics as the recovery of repressed femininity?

If some postulates of new French feminist theory seem ill-suited to our present political moment, we might ask why they have proved so appealing. Could it be that assumptions about the totally bankrupt, seamlessly patriarchal character of culture that were radicalizing and energizing in the heyday of the New Left take on a different valence today? Is it possible that the experience of living through the rise of the New Right has disposed many of us to accept the idea of a global and suffocating Paternal Law? In so doing, are we inflating a pessimism that is rooted in a historically specific situation into a much more grandiose and ahistorical theory that could prove politically disabling?

Whatever we conclude about the continuing appeal of some seemingly dated dimensions of deconstructive-psychoanalytic French feminist theories, other postulates of these theories remain incontrovertibly relevant. Among the latter, surely, is the identification of language as a constitutive aspect of social reality and, therefore, a crucial arena for feminist intervention. Equally to the point today is the characteristic emphasis on gendered subjectivity as a medium of subordination and, perforce, a terrain of feminist contestation. Finally, we have yet to exhaust the possibilities in the view that those two problematics are connected—the view, in other words, that language is a formative force in the construction, and hopefully reconstruction, of gendered forms of subjectivity. All these quintessentially "new French feminist" postulates are continuing to bear fruit today in feminist theory, feminist culture, and feminist politics.

Revaluing French feminism today, therefore, means sorting the conceptual wheat from the chaff. This in turn requires sensitivity to context and situation. We might ask: What problems have English-speaking feminists met in attempting to apply paradigms derived from a radical, countercultural phase of struggle to the more heterogeneous processes of the present? Should we write off these paradigms as irreparably unsuited to current concerns? Or are they adaptable, and indeed, are we already engaged in adapting them? In that case, and if so, what sorts of modifications are needed in order to render deconstructive-psychoanalytic French feminist theory viable for feminists today?

Questions like these form the backdrop for the present volume. They inform the content and the method of the individual essays, as well as the overall organization. The volume opens with two wide-ranging, late interviews with Simone de Beauvoir that contain her final, rather negative appraisal of some new French feminist paradigms. Next come two important instances of new French feminist philosophy: Sarah Kofman's spirited critique of the naturalization of gender in the philosophy of Rousseau and Luce Irigaray's deconstruction of the metaphysics of love in Plato's *Symposium*. Finally, in the remaining six essays, North American feminists subject some versions of deconstructive and psychoanalytic French feminism to extended critical scrutiny. In each case, the critic surveys a large body of difficult and often elusive theoretical writing; she reconstructs the French theorist's principal line of argument, identifies the evidence and assumptions on which it rests, and assesses its cogency.

The volume as a whole, then, is a revaluing of French feminism. It concentrates on theoretical arguments—reflecting the disciplinary training in philosophy of most of the contributors. However, the philosophizing found here is not disengaged from practice. On the contrary, these essays share the presupposition that the point of feminist philosophy is to change the world, not merely to theorize it. The North American contributions, especially, reflect this orientation. They center their respective assessments of the cogency of French feminist theory on the question of its present usefulness for feminist practice.

One cluster of themes that is central to these essays is the triad *identity, difference,* and *femininity.* These themes have become foci of intense controversy in feminist theory in the wake of a number of developments. In the earliest phase of the Second Wave, many feminists believed that femininity was a patriarchal construction that functioned to confine women to a separate sphere and to inhibit our full development as human beings. We also believed that what the larger sexist culture understood as sex differences were either simply misogynist lies about women or the socially constructed results of oppression. In either case, the consensus was that the goal of women's liberation was to throw off the shackles of femininity, eliminate gender differences, and become universal human subjects. Thus, from a perspective that Iris Young (1985) has called "humanist feminism," "difference" and "femininity" carried negative connotations, while the idea of a universal human identity to which all should have access was positive and unproblematical.

However, in the late seventies and early eighties, this humanist feminist consensus was shattered. The status of universal subject, which humanist feminist women had wished to claim, was now rejected as masculinist ideology. One factor was the rise of what Young (1985) has called "gynocentric feminism," which undertook to revalue femininity and difference. Feminists sympathetic to this orientation sought to establish that, in some respects, women really were different from men, and that the differences were to women's credit. Accordingly, writers like Nancy Chodorow (1978) and Carol Gilligan (1982) elaborated detailed conceptions of gender identity in which femininity and masculinity were contrasted. Now, "femininity" and "difference" (in the sense of gender difference) became positive notions, and the thesis that all women shared a common gender identity was held to underpin the possibility of sisterhood.

However, that thesis has itself been rendered problematic as differences among women have proved increasingly salient. Many lesbians, women of color, and working class women have rejected accounts of femininity that had a heterosexual, white middle class point of reference.[6] In addition, the quasi-prescriptive character of definitions that closely resembled traditional gender stereotypes has rankled many feminists.[7] Finally, it is no longer clear that the posit of a shared gender identity really does promote solidarity, when so many women fail, as a matter of fact, so to identify. The upshot is that "femininity" has become problematic again, as have "gender identity" and "difference" in the singular.[8] Instead, it has become common among North American feminists to speak of "identities" and "differences" in the plural. The latter term especially often carries positive connotations, reflecting the shift in emphasis from the single divide between masculine and feminine to the many different differences among women (and men), including class, color, ethnicity, and sexual orientation.

However, there are signs that even this new, anti-essentialist orientation is proving unstable as we ponder its implications for practice. An uncritical valorization of "differences" is seen by writers like Linda Gordon (1991) as threatening to forestall efforts to theorize those pernicious social processes that differentiate women, enabling some of us to dominate others. In addition, the stress on "differences" is provoking worries about whether women share any common conditions or common interests at all and, if not, about whether any common action is possible. Feminists like Denise Riley (1988) now entertain doubts as to whether the very categories of "woman" and "women" are meaningful, even while acknowledging that we cannot do without them. The deepest fear is that we are backing ourselves so far into an anti-essentialist corner that feminism itself will become impossible.

It is in the light of this explosive mix of contested concepts and practical conundrums that new French feminist theories now warrant revaluation. One important current, represented by Colette Guillaumin (1987), Monique

Wittig (1980, 1981, 1983, 1984, 1985, 1989), and the journals *Questions féministes* and *Nouvelles questions féministes*, retains a humanist feminist commitment to universalism and a negative view of difference. However, the deconstructive-psychoanalytic theories that are best known in the United States often seem closer to our own gynocentric feminisms, since they reject universalism and endorse difference in the sense of gender difference. This is especially true of those theorists, such as Luce Irigaray (1985b) and Hélène Cixous (1976), who have elaborated positive conceptions of femininity. These conceptions, in turn, have given rise to charges of essentialism and biologism, since they are adumbrated in terms that refer to features and capacities said to be specific to the female body.

However, there is also another, anti-essentialist side of these theories, the side that Linda Alcoff (1988) has labeled "nominalist." This side, which is especially pronounced in the work of Julia Kristeva (1980, 1982, 1984, 1986), rejects the very idea of a stable, centered identity as a repressive fiction. Perhaps its most extreme and controversial expression is Kristeva's (1986) claim that "woman" does not exist and that in so far as feminism assumes that she does or should, it threatens to become metaphysical, religious, and totalitarian.

In their more utopian moments, some deconstructive-psychoanalytic French feminists have projected a nominalist vision of liberation as liberation *from* identity. Yet, in a reprise of the gynocentric motif, they often figure that liberated state as the recovery of repressed femininity. Here femininity is a condition of dispersed and destabilized identity that is associated with the pre-Oedipal phase of individual development. Thus, in paradoxical formulations that fuse gynocentric and nominalist themes, femininity is held to be a force that eludes definition, even as it is defined as such and contrasted with masculinity.

Understandably, this strange mix of ideas has been the subject of considerable controversy. To some feminists it has seemed to combine the worst essentializing aspects of gynocentrism with the worst depoliticizing aspects of nominalism, all the while maintaining a wholesale insensitivity to differences among women. To others, in contrast, pychoanalytic-deconstructive views of identity, difference, and femininity have seemed to provide precisely the nuanced understandings we need in order to move beyond current impasses.[9]

The essays collected here offer a spectrum of conflicting assessments. In her interviews with Margaret A. Simons, Simone de Beauvoir criticizes gynocentric and essentialist tendencies in new French feminist theory. Instead she reaffirms her longstanding humanist feminist commitment to a view of human being that transcends gender difference. Rejecting the misleading translation by Howard M. Parshley in *The Second Sex* of "la réalité humaine" as "human nature," she upholds the existentialist insistence on the priority of social situation over essence or nature. It is this philosophical commitment that informs her response to Simons's questions about "feminine identity." Gynocentric feminists, claims Beauvoir, "come back to men's mythologies . . . that woman is a being apart." It is women's situation, not women's identity, that is the proper focus of feminist scrutiny.

However, it is possible that gynocentric influences led Beauvoir to revise her views in one important way. In these interviews, she softens the harsh stand against motherhood that she took in *The Second Sex*. Denying that she ever wrote that "motherhood does not support human meaning," she now affirms it to be a perfectly "valid choice," albeit one that is "very dangerous today because all the responsibility falls on the shoulders of the woman." Here the diagnosis of the ills of motherhood shifts from the ontological to the institutional: it is no longer anything intrinsic to the enterprise of bearing and raising children that makes problems for the second sex; it is rather the current social organization of that enterprise as "enslaved motherhood."

This shift in Beauvoir's analysis, if indeed it is a shift, suggests the ability of humanist feminism to absorb some elements of gynocentric feminism without having to posit a feminine essence. It suggests the possibility of keeping the humanist focus on the capacities shared by women and men alike, and on the institutional arrangements that deny women the chance to realize many of those capacities, while refusing to buy into androcentric valuations that privilege traditionally male-dominated activities over traditionally female-associated ones. This would certainly be a stronger, more consistent, and more critical humanist feminism, one with a broader potential appeal.

Interestingly, Beauvoir's stance finds an echo of sorts in the next essay in this collection, Sarah Kofman's "Rousseau's Phallocratic Ends." Although Kofman is a deconstructive philosopher and therefore an unlikely ally for an existentialist, she shares Beauvoir's suspicion of views that define femininity in terms of maternity and insist too strongly on gender difference. She gives us a veritable object lesson in the dangers of such approaches through a close reading of the various moves by which Rousseau prescribes a maternal destiny for women. Notoriously, the author of *Emile* grounds the sociopolitical gender arrangements he proposes on appeals to "Nature." But, claims Kofman, these appeals to "the ends of Nature" actually dissimulate "the ends of man."

Kofman scrutinizes Rousseau's claims to found separate spheres for men and women on "natural differences." She demonstrates that what he casts as gender complementarity is actually gender hierarchy and that what he portrays as simple difference is actually inequality. In addition, she exposes a number of contradictions in Rousseau, points where what were supposed to be supplemental elaborations of primary claims turn out instead to undercut them. In the process, Kofman in effect poses a series of devastating questions. Why, when he explicitly holds women to be the weaker sex, does Rousseau implicitly cast us as the stronger? Why, when he claims we are "naturally reserved," does he deem it necessary to confine us forcibly to a "domestic reservation"? Why does it turn out to be men who are the principal beneficiaries of "Nature's gift" of shame to women? Why, if indeed our natural destiny is motherhood, do we require the whip of shame and related social sanctions to ensure that we perform it? Finally, why, if men and women are really so natu-rally different, are elaborate institutional arrangements needed in order to en-force that difference?

Kofman's essay can also be read as an implicit challenge to the gynocen-trism of some other deconstructive feminists. Whereas they understand difference as a condition to be celebrated, she sees it as a construct of domi-nation to be demystified.[10] In fact, Kofman offers a synthesis of elements that is unusual in new French feminist theory: she links an anti-essentialist, deconstructive methodological stance to a political orientation that has more in common with the humanist feminism of Simone de Beauvoir than with the gynocentric feminism of Luce Irigaray.

The debate about difference is joined from the other side in the next essay in this volume, Irigaray's "Sorcerer Love." This essay proposes an analysis of patriarchal metaphysics that is the direct antithesis of Sarah Kofman's. Whereas Kofman claims that Rousseau's philosophy enacts a fear of being confounded with women and a need to insist on gender difference, Irigaray holds that the deep structure of Western philosophy is man's fear of difference and desire for the same.

"Sorcerer Love" belongs to the critical, as opposed to the utopian, side of Irigaray's multifaceted oeuvre. It offers a re-reading of Plato's *Symposium* that is focused on the only woman whose words appear in a Platonic dialogue. Irigaray reads Diotima's speech on love as an early exercise in patriarchal metaphysics. She identifies the founding gesture of this metaphysics as the substitution of a teleological view of love as an instrument in the service of procreation for a processual view of love as a "demon" or "intermediary." The upshot, according to Irigaray, is a set of hierarchical oppositions wherein be-ing takes precedence over becoming, the immortal is privileged over the mor-tal, and the soul is deemed superior to the body. Moreover, once love is seen in terms of product rather than process, the way is opened for a hierarchy of better and worse products and of higher and lower loves. Irigaray suggests that that move provides the conceptual basis for the Greek devaluation of women and of heterosexual relations.

This reading of Diotima's speech belongs to a genre of Irigarayan critique familiar to readers of her book *Speculum of the Other Woman* (1985a). There she reads an impressive array of classical philosophical and psychoanalytic texts as providing the constitutive metaphysics of a phallocentric Western symbolic order. This order, in her view, is premised on the repression of the feminine; no genuine feminine difference can be represented there. What passes for femininity in Western culture is actually pseudofemininity, the specular construction of woman by man as his own mirror image, his negative

complement or inferior copy. Diotima's speech on love, therefore, is an early
and formative move in the construction of a symbolic order that banishes sexual difference and feminine specificity.

In the essay that follows, Andrea Nye takes issue with Irigaray's reading of
Diotima and with the larger cultural diagnosis of which it is a part. Nye offers
another Diotima, a powerful priestess who is "The Hidden Host" of the *Symposium* and the exponent of the pre-Classical worldview on which Platonic
metaphysics feeds. This Diotima draws on earlier cultural representations of
female fecundity in order to figure social life as a continuum of love-inspired,
generative activities. On this continuum, activities like statecraft, friendship, and philosophy are modeled on childbearing and childrearing. Thus, far
from marginalizing and denigrating the feminine, Diotima's philosophy actually celebrates it, drawing on pre-Platonic religious traditions that allowed for
female power.

Nye in effect rejects the view of the history of Western metaphysics as always and everywhere excluding "the feminine." She implies that Irigaray's
view imposes a false homogeneity on the tradition, thereby occluding
women's contributions. In actuality, it is the second-order ideological construction of tradition, rather than the record of cultural production per se,
that "represses the feminine."[11] On Nye's view, then, it is Irigaray herself
who, by drawing Diotima into the supposedly all-encompassing closure of
phallocentric metaphysics, suppresses her "difference." Ironically, then, the
feminist critic of phallocentrism unwittingly extends it.[12]

Nye's essay raises important questions about the general diagnosis that underlies the critical side of Irigaray's theory. Yet it need not entail a complete
rejection of Irigarayan critique. On the contrary, it holds out the appealing
prospect of having our cake and eating it too. We might embrace Irigaray's
brilliant critical readings of specific androcentric texts while demurring from
her global hypothesis about their collective import. For example, feminists
could applaud her stunning deconstruction of Freud's essay on "Femininity"
without accepting her view that the logic deconstructed there underpins all
symbolic expression in Western culture.[13] Then, it would be possible to replace the view that phallocentrism is coextensive with *all* extant Western
culture with a more complicated story about how the *cultural hegemony* of
phallocentric thinking has been, so to speak, erected.[14]

If the preceding is a promising way of approaching Irigaray's critical side,
then what should we make of her utopian side? This hotly contested issue is
the focus of Diana J. Fuss's essay, "'Essentially Speaking.'" Fuss examines
Irigaray's attempts to conjure up an "other woman," a woman who would in-
carnate neither the patriarchal femininity of Freudian theory nor the male-
defined specularity of phallocentric metaphysics. This new woman, rather,
would be beyond phallocentrism; she would deploy a new, feminine syntax to
give symbolic expression to her specificity and difference.

Irigaray's most striking attempts to release, conjure up, or invent this other woman are lyrical evocations of a nonphallic feminine sexuality. These attempts, found in essays like "This Sex Which Is Not One" and "When Our Lips Speak Together,"[15] evoke an eroticism premised on the continual self-touching of "two lips." Neither clitoral nor vaginal, requiring the interposition neither of hand nor of penis, this would be a feminine pleasure that escapes the phallocentric economy. Moreover, certain characteristics of this pleasure—the way it exceeds the opposition activity/passivity, for example—suggest features of a postphallocentric way of thinking and speaking. Thus, like her fellow gynocentrist Hélène Cixous, Irigaray connects the specificity of women's bodies not only to the specificity of our sexual desires and sexual pleasures but also to putatively specific feminine modes of symbolic expression.

As Fuss's paper indicates, the utopian side of Irigaray has proved extremely controversial. Many American readers have accused her of biologism and essentialism.[16] And yet, argues Fuss, these readers appear to have missed the *figurative* character of Irigaray's body language. They have failed to register the fact that her project is less to reduce social meanings to biology than to create new, empowering social meanings for our bodies and pleasures. Since Irigaray's aim is to *re-metaphorize* the female body, the charge of biologism misses the mark.

The charge of essentialism, on the other hand, is harder to assess. Fuss offers an original and interesting defense of Irigaray on the grounds that her essentialism is strategic, politically enabling, and therefore worth the risk. By laying claim on behalf of women to an essence of our own, Irigaray disrupts those androcentric metaphysical systems that deny our access to "the essential." Moreover, according to Fuss, the posit of a feminine essence may be essential to feminist politics. After all, its function within Irigaray's philosophy is precisely to provide a point of leverage for feminist critique and political practice. "An essentialist definition of 'woman' implies that there will always remain some part of 'woman' which resists masculine imprinting and socialization . . . that a woman will never be a woman solely in masculine terms, never be wholly and permanently annihilated in a masculine order." Here Fuss implies that unless we assume a point that escapes the culture that constructs us, we have no way of conceiving ourselves as anything other than obedient constructs of that culture.[17] Irigarayan essence, in her view, provides us with such a point.

Fuss's essay raises the feminist debate about essentialism to a new level of sophistication. It shifts the burden of argument back onto the anti-essentialists, requiring them to show that it is possible to conceive feminist opposition to sexism and feminist solidarity among women without presupposing a feminine essence. The remaining essays in this volume can be read as attempts to do just that.[18]

Dorothy Leland's paper, "Lacanian Psychoanalysis and French Feminism: Toward an Adequate Political Psychology," concerns precisely this issue. Leland's focus is the problem of "internalized oppression," the inculcation in women in male-dominated societies of sexist and androcentric schemas of thought, feeling, and valuation. What sort of theory, she asks, can provide an account of internalized oppression that acknowledges its depth and power while still allowing for the possibility in principle of political resistance and social change? Her answer, in brief, is no theory that accepts the basic postulates of Lacanian psychoanalysis.

Leland criticizes both Irigaray and Kristeva for failing to break fully enough with Jacques Lacan. She argues that, because Lacan's account of the Oedipal complex prescribes contours of socialization that are independent of any historically specific social relations, it casts women's internalized oppression as inevitable and irreversible. The result is a psychological determinism so absolute that no feminist political practice is even conceivable.

Now, it was as a counter to just this sort of theory that Fuss defended the strategic essentialism of Luce Irigaray. But this is not Leland's tack. Rather than oppose one exorbitant construct to another, she opts to debunk the initial Lacanian postulate of an autonomous, all-embracing Oedipal structuring of subjectivity. Writing from a socialist-feminist perspective, Leland rejects the autonomy of psychology. Instead, she proposes to explain internalized oppression by reference to specific, historically variable social relations and institutions, and therefore to build in the possibility of change. In Leland's view, it is Irigaray's tacit continuation of the Lacanian tendency to bypass historical and sociological analysis that creates problems for her theory. Because she does not ground internalized oppression in variable cultural practices, Irigaray ends up without a tenable foundation for her commitment to change.

If Irigaray's problem is her failure to develop the theoretical resources needed to underpin her political optimism, then Kristeva's problem, according to Leland, is her surrender to "political pessimism." Here, too, the root of the trouble is misplaced fidelity to Lacan. In fact, Kristeva outdoes Irigaray in this respect, even accepting the Lacanian claim that the phallocentric symbolic order is not susceptible to change. With change ruled out, the best one can hope for is a series of endless and fruitless skirmishes in which asocial "semiotic" instinctual drives—"feminine" vestiges of the pre-Oedipal past—disrupt but never overthrow the power of "The Father's Law." Moreover, like Irigaray, Kristeva also accepts the Lacanian assumption, earlier challenged by Nye, that "patriarchal representations . . . exhaust the entire symbolic dimension that mediates experience." According to Leland, then, because she assumes a monolithically phallocentric symbolic order that is wholly impervious to change, "Kristeva rejects too much and hopes for too little."

Leland's essay examines the accounts of internalized oppression in psycho-analytic feminist theories, their ability to explain how gender becomes entrenched. The next essay, by contrast, examines the accounts of women's agency in psychoanalytic feminist theories, their ability to envision how gender could be transformed. In "The Subversion of Women's Agency in Psychoanalytic Feminism," Diana T. Meyers considers the crucial but relatively neglected issue of "what shape women's personalities might assume in an egalitarian world." She takes the measure of Kristeva's handling of this issue in the context of an ambitious, comparative inquiry that also assesses the object relations theories of Nancy Chodorow and Jane Flax.

In Meyers's interpretation, Chodorow and Flax use single-pronged but opposite strategies for re-visioning women's agency. Chodorow takes the gynocentric tack of seeking the makings of a new, ideal "relational autonomy" in traditional feminine qualities of "relationality" and "(self-) nurturance." Flax, on the other hand, takes the humanist approach of looking to recover elements of a traditionally masculine autonomy that women have repressed. But in neither case, argues Meyers, is the result satisfactory. Chodorow's approach fails to provide women with critical, oppositional capacities, while Flax neglects to show how "masculine" autonomy is compatible with "feminine" connectedness. Both problems, according to Meyers, have a common root in the theorists' shared failure to overcome the gender coding of human capacities that is endemic to psychoanalysis.

Meyers finds Kristeva's approach more complex and, hence, more promising. It combines a gynocentric moment aimed at revaluing femininity with a humanist moment aimed at securing for women stereotypically masculine capacities of critical distance from societal norms. In addition, Kristeva incorporates a third, potentially transformative element in her theoretical strategy: she tries at times to scramble standard Freudian alignments of unconscious forces with either masculinity or femininity and to "demassify" gender difference. This innovative combination of tactics appears most clearly, in Meyers's view, in Kristeva's account of femininity. First, Kristeva reclaims what misogynists have denigrated as women's "emotional irrationality," and she renames it "heterogeneity." Then, she links heterogeneity with the destabilization of fixed social identity and the capacity for critical "dissidence." This series of moves in effect redefines femininity as a source of critical, oppositional capacities, thereby breaking the traditional association of agency with masculinity and avoiding a principal weakness of Chodorow's theory. In addition, Kristeva improves on Flax by frankly acknowledging tensions between the decentering of identity associated with femininity, on the one hand, and the provisional unity of self required by the "social symbolic contract," on the other hand. Rather than seek an impossible synthesis of contradictories, Kristeva recommends as ideal the self who can alternate fruitfully between these two poles.

Yet for all its promising complexity, this theory, too, ultimately fails to sustain a conception of agency that feminists can endorse. The sticking point, according to Meyers, is that in order to ensure that "dissidence" will be ethically responsible, Kristeva needs a functional equivalent for Freud's paternal superego. The best she can come up with, alas, is an image of maternity that is conventional, sentimental, and prescriptive. Thus, Kristeva, too, falls prey to gender dichotomies. The stereotypes she excludes from one level of her theory return to vitiate it at another.

Meyers claims it is no mere coincidence that all three psychoanalytic feminisms fail to re-vision women's agency. She argues that the structure of psychoanalysis as we currently know it presents obstacles to that task. These obstacles include the relentless gendering of explanatory concepts and the presumption that gender identities tied to procreative heterosexuality are the telos of psychic development. Meyers concludes that "psychoanalytic feminism will be barred from directly describing a feminist vision of agency until it reformulates its account of psychic forces and liberalizes its assumptions about the ends of human development."

Whereas Meyers's essay suggests that Kristeva's stated aim of "demassifying" difference runs aground on gender stereotypes, the following essay locates the problem in the French writer's theoretical views about the relation between culture and bodily drives. In "The Body Politics of Julia Kristeva," Judith Butler argues that "the maternal body" plays a role in Kristeva's theory not unlike that which Fuss attributes to Irigarayan essence: it harbors an extra-cultural source of cultural subversion. But, claims Butler, the result is anything but emancipatory. While purporting to reveal the repressed foundations of culture in the libidinal multiplicity of infants' primary relations to their mothers' bodies, Kristeva actually constructs an ideological legitimation of compulsory motherhood for women.

Butler carefully elaborates the steps in this construction. She identifies the figure of the lesbian as the stress point in Kristeva's theory, the point where various anxieties and contradictions condense. For Kristeva, lesbianism is a way in which women re-experience their pre-Oedipal relation to their mothers' bodies. In this respect, it is like avant-garde poetic practice and maternity itself, since all three are seen by Kristeva as practices in which the subject's identity is put "on trial" as the repressed semiotic, feminine foundations of culture burst onto the paternally sanctioned symbolic scene. However, Kristeva does not value the three practices equally. Rather, she reserves her approval for motherhood and poetry, claiming that in them alone semiotic multiplicity finds *symbolic* expression. Lesbianism, by contrast, she assimilates to psychosis, an escapist flight from the symbolic and a regression beneath culture.

In Butler's reading, Kristeva's homophobia is symptomatic of deep theoretical and political difficulties. Kristeva accepts the structuralist and Lacanian dogmas equating heterosexuality with the founding of culture, culture with the symbolic, and the symbolic with "the Father's Law." It follows, argues Butler, that the lesbian can only appear as the "other" of culture, an archaic and chaotic force that is intrinsically unintelligible. But "this says more about the fantasies that a fearful heterosexist culture produces to defend against its own homosexual possibilities than about lesbian experience itself." In failing to treat lesbianism as an alternative possibility *within* culture, Kristeva refuses to take up the challenge it poses to her restricted view of culture as wholly and necessarily paternal.

Butler goes on to challenge Kristeva's view of the relation between libidinal drives, language, and the law. To Kristeva's naturalistic understanding of drives as prediscursive things-in-themselves Butler counterposes a Foucauldian view according to which "drives" are actually discursive constructs. Thus, she argues, contra gynocentric essentialists, that we should not anchor our hopes for women's liberation on a concept of the feminine seen as external to a culture that represses it. Nor should we dream of liberating a natural female body from the shackles of cultural construction. Rather, we should think in terms of exploiting oppositions and contradictions within male-dominated culture. And we should situate the project of liberating our bodies in the horizon of "an open future of cultural possibilities."

Both Butler's essay and the final essay in this anthology combine anti-essentialist critiques of gynocentrism with political orientations that stress cultural conflict. But whereas Butler's argument is inspired by the nominalist philosophy of Michel Foucault, mine draws on the cultural Marxism of Antonio Gramsci and the pragmatic tradition in the philosophy of language.

In "The Uses and Abuses of French Discourse Theories for Feminist Politics," I propose that feminists evaluate theories of discourse in terms of four desiderata: First, can the theory help us understand how people's social identities are fashioned and altered over time? Second, can it help clarify how, under conditions of inequality, social groups in the sense of collective agents are formed and dissolved? Third, can the theory illuminate how the cultural hegemony of dominant groups in society is secured and contested? Finally, can it shed light on the prospects for emancipatory social change and political practice? I then assess the relative merits of structuralist and pragmatic approaches to the study of language in terms of these four criteria. I argue that structuralist approaches are less useful than pragmatic approaches because, by focusing on symbolic systems or codes, they bracket the social practice and social context of communication. Consequently, structuralist models cannot easily deal with power, inequality, and discursive conflict.

My essay elaborates these objections to structuralism via critical discussions of Lacan and Kristeva. Although both theorists are widely thought of as "poststructuralists," I contend that in important respects they continue the structuralist legacy. In Lacan's case, this takes the form of what I call "symbolicism": "the homogenizing reification of diverse signifying practices into a monolithic and all-pervasive 'symbolic order.'" In Kristeva's case, the problem is an "additive" approach to theorizing: rather than eliminate or transform untenable structuralist notions, she simply adds antistructuralist notions alongside of them. For example, she conjoins the abstractly anti-structuralist "semiotic" to the unreconstructedly structuralist "symbolic" to generate an amalgam of structure and antistructure. Likewise, in her thinking about identity, difference, and femininity, she alternates essentialist gynocentric moments with anti-essentialist nominalist moments—moments that consolidate an ahistorical, undifferentiated, maternal feminine gender identity with moments that repudiate women's social identities altogether. In my view, neither of these alternating moments is adequate in itself, however; nor is a compound in which the two are forever locked together in antithetical oscillation, without ever getting to anything else.

In contrast, I suggest that a consistently pragmatic approach to the study of discourse could help obviate Kristeva's difficulties. A pragmatic approach would study discourses—in the plural—as historically changing signifying practices located in and around specific social institutions. Consequently, it would enable feminists to think of social identities as complex, changing, and discursively constructed. That in turn would "permit us to navigate safely between the twin shoals of essentialism and nominalism, between reifying women's social identities under stereotypes of femininity, on the one hand, and dissolving them into sheer nullity and oblivion, on the other." Thus, we could accept the critique of essentialism without becoming "postfeminists."

Read together, these essays point to a paradoxical logic in some French feminist philosophies. Insofar as the theorist posits the patriarchal constitution of culture and of subjectivity as total and all-pervasive, she effectively liquidates the possibility of any socially situated female resistance. But then, in order to avoid the pessimistic conclusion that we are trapped forever in a patriarchal iron cage, she is driven to posit a hyperbolic capacity for action, since in order to act at all we must act against absolutely everything. This, in turn, leads the theorist to look for an extra-cultural source of energy powerful enough to fuel such hyperbolic action, say, an extra-cultural feminine essence or a set of prediscursive bodily drives. In either case, the aim is to show that women formed in a univocally patriarchal culture are nonetheless able to act against it, whether by creating ex nihilo an entirely new, feminine culture or, more modestly, by periodically jolting existing culture with shockwaves of bodily negativity.

This formulation helps explain why the problem of *agency* appears so frequently in these essays. Agency has become a problem in recent feminist theory because of the cross-pull of two equally important imperatives. On the one hand, feminists have sought to establish the seriousness of our struggle by establishing the pervasiveness and systematicity of male dominance. Accordingly, we have often opted for theories that emphasize the constraining power of gender structures and norms, while downplaying the resisting capacities of individuals and groups. On the other hand, feminists have also sought to inspire women's activism by recovering lost or socially invisible traditions of resistance in the past and present. Under the sway of this imperative, we have often supposed quasi-voluntarist models of change. The net result of these conflicting tendencies is the following dilemma: *either* we limn the structural constraints of gender so well that we deny women any agency *or* we portray women's agency so glowingly that the power of subordination evaporates. Either way, what we often seem to lack is a coherent, integrated, balanced conception of agency, a conception that can accommodate both the power of social constraints and the capacity to act situatedly against them.

We encounter this problem in this volume in the interviews with Simone de Beauvoir, where she wrestles with the question of whether the voluntarist orientation of existentialism is not finally irreconcilable with a theory of women's oppression, since it seems to imply that women are responsible as individuals for tolerating their situations. We find it also in Sarah Kofman's demonstration that Rousseau's philosophy is a veritable morass of contradictory ideas about women's powers as agents[19] and in Diana Fuss's defense of Irigaray's essentialism on the ground that it enables women's agency. However, the most explicit and extended treatment is Diana Meyers's examination of structural barriers to conceiving women's agency in psychoanalytic feminist theory.

In addition, several other essays in this volume link the problem of agency to yet another cluster of recurrent themes, namely, *culture, language,* and *the nature of patriarchy*. Clearly, some French feminist philosophies invite us to ask, how far down does cultural construction go? Are we patriarchally formed to the innermost depths of our psyches or is there something in us that escapes construction? However, this way of posing the question presupposes a prior thesis about the nature of culture: the thesis, associated with Lacan, that culture is wholly and seamlessly phallocentric. That thesis is reinforced, we have seen, if culture is identified with a single overarching symbolic order, if that symbolic order is held to be ordered in accordance with the deep structure of language, and if the deep structure of language, in turn, is held to be phallocentric.

We have already seen that Luce Irigaray appears to endorse the wholly phallocentric view of culture in her reading of Diotima's philosophy of love, as it is reported in Plato's *Symposium*. We have also seen that Andrea Nye rejects that view and constructs a counterreading of the dialogue according to which an emergent, patriarchal strand of culture struggles to displace a residual, prepatriarchal strand, eventually to become the cultural dominant.[20] For Irigaray and Nye, then, the Greek world of Plato's time becomes in effect a test case for deciding between two antithetical conceptions of culture. One is a view of culture as monolithically phallocentric, everywhere instantiating the same hierarchical binary oppositions and eternally repressing feminine difference. The other is a view of culture as male-dominated but plurivocal and contested, a multivalent weave of dominant, residual, and emergent strands that are often in tension with one another.

Which of these two models of culture is best suited to feminist practice today? Which is most theoretically defensible? Several contributors to this volume challenge the former, monolithic view by scrutinizing its theoretical underpinnings. Dorothy Leland refutes the postulate, derived from anthropologist Claude Lévi-Strauss, and accepted by Irigaray and Kristeva, that the exchange of women by men is the original and continuing structural foundation of culture. Likewise, Judith Butler challenges the assumptions about language, drives, and "the Father's Law" that lead Kristeva to expel lesbian cultural practices into a wilderness outside of culture, and she proposes an alternative conception of culture as a terrain of contestation. Finally, my essay challenges the structuralist linguistic approach that underlies the Lacanian concept of "the symbolic order" and defends an alternative, pragmatic approach that can focalize cultural fault lines and discursive conflicts.

Can we read in these essays the makings of a new feminist consensus for the nineties? Certainly, a majority of contributors to this volume oppose the view of culture as monolithically patriarchal, but there is no unanimity on this issue. Likewise, while all the contributors seek to understand male dominance in ways that are compatible with women's agency, there is no agreement as to how this is best done. To be sure, many contributors share a commitment to reconceptualizing agency, but their programmatic orientations diverge. Finally, with respect to identity, difference, and femininity, these essays clarify but do not fully untie the conceptual knots. We are still struggling, it seems, to juggle at least four seemingly conflicting political imperatives: 1) the need to criticize forms of male dominance that consist in excluding women from participating in valuable activities and from developing desirable capacities; 2) the need to reclaim aspects of women's lives that misogynist culture has denigrated and to decenter androcentric values and norms; 3) the need to understand women's lives in their full complexity and diversity by theorizing the intersection of gender with class, color, ethnicity, and sexual orientation; and 4) the need to think programmatically about such "differences" in ways that promote movements and coalitions capable of effecting fundamental social change.

On the other hand, there is one issue that compels universal agreement in this volume, namely, the rejection of compulsory motherhood. That is a theme that reverberates through virtually every essay. It appears in Beauvoir's objections to "enslaved motherhood," in Kofman's deconstruction of obligatory maternity in Rousseau, in Irigaray's deconstruction of teleological, procreation-driven love in Plato,[21] and in the various critiques of Kristeva's maternalist essentialism by Leland, Meyers, Butler, and me. Thus, opposition to forced childbearing and to prescriptive maternalist conceptions of femininity unites existentialist-humanists like Beauvoir, deconstructive anti-essentialists like Kofman, gynocentric essentialists like Fuss and Irigaray, and the rest of the North American contributors.

Given the problems concerning political context with which I began this introduction, it is fitting that opposition to forced childbearing should be the point at which a consensus emerges from amidst the theoretical dissension. Today women everywhere are being bombarded with a barrage of neomaternalist images and rhetorics, and reproductive freedoms are once again under open attack. Indeed, this issue seems to epitomize many of the political contradictions of the present. On the one hand, it positions feminists on the defensive on a terrain defined by the New Right; but on the other hand, it calls forth our strength, depth, and breadth as a variegated and genuinely organic social movement. In addition, the struggle for reproductive freedom poses the challenge of dealing with differences in its starkest and most pressing form: are we capable of developing theories, practices, and rhetorics of contestation that can speak to the full array of women's reproductive needs, as these arise from, and are discursively constructed in response to, the diversity of our situations? As we enter a new decade of feminist politics, perhaps the battle for reproductive freedom will be one important site at which we can utilize French feminist insights about the formative force of language in social life, while forswearing those aspects of these theories that are counterproductive for the struggles ahead.

NOTES

I am grateful for helpful comments from Sandra Bartky, Gerald Graff, Linda J. Nicholson, and Diana T. Meyers.

1. Translations that predated the appearance of Marks and de Courtivron (1980) include Cixous (1976), Delphy (1977), Féral (1978), Irigaray (1977), Kristeva (1977), and Wittig (1971, 1976). Early secondary discussions in English include Burke (1978), Conley (1975,1977), Jardine (1980), and Marks (1978).

2. I say "relatively catholic" because of the underrepresentation of materials representing "syndicalist feminism" and feminist currents within leftwing parties. These currents became increasingly important during the eighties, when the Socialist Party came to power and when the two major labor federations, the CGT and the CDFT, broadened their field of action to encompass issues of social reproduction and the distinctive needs and problems of women workers. For an account of these important but understudied currents of "French feminism," see Jane Jenson (1990).

3. We could doubtless learn much about the workings of our culture and its institutions if we could reconstruct the precise process of this synecdochic reduction. It is all the more striking in that it occurred despite the strenuous protests of Monique Wittig, Simone de Beauvoir, and the editors of the journal Feminist Questions.

4. For the general ethos of 1968 and its aftermath, see Hamon and Rotman (1982, 1988), Ross and Frader (1988), and Turkle (1978). For the continuation of the ethos of '68 in the

French women's liberation movement in the seventies, see Delphy (1984), Duchen (1986), Jenson (1990), Léger (1982), Picq (1987), and Pisan and Tristan (1977).

5. It would be a mistake to think that the changes I have been sketching are specific to feminist movements in Anglophone countries. In France, too, we can find many analogous transformations. The ascension to power of a Socialist government in 1981 crystallized an already developing sea-change in the relationship of French women's movements to institutions, a change graphically symbolized in the establishment of a state Ministry for Women's Rights. Such developments presented French feminists a new set of opportunities, dangers, and challenges, fundamentally altering the terms of political practice. See Duchen (1986) and Jenson (1990).

6. See, for example, Frye (1983), Hooks (1984), Joseph (1981), Lord (1981), Lugones and Spelman (1983), Rich (1980), and Spelman (1988).

7. See Echols (1983).

8. See Fraser and Nicholson (1988).

9. For negative assessments, see Jones (1981, 1984), Moi on Irigaray (1985), Nye (1987), Plaza (1980), Spivak (1981), Stanton (1986), Stone (1983), and Weedon (1987). For more positive assessments, see Grosz (1989), Jardine (1986), Moi on Kristeva (1985), Rose (1986), Schor (1989), and Young (1990). For mixed assessments, see Butler (1990) and Gallop (1982).

10. In this respect, though not in others, both Kofman and Beauvoir have affinities with the leading American exponent of this position, Catharine A. MacKinnon (1987), who argues that gender difference is just gender domination.

11. For a parallel argument concerning the repression of African and Semitic influences in the construction of an "Aryan" model of the sources of Greek civilization, see Martin Bernal (1987).

12. A similar objection could be made against Derrida insofar as he posits a totally "phallogocentric" cultural order. Revealingly, the evidence he adduces in support of this view comes entirely from texts by men. For example, in a recent (1988) paper he argues that "the" Western concept of friendship is male. Yet the only support he offers for this claim is a reading of a text by Aristotle. The result is to render invisible the large and interesting cultural record of female friendship that has been documented by feminist scholars like Carroll Smith-Rosenberg (1975).

13. See "The Blind Spot of an Old Dream of Symmetry," in Irigaray (1985a).

14. Again, the most extensive and persuasive exemplar of this sort of approach is Bernal (1987).

15. Both of these essays appear in Irigaray (1985b).

16. Early and influential arguments to this effect were offered by Jones (1981) and Plaza (1980).

17. This assumption appears to be dependent on a prior acceptance of Irigaray's view of Western culture as monolithically phallocentric. If one follows Nye in refusing that assumption, then the problem of how opposition is possible looks very different. On Nye's view, resistance to male dominance involves pitting some elements of the tradition against others that contradict them. This alternative will be discussed below.

18. There have of course been other attempts to answer the sort of challenge posed by Fuss. Among the most interesting and compelling of these is Denise Riley's (1988) book. See also Linda Alcoff (1988) and Nancy Fraser and Linda Nicholson (1988).

19. In Kofman's reading, Rousseau claims, on the one hand, that women are naturally subordinate and reserved, and on the other hand, that we are everywhere insubordinate, shamelessly vying with men for power and position. In addition, he argues that if only we would return to our natural state of subordination and confinement, we would inherit a veritable empire and rule thoroughly, if unobtrusively, over men!

20. The terms residual, emergent, and dominant are not used by Nye herself, although they fit her account very nicely. They are associated with the late Marxist critic Raymond Williams (1977), who argued that at any point in time a culture is an unstable, contested amalgam of dominant, residual, and emergent strands.

21. Although Irigaray sometimes seems like the odd woman out in this volume, it is a basic intention of her philosophy to contest maternalist constructions of femininity. That is precisely the point of her counterconstruction of a feminine eros detached from procreation.

BIBLIOGRAPHY

Alcoff, Linda. 1988. Cultural feminism versus poststructuralism: The identity crisis in feminist theory. *Signs: Journal of women in culture and society* 13(3): 405-36.

Bernal, Martin. 1987. *Black Athena*. New Brunswick, NJ: Rutgers University Press.

Burke, Carolyn Greenstein. 1978. Report from Paris: Women's writing and the women's movement. *Signs: Journal of women in culture and society* 3(4): 843-55.

Butler, Judith. 1990. *Gender trouble: Feminism and the subversion of identity.* New York: Routledge, Chapman and Hall.

Chodorow, Nancy. 1978. *The reproduction of mothering: Psychoanalysis and the sociology of gender.* Berkeley: University of California Press.

Cixous, Hélène. 1976. The laugh of the Medusa. Trans. Keith Cohen and Paula Cohen. *Signs: Journal of women in culture and society* 1: 875-93.

Conley, Verena. 1975. Kristeva's China. *Diacritics* 25-30.

———. 1977. Missexual misstery. *Diacritics* (Summer): 70-82.

Delphy, Christine. 1977. *The main enemy.* trans. Lucy ap Roberts and Diana Leonard Baker. London: Women's Research and Resources Center Publications.

———. 1984. Les femmes et l'état. *Nouvelles questions féministes* 6-7: 5-19.

Derrida, Jacques. 1988. The politics of friendship. Paper delivered at the meeting of the American Philosophical Association, Eastern Division, Washington, D.C., December 30.

Duchen, Claire. 1986. *Feminism in France: From May '68 to Mitterrand.* London: Routledge and Kegan Paul.

———. 1987. *French connections: Voices from the women's movement in France.* Amherst: University of Massachusetts Press.

Echols, Alice. 1983. The new feminism of yin and yang. In *Powers of desire: The politics of sexuality,* ed. Ann Snitow, Christine Stansell, and Sharon Thompson. New York: Monthly Review Press.

Féral, Josette. 1978. Antigone or the irony of the tribe. Trans. Alice Jardine and Tom Gora. *Diacritics* Fall: 2-14.

Fraser, Nancy and Linda Nicholson. 1988. Social criticism without philosophy: An encounter between feminism and postmodernism. *Theory, Culture and Society* 5(2-3): 373-94.

Frye, Marilyn. 1983. *The politics of reality: Essays in feminist theory.* Trumansburg, NY: The Crossing Press.

Gallop, Jane. 1982. *The daughter's seduction: Feminism and psychoanalysis.* Ithaca, NY: Cornell University Press.

Gilligan, Carol. 1982. *In a different voice: Psychological theory and women's development.* Cambridge, MA: Harvard University Press.

Gordon, Linda. 1991. On "difference." *Genders* (Autumn).

Grosz, Elizabeth. 1989. *Sexual subversions: Three French feminists.* Sydney: Allen and Unwin.

Guillaumin, Colette. 1987. The question of difference. In *French connections: Voices from the women's movement in France,* ed. Claire Duchen. Amherst: University of Massachusetts Press.

Hamon, Hervé and Patrick Rotman. 1982. *La deuxième gauche.* Paris: Seuil.

———. 1988. *Génération.* Paris: Seuil.

Hooks, Bell. 1984. *Feminist theory from margin to center.* Boston: South End Press.

Irigaray, Luce. 1977. Women's exile. *Ideology and consciousness.* 1: 62-76.

———. 1985a. *Speculum of the other woman.* Trans. Gillian C. Gill. Ithaca: Cornell University Press.

———. 1985b. *This sex which is not one.* Trans. Catherine Porter. Ithaca: Cornell University Press.

Jardine, Alice. 1980. Theories of the feminine: Kristeva. *enclitic* 4(2).

———. 1986. Opaque texts and transparent contexts: The political difference of Julia Kristeva. In *The poetics of gender,* ed. Nancy K. Miller. New York: Columbia University Press.

Jenson, Jane. 1990. Representations of difference: The varieties of French feminism. *New Left Review* (180): 127-60.

Jones, Ann Rosalind. 1981. Writing the body: Toward an understanding of *l'écriture féminine. Feminist Studies* 7(2): 247-63.

———. 1984. Julia Kristeva on femininity: The limits of a semiotic politics. *Feminist Review* 18: 56-73.

Joseph, Gloria. 1981. The incompatible menage à trois: Marxism, feminism and racism. *Women and revolution.* Ed. Lydia Sargent. Boston: South End Press. 91-107.

Kristeva, Julia. 1977. *About Chinese women.* Trans. Anita Barrows. Urizen Books.

———. 1980. *Desire in language: A semiotic approach to art and literature.* Ed. Leon S. Roudiez, trans. Alice Jardine, Thomas Gora, and Leon Roudiez. New York: Columbia University Press.

———. 1982. *Powers of horror: An essay on abjection.* Trans. Leon S. Roudiez. New York: Columbia University Press.

———. 1984. *Revolution in poetic language.* Trans. Margaret Waller. New York: Columbia University Press.

———. 1986. *The Kristeva reader.* Ed. Toril Moi. New York: Columbia University Press.

Léger, Daniele. 1982. *Le féminisme en France.* Paris: Le Sycomore.

Lord, Audre. 1981. An open letter to Mary Daly. In *This bridge called my back: Writings by radical women of color,* ed. Cherrie Moraga and Gloria Anzaldua. Watertown, MA: Persephone Press. 94-97.

Lugones, Maria C., and Elizabeth V. Spelman. 1983. Have we got a theory for you! Feminist theory, cultural imperialism and the demand for the woman's voice. *Hypatia*, published as a special issue of *Women's Studies International Forum*, 6(6): 578-81.

MacKinnon, Catharine A. 1987. *Feminism unmodified*, Cambridge MA: Harvard University Press.

Marks, Elaine. 1978. Review essay: Women and literature in France. *Signs: Journal of women in culture and society* 3(4): 832-42.

—— and Isabelle de Courtivron, ed. 1980. *New French feminisms*. Amherst: University of Massachusetts Press.

Moi, Toril. 1985. *Sexual/textual politics*. London: Methuen.

Nye, Andrea. 1987. Woman clothed with the sun. *Signs: Journal of women in culture and society* 12(4): 664-86.

Picq, Françoise. 1987. *Le mouvement de libération des femmes et ses effets sociaux*. Paris: ATP Recherches féministes et recherches sur les femmes.

Pisan, Annie de, and Anne Tristan. 1977. *Histoires du MLF*. Paris: Calmann-Lévy.

Plaza, Monique. 1980. "Phallomorphic" power and the psychology of "woman." *Feminist Issues* 1(1): 71-102.

Rich, Adrienne. 1980. "Compulsory heterosexuality and lesbian existence." *Signs: Journal of women in culture and society* 5(4): 631-60.

Riley, Denise. 1988. *"Am I that name?" Feminism and the category of "women" in history*. Minneapolis: University of Minnesota Press.

Rose, Jacqueline. 1986. *Sexuality in the field of vision*. London: Verso.

Ross, George, and Laura Frader. 1988. The May generation: From Mao to Mitterrand. *Socialist Review* 18(4): 105-16.

Schor, Naomi. 1989. This essentialism which is not one: Coming to grips with Irigaray. *Differences* 1(2): 38-58.

Smith-Rosenberg, Carroll. 1975. The female world of love and ritual: Relations between women in 19th century America. *Signs: Journal of women in culture and society* 1(1): 1-29.

Spelman, Elizabeth V. 1988. *Inessential woman*. Boston: Deacon Press.

Spivak, Gayatri C. 1981. French feminism in an international frame. *Yale French Studies* 62: 154-84.

Stanton, Domna C. 1986. Difference on trial: A critique of the maternal metaphor in Cixous, Irigaray and Kristeva. In *The poetics of gender*, ed. Nancy K. Miller. New York: Columbia University Press.

Stone, Jennifer. 1983. The horrors of power: A critique of Kristeva. In *The politics of theory: Proceedings of the Essex conference on the sociology of literature*, ed. Francis Barker, et al. Colchester: University of Essex. 38-48.

Turkle, Sherry. 1978. *Psychoanalytic politics: Freud's French revolution*. New York: Basic Books.

Weedon, Chris. 1987. *Feminist practice and poststructuralist theory*. London: Basil Blackwell.

Williams, Raymond. 1977. *Marxism and literature*. Oxford: Oxford University Press.

Wittig, Monique. 1971. *Les guérillières*. Trans. David Le Vay. New York: Viking.

———. 1976. *The lesbian body*. Trans. Peter Owen. New York: Avon.

———. 1980. The straight mind. *Feminist Issues* 1(1):103-11.

———. 1981. One is not born a woman. *Feminist Issues* 1(2): 47-54.

———. 1983. The point of view: Universal or particular? *Feminist Issues* 3(2): 63-69.

———. 1984. The Trojan horse. *Feminist Issues* 4(2): 45-49.

———. 1985. The mark of gender. *Feminist Issues* 5(2): 3-12.

———. 1989. The social contract. *Feminist Issues* 9(1): 3-12.

Young, Iris. 1985. Humanism, gynocentrism and feminist politics. *Hypatia* 3, published as a special issue of *Women's Studies International Forum* 8(3): 173-83.

———. 1990. Abjection and oppression: Unconscious dynamics of racism, sexism, and homophobia. In *The crisis in continental philosophy*, ed. Arleen Dallery and Charles Scott. New York: SUNY Press.

Two Interviews with Simone de Beauvoir

MARGARET A. SIMONS
Transcribed and translated by JANE MARIE TODD

In these interviews from 1982 and 1985, I ask Beauvoir about her philosophical differences with Jean-Paul Sartre on the issues of voluntarism vs social conditioning and embodiment, individualism vs reciprocity, and ontology vs ethics. We also discuss her influence on Sartre's work, the problems with the current English translation of The Second Sex, *her analyses of motherhood and feminist concepts of woman-identity, and her own experience of sexism.*

I. Introduction

In May of 1982 and September of 1985, I had my last interviews with Simone de Beauvoir. My first was in the autumn of 1972. I had come to Paris on a grant to do doctoral research with Beauvoir on her philosophy in *The Second Sex*. Developments in the women's liberation movement had left me searching for direction and I hoped that returning to the theoretical foundations of feminism as Beauvoir developed them in *The Second Sex* would help me find my way again.

The Second Sex had inspired radicals like Ti-Grace Atkinson, Shulamith Firestone, and Kate Millett, as well as liberals like Betty Friedan, and socialists like Juliet Mitchell. Criticizing the male bias in traditional philosophy, religion, psychology, and Marxism, Beauvoir based her understanding of women's situation on descriptions of women's own "lived experience." She rejected essentialist definitions of woman that reflected the oppressive myth of woman as Other. Only women acting together, she argued, could secure independence for all women and replace oppression with relationships of genuine reciprocity between men and women.

But Beauvoir wrote *The Second Sex* in 1948-9, between the first and second waves of the women's movement. I was interested then, as now and through-

I am indebted to the editors of this volume, Nancy Fraser and Sandra Bartky, for their encouragement and helpful suggestions during the long process of preparing these interviews for publication; to Jane Marie Todd, for undertaking the tasks of transcribing them from the tape, translating, and editing them; to the Graduate School of Southern Illinois University at Edwardsville, for supporting my travel to France; and to Simone de Beauvoir for generously agreeing to meet with me and respond to my questions.

Hypatia vol. 3, no. 3 (Winter 1989) © by Margaret A. Simons

out my relationship with her, in how her experience of the contemporary movement had changed her perspective. In the interviews that follow, I ask her about her response to the new form of feminist essentialism, the search for our "woman-identity" and about motherhood, an experience central to the traditonal definition of womanhood, and thus one charged with emotional ambivalence for many feminists. In *The Second Sex*, she describes motherhood in negative terms, as "enslavement to the species," a barrier to authentic human experience, and a burden for women that only society could lighten. Would she still define motherhood in such a negative way or has her philosophical position changed?

A student of Beauvoir's philosophy must overcome several difficulties. One posed by our cultural differences is that of translation. In these interviews we discuss the need for a scholarly translation of *The Second Sex*. The only translation currently available to English readers is by Howard M. Parshley, a zoologist who authored a 1930's text on sex differences. In response to demands from the publisher, Parshley made extensive cuts, eliminating almost ten percent of the original French text of *The Second Sex*, including half of one chapter on history and the names of 78 women in history. Unfortunately Parshley lacked any expertise in philosophy, or familiarity with existential phenomenology, the philosophical tradition within which Beauvoir was working. As a consequence, he gave mistranslations of philosophical terms crucial to an understanding of Beauvoir's philosophical perspective.

Few chroniclers of continental philosophy or existential phenomenology mention Beauvoir's work, which may lead one to wonder whether she is a philosopher at all. This poses another problem for scholars interested in her work. When histories of philosophy deal with her at all, they ignore *The Second Sex*, commonly describing Beauvoir as a follower of Sartre. But Sartre was no feminist, and his attempt in *Being and Nothingness* to construct an existential social philosophy was convincing on neither theoretical nor practical grounds. In *The Second Sex* Beauvoir rejected the Sartrean assumptions of absolute freedom and radical individualism. Grounded epistemologically in women's experience of oppression within historically defined relationships with men, *The Second Sex* represented an important theoretical advance for existentialism as well as feminism, and inspired women around the world to challenge their traditional roles.

In these interviews with Beauvoir, I explore themes in her philosophy that differentiate it from Sartre's. I am also interested in her influence on him. We discuss specific areas of disagreement between Beauvoir and Sartre, for example, voluntarism vs. emphasis on social conditions and embodiment; individualism vs. emphasis on reciprocity; ontology vs. ethics. I also raise the questions of philosophical influence: whether Beauvoir considered the reconciling of a Sartrean "choice" with her understanding of woman's oppression a problem in *The Second Sex*; and whether Sartre's later work, for example, on Genet and Flaubert, was influenced by *The Second Sex*.

Beauvoir was not always receptive to these questions. When we first met in 1972, Beauvoir seemed angered by my questions about her philosophy in *The Second Sex*, despite her support for my Fulbright proposal which was precisely to examine this philosophy. "I am not a philosopher," she insisted, "but a literary writer; Sartre is the philosopher. How could I have influenced him?" When I asked about the importance of Hegel's *Phenomenology* on *The Second Sex*, she angrily replied that, the only important influence on *The Second Sex* was *Being and Nothingness* by Jean-Paul Sartre. This was certainly an odd response, given that she tells us in her memoirs that immediately prior to writing *The Second Sex* she had made a careful and extensive study of Hegel. Understanding her response became a continuing topic in my research and interviews with Beauvoir.

Beauvoir was a philosopher by training. She taught philosophy for several years. In her memoirs she describes her philosophical work on the "existentialist ethics" that forms the theoretical framework of *The Second Sex*. How was I to understand her statement that she, unlike Sartre, was "not a philosopher" but a "literary writer"?

Her identification as a literary writer might be understood as a philosophical stance, confirming the priority of the concrete and experiential over the abstract and ahistorical. Her goal, shaped during the period of her most intense philosophical work in the 1940's, was to ground existential ethics in history and concrete relationships rather than in abstractions. In *The Second Sex* she locates her ethical enquiry within the context of specific historical relationships, and asks how, given man's historical definition of woman as Other, authentic relationships between men and women are possible. Philosophers like Kant, Hegel, and Sartre (to use her example) build abstract systems, meant to transcend history. Meaning, for Beauvoir, is always situated and historical.

This is a substantive philosophical claim. Then why did Beauvoir insist she was not a philosopher? Why did she assume a position outside of philosophy for her critique? Why did she relinquish the right of every philosopher to redefine philosophy itself? Her memoirs suggest that her identification with a literary tradition that had included women, rather than with a philosophical tradition that had excluded them, is connected with a sense of inferiority that she herself connects with the "feminine condition."

"Why not try my hand at philosophy?" she asks herself in 1935. "Sartre says that I understand philosophical doctrines, Husserl's among others, more quickly and more exactly than he. . . . In brief, I have few solid powers of assimilation, a developed critical sense, and philosophy is for me a living reality. I'll never tire of its satisfactions.

"However, I don't consider myself a philosopher. I know very well that my ease in entering into a text comes precisely from my lack of inventiveness. In this domain, the truly creative spirits are so rare that it is idle of me to ask why I cannot try to join their ranks. It's necessary rather to explain how certain individuals are capable of pulling off this concerted delirium which is a system, and whence comes the stubborness which gives to their insights the value of universal keys. I have said already that the feminine condition does not dispose one to this kind of obstinacy" (1960, 228-9).

When invited in 1943 to contribute an article on existentialism to an anthology on recent work in philosophy, Beauvoir writes that, "at first I refused, I said that where philosophy was concerned I knew my own limitations" (1960, 562).

In the interviews that follow I ask Beauvoir about the educational experiences that might have contributed to this attitude. She denies ever having suffered from discrimination as a woman and claims to have escaped woman's traditional role. But her autobiographies tell a different story. Consider this description of her education in a Catholic girl's school: "My upbringing had convinced me of my sex's intellectual inferiority, a fact admitted by many women. 'A lady cannot hope to pass the selective examination before the fifth or sixth attempt,' " one of her teachers, who already had made two attempts, had told her (1974, 295). In the university her experience was that of a token woman. She felt "privileged" by her access to the male domain of philosophy, but I learned that her access had not been on equal terms with men.

On the day before my 1985 interview with Beauvoir, Michele LeDoeuff, the French feminist philosopher, told me about a conversation she had once had with Beauvoir about philosophy. According to LeDoeuff, it *had* been significant to Beauvoir that she had not been a student at the prestigious École Normale Supérieure (ENS). In the highly centralized French university system, the Sorbonne, where Beauvoir was enrolled, provided higher education for the mass of French students. The École Normale Supérieure, which was open only to men, trains the elite of the academic professoriate, and provides its students with the contacts necessary for major academic appointments. Both Sartre and Maurice Merleau-Ponty had won entrance to the ENS. Beauvoir was not permitted to matriculate there, although she did attend lectures there in preparation for the standardized competitive examinations, the "agrégation" in philosophy.

Sartre, who was a year ahead of her, was preparing to take his exams a second time, after having failed on his first attempt. Beauvoir's thesis on Leibniz won her an invitation to join his study group. When they took the exams at the end of that year, Sartre placed first and Beauvoir second, making her the youngest student ever to pass the exams. But this success apparently could not overcome Beauvoir's sense of intellectual inferiority. She saw her youth not as a sign of her brilliance, but rather as another marker of her inferiority. She claims that she often assumed a passive role in philosophical discussions among Sartre's male friends, offering criticism or remaining silent, feeling that she "did not think fast enough" (1960, 35).

Beauvoir's responses to my questions about her experience of sexism in her education and in her relationship with Sartre are often ambiguous. They point out the difficulties in any attempt to interpret another person's life. But they also shed light on Beauvoir's experience as a "token woman" and on her innovative response to that experience. Feeling inferior in the male-dominated domain of philosophy, she identified instead with a literary tradition more hospitable to women and transformed her "lack of inventiveness" into a critique of philosophy and a profoundly philosophical reflection on the situation of women.

II. PARIS; MAY 11, 1982

MS: I have a question about Sartre's influence on *The Second Sex*. You wrote in *The Prime of Life* that Sartre's questions about your childhood, about the fact that you were raised as a girl, not a boy, are what gave you the idea for *The Second Sex*.

SB: No, not exactly. I had begun—well, he was the one who actually told me. . . . I wanted to write about myself and he said, "Don't forget to explain first of all what it is to be a women." And I told him, "But that never bothered me, I was always equal to men," and he said, "yes, but even so, you were raised differently, with different myths and a different view of the world." And I told him, "that's true". And that's how I began to work on the myths. And then, he encouraged me by saying that, in order to understand the myths, one had to understand the reality. So I had to come back to reality, all of it, physiological, historical, etc. Then afterwards, I continued on my own on women's situation as I saw it.

MS: You wrote somewhere that you never suffered from being female in your childhood.

SB: No, I never suffered.

MS: But, was not your childhood different from a boy's? When you did the research for *The Second Sex*, did that change your interpretation of your childhood?

SB: Not of my own childhood, but I interpret differently other people's childhood. I see many women whose childhood was unfavorable compared to that of a boy. But for me my childhood was not unfavorable.

MS: I remember a passage from *Memoirs of a Dutiful Daughter*. You were walking past a [boy's] high school. . . .

SB: Ah yes, near the College Stanislas. And I thought that they had a superior education, that's true. But in the end, I adapted to mine because I thought that later on I would be able to go on to higher education. But at that moment, yes, I thought that there was something there that was more intellectual than our course of study.

MS: And this was the case?

SB: Yes, it was true.

MS: In your autobiography, you wrote that there was a disagreement between you and Sartre concerning literature and philosophy, and life. He did one before the other, and you did the reverse?

SB: Yes, that's right.

MS: And somewhere you described sexuality and passion as overwhelming you when you were young. He always thought that it was a question of will, an act of will. And you thought that the body, that passion, could overwhelm. . . . That's a difference between the two of you.

SB: Yes, Sartre was much more voluntarist. But he also thought that about seasickness. He thought if you got seasick, it was because you had let it happen and with willpower, you could conquer seasickness.

MS: I thought that perhaps that might be a problem in *The Second Sex*. You used Sartre's philosophy, which is voluntarist, but you studied the body, and passion, and the training of girls. And you questioned whether there is a choice. . . .

SB: All the same, there's a choice in the Sartrean sense, that is, choices are always made in a certain situation and, starting from the same situation, one can choose this or that. One can have different choices in a single situation. That is, granted, one is a girl with a certain physical training, and a certain social training but starting from that, one can choose to accept it or to escape it or to. . . . Well, naturally, the choice itself depends upon a number of things. But after all, there is still some freedom or choice, even in resignation of course.

MS: But you didn't think that was a great problem for you, to reconcile the Sartrean philosophical foundation with your research in biology, on the body?

SB: But Sartre was not so voluntarist. In *Being and Nothingness*, there was a lot of things about the body.

MS: And in 1949, he also changed his ideas.

SB: Oh no, *Being and Nothingness*, which he wrote well before that, is full of texts about the body. The body always had a lot of importance for him.

MS: But not exactly the same importance as for you.

SB: When, in *Being and Nothingness*, he speaks of masochism as well as sadism, of love etc., the body plays a very great role for Sartre also. Yes, always.

MS: And that wasn't a problem for you?

SB: No, not at all.

MS: And you don't think he changed his ideas at that time?

SB: No.

MS: How did he react to your book *(The Second Sex)*?

SB: He read it along the way, as I was writing it, as we always read each other's work. From time to time, after reading a chapter, he would tell me that there were corrections to make, as I would sometimes tell him. So that book too, he read it as I wrote it. So he was not at all surprised by the book. He was in complete agreement with me.

MS: Not long before you wrote *The Second Sex*, he wrote *Baudelaire*, mentioning very little about Baudelaire's childhood. And afterwards, in *Saint Genet*, he wrote a lot about Genet's childhood. Perhaps your interest in childhood experience might have interested him in it as well.

SB: No, I don't think so. I think that was a development. *Baudelaire* was written very quickly and for Genet he wanted to do something more extensive. And then, Genet himself speaks a lot about his childhood and about children so it's the subject Genet which required that one speak a lot about childhood. . . .

MS: I see differences between your perspective in *The Second Sex* and Sartre's perspective in *Being and Nothingness*. You have said that in social relations one ought to look for reciprocity. That's a kind of optimism that was not in

Being and Nothingness. Do you agree? Is there a difference, at least in attitude if not in philosophy?

SB: Yes, in effect, I think that the idea of reciprocity came later for Sartre. He had it in *The Critique.* In *Being and Nothingness,* reciprocity is not his subject. But that doesn't mean that he didn't believe that reciprocity was the best way after all to live out human relationships. That *was* what he believed. It's just that it wasn't his subject in *Being and Nothingness,* because in *Being and Nothingness* he's concerned with the individual and not so much with the relations among individuals. . . .

That is, in *The Second Sex,* I place myself much more on a moral plane whereas Sartre dealt with morality later on. In fact, he never exactly dealt with morality. In *Being and Nothingness,* he's not looking for the moral, he's seeking a description of what existence is. . . . It's more an ontology than a morality.

MS: Now a final question on motherhood. You opened your discussion of motherhood in *The Second Sex* with a study of abortion and you described motherhood as something rather negative, as an inhuman activity.

SB: No, I didn't say that exactly. I said that there could be a human relation, even a completely interesting and privileged relation between mother and child but that, in many cases, it was on the order of narcissism or tyranny or something like that. But I didn't say that motherhood in itself was always something to be condemned, no, I didn't say that. No, something that has dangers, but obviously, any human adventure has its dangers, such as love or anything. I didn't say that motherhood was something negative.

MS: I thought that you said that it did not support human meaning.

SB: No, oh no, I didn't say that motherhood does not support human meaning. No, I am sure that I never said that.

MS: Is this a question that interests you now?

SB: Oh yes, of course, motherhood interests me a great deal, because one also discusses it a lot in feminist quarters. There are feminists who are mothers and, of course, just because one is for abortion—naturally, all feminists are for abortion—but that doesn't mean that there aren't some who have chosen to have children. And I find that that can be a completely valid choice, which is very dangerous today because all the responsibility falls on the shoulders of the woman, because in general it's enslaved motherhood. One of my friends has written a book called *Enslaved Motherhood* [Les Chimères, 1975]. But motherhood in itself is not something negative or something inhuman.

No, I certainly didn't write that motherhood had no human meaning. I may have said that one had to give it one or that the embryo, as long as it is not yet considered human, as long as it is not a being with human relationships with its mother or its father, it's nothing, one can eliminate the embryo. But I never said that the relation to the child was not a human relation. No, no, reread the text, I don't have it here.

Listen, I'm very happy [that you are undertaking the new translation of *The Second Sex*, and correcting mistranslation of "*la réalité humaine*" as "the real nature of man"] since the base of existentialism is precisely that there is no human nature, and thus no "feminine nature." It's not something given. There is a presence to the world, which is the presence which defines man, who is defined by his presence to the world, his consciousness and not a nature that grants him *a priori* certain characteristics. That's a gross error to have translated it in that way.

MS: "Woman-identity" is an important issue in America, now, with many feminists searching for a feminine nature.

SB: There are also women in France who do that, but I am completely against it because in the end they come back to men's mythologies, that is, that woman is a being apart, and I find that completely in error. Better that she identify herself as a human being who happens to be a woman. It's a certain situation which is not the same as men's situation of course, but she shouldn't identify herself as a woman.

MS: In America the question of woman-identity is often connected with motherhood; a woman sometimes becomes pregnant when she is insecure of her identity. Was it rather difficult for you because almost all women of your generation, all of your friends were mothers?

SB: No, in general, my friends are not mothers. Most of my friends don't have children. Of course, I have friends with children but I have many friends without children. My sister doesn't have any children; my friend Olga has no children, many, many women I know have no children. There are some who have a child and it's no big deal. They don't consider themselves mothers. They work in addition. Almost all the women I'm connected with work. Either they're actresses, or they're lawyers. They do things besides having children.

III. PARIS; SEPTEMBER 10, 1985

MS: You know that in my critical study of the Parshley translation [of *The Second Sex*], I've uncovered numerous deletions, almost a hundred pages were cut from the original French edition. This is an important issue for the study of your philosophy—for me it's a philosophy—because the translation destroys the philosophical integrity of your work. But you've told me many times that you are not a philosopher. Well, he's done a popular [non-philosophical] translation of your book. What do you think of this translation?

SB: Well, I think that it's very bad to suppress the philosophical aspect because while I say that I'm not a philosopher in the sense that I'm not the creator of a system, I'm still a philosopher in the sense that I've studied a lot of philosophy, I have a degree in philosophy, I've taught philosophy, I'm infused with philosophy, and when I put philosophy into my books it's because that's a way for me to view the world and I can't allow them to eliminate that way of viewing the world, that dimension of my approach to women, as Mr. Parshley has done. I'm altogether against the principle of gaps, omissions, condensations which have the effect, among other things of suppressing the whole philosophical aspect of the book.

MS: You accepted this translation in 1952.

SB: I accepted it to the extent that . . . you know, I had a lot of things to do, a creative work to write, and I was not going to read from beginning to end all the translations that were being done of my work. But when I found out that Mr. Parshley was omitting things, I asked him to indicate the omissions to me, and I wrote to tell him that I was absolutely against them, and since he insisted on the omissions on the pretext that otherwise the book would be too long, I asked him to say in a preface that I was against the omissions, the condensation. And I don't believe that he did that, which I begrudge him a great deal.

MS: Yes, it's awful. We've been studying this book for more than [thirty] years, a book which is very different from the book you wrote.

SB: I would like very much for an unabridged translation to be done today. An honest translation, with the philosophical dimension and with all the parts that Mr. Parshley judged pointless and which I consider to have a point, very much so. . . . From certain things that you've told me, I think that one will have to look at passages that weren't cut as well to see if there are not mistranslations, misrepresentations. For example, you tell me that he speaks of human nature whereas I have never believed—nor Sartre either, and on this point I am his disciple—we never believed in human nature. So it's a serious mistake to speak of "human nature" instead of "human reality," which is a Heideggerian term. I was infused with Heidegger's philosophy and when I speak about human reality that is, about man's presence in the world, I'm not speaking about human nature, it's completely different.

MS: Yes, exactly. These translation problems have been quite significant in feminist debate. American feminists have criticized your analysis of history and of marriage. But those discussions in *The Second Sex* contain the most extensive deletions. Parshley cut out the names of seventy-eight women from history, and almost thirty-five pages from the chapter on marriage. You did a very good study of the letters of Sophie Tolstoy and he cut almost all of it.

SB: That's too bad because really I liked that very much. It was Sophie Tolstoy's journal, not her letters. It's the journal, well the whole relationship was very strange, no, not very strange, on the contrary, one could say it was very banal, very typical of Tolstoy with his wife. At the same time, she is odious, but he even more odious. There. I'm enormously sorry that they cut out that passage. . . . I would like very much for another translation of *The Second Sex* to be done, one that is much more faithful, more complete and more faithful.

MS: I have another question. A French philosopher friend explained to me your experience at the École Normale Supérieure [the institution responsible, under the highly centralized French university system, for training the elite professoriate, as opposed to the Sorbonne, a more mass institution].

SB: I was never at the ENS. That's false.

MS: Just a year as auditor. . .?

SB: No, No, never, never.

MS: You didn't. . . .

SB: I took courses at the ENS like everyone else, I took courses there when I was preparing my *agrégation*. When you are preparing an *agrégation*, you have the right to take courses there, but I was never enrolled.

MS: But Sartre was [enrolled] there.

SB: Yes, he was a student there.

MS: And Merleau-Ponty?

SB: Yes, he as well.

MS: Were there other women who were regular students there?

SB: There were some for a year or two. There was Simone Weil, Simone Petrement, but that was after me. I was already *agrégée*, that is, I had already finished my studies, when they were at the ENS.

MS: It was a normal thing for a woman to take courses, but not to be a regular student.

SB: No, but taking courses was normal. At the time one was preparing for the *agrégation*, one could take certain courses at the ENS. That was completely normal.

MS: Was it forbidden for women to be regular students at the ENS at that time?

SB: No. Yes, it was forbidden and then it was allowed for a year or two and it was just at that moment that Simone Weil, Simone Petrement, perhaps even another woman, were regular students. All that is not very pertinent between us, that is.

MS: Was it an important exclusion for you not to. . . ?

SB: Absolutely not. I could have gone to Sèvres if I had wanted to. But I preferred to stay, not that I loved my family, but I preferred. . . . Well, it wasn't even a matter of that . . . I didn't want to live on campus anywhere. That would have bothered me a lot. No, it wasn't exclusion. Well, it was completely normal. You studied at the Sorbonne and that was it. That didn't prevent me from getting my *agrégation* at a very young age; that didn't bother me at all.

MS: I once remarked to a colleague that you describe Sartre as a philosopher, and yourself as a literary writer, and he replied: "Simone de Beauvoir said that she is a literary writer and Sartre is the philosopher? Ah, that's funny, *he* would prefer to be a literary writer". Is that true?

SB: No, it's not exactly that. He thought that among his works, he was perhaps more attached to his literary works than to his philosophical ones, because a literary work remains yours [*en soi*], and a philosophical work is always taken up and revised by posterity, it's changed and criticized, etc.

MS: When I started my studies with you, I was especially looking for an independent woman. It was very important to find a role model. And I looked for this role model in you. And I was angry that men said "The Great Sartreuse."

SB: Oh, but that, that's a joke.

MS: Yes, a joke. But a lot of people told me, "Why are you working with her? Why not the man himself? She is just a follower."

SB: My books are completely personal. Sartre never interfered. *She Came To Stay, The Mandarins,* all of that is mine. And *The Second Sex* is mine. Sartre was hardly interested at all in the education of women. . . . Feminists understand very well that feminism is me and not Sartre.

MS: I heard that in 1968 or 1970, French feminists were very unhappy with *The Woman Destroyed* because they thought that it was against women.

SB: There were critiques by certain feminists about it, but it was completely false because—well, I don't like "thesis" books, but—the story was that a woman should be independent. The heroine of *The Woman Destroyed* is completely destroyed because she lived only for her husband and children. So it's a very feminist book in a sense since it proves finally that a woman who only lives for marriage and motherhood is miserable.

MS: Now, this book is being read favorably by American feminists who see it reflecting your own experience.

SB: Well, of course, one puts part of oneself into any book, but it's not at all autobiographical.

MS: They refer to the rage, the fear of losing your sensuality or your tendency to sacrifice yourself, they found all those themes in that book in you.

SB: But I never had the idea of sacrificing myself, all of that doesn't exist. They're wrong. It's hardly autobiographical at all. When one says that it's autobiographical, it's that I put in settings that I liked, that I place the story in places, etc. But the whole story of the good wife who has sacrificed everything for her marriage and daughters, that's just the opposite. I'm completely against that, the idea of sacrificing oneself for a good husband and children. I'm completely adverse, the enemy of that idea.

MS: But you don't find that in your relation to Sartre.

SB: No, not at all . . . I never sacrificed myself for Sartre, any more than he sacrificed himself for me.

MS: Have you read the review by Michele LeDoeuff [1984] of your edited collection of Sartre's letters, *Les Lettres au Castor?*

SB: There were so many articles.

MS: LeDoeuff refers to Sartre as "the only speaking subject" in the relationship.

SB: Does that mean that I didn't give them my letters?

MS: No, it's not that. It's that Sartre really dominated the relationship.

SB: No, that's not true. He's writing to me, so, one doesn't see my own stories, one doesn't see me, my personal life in his letters. One only sees Sartre's. That's all.

MS: So it's really Sartre who is speaking.

SB: In his letters, yes. If I published my own, I would be the one speaking. But in my lifetime, I won't publish my letters.

MS: A friend, an American philsopher, once told me, "I am completely angry at this Simone de Beauvoir—"we, we, we"—she always says "we" in her autobiography. Where is *she*? She had completely disappeared".

SB: I'm the one speaking. Obviously, Sartre didn't write his autobiography [covering the period of our relationship]. If he had, he would have had to say "we" also.

MS: Yes, you begin a sentence and he finishes it, and afterwards you think together.

SB: Yes, but it's the same thing. If I begin it, he finishes it; if he begins it, I finish it, afterwards, there's a moment. . . . Yes, we were very, very close. But that's nothing contrary to feminism. Because I believe one can be close to a man and be a feminist. Obviously, there are feminists, especially lesbian feminists, who would not at all agree. But that's my own feminism.

MS: I am surprised that you don't say that you find the tendency to sacrifice yourself in your inner life. Because I think I saw it in your books.

SB: Not in my memoirs. In my memoirs, there is no tendency to self-sacrifice, whereas in my novels, I described women who perhaps had a tendency to self-sacrifice. Because I'm not speaking only about myself, I'm also speaking about other women.

MS: And yet, you have told me, "Yes, when I was very young, just before leaving for Marseilles, I had a crisis of consciousness". [This question refers to Beauvoir's experience of losing a sense of direction in her life, in the early years of her intimate relationship with Sartre, after finishing her graduate study and before beginning her first position in Marseilles.]

SB: Well, in fact, I refused to marry him after all. Thus, I remained feminist. I did not at all want to attach myself to a man by the ties of marriage. I refused marriage. I was the one who refused. Sartre proposed to me.

MS: You chose that relationship with Sartre? When one reads the memoirs, it seems that it was he who defined the relationship.

SB: No, not at all. I also chose Sartre. I was the one who chose him. I saw a lot of other men, I even saw men who later became famous, like Merleau-Ponty, like Levi-Strauss etc., etc. But I was never tempted to live with them, to make a life together. I was the one who chose Sartre, well, we chose each other.

MS: I have a question about choice. There is a theoretical tension in *The Second Sex* on the question of choice and oppression. In one chapter you wrote that women are not oppressed as a group. But in the next chapter, you wrote, "Yes, women are truly oppressed as a group." In another chapter, you questioned whether one can say that a girl raised to be the Other ever chooses to be the Other. But you also say that the woman is in complicity with her oppression. I find that there's a tension there. It remains even today in feminism, between choice and oppression.

SB: I think that on the whole women are oppressed. But at the heart of their oppression—sometimes, they choose it because it's convenient for a bourgeois woman who has a little bit of money to marry a man who has even more money than she has and who will take care of evrything so that she can do nothing. There is a complicity on the part of women. Very often, not always. They often find it easier to get married than to have a career, to work and be independent.

MS: And the women who are not rich, not at all rich, and I'm thinking about young girls who were [victims of] incest. Can one say that these women have the choice to be. . . ?

SB: No, I think that they had very little choice. But all the same, there is a way of choosing at a certain moment, as soon as they get a little older, of choosing to stay in that incest situation or of refusing and even bringing their father to court.

MS: I think that many feminists understand women as victims of an absolute patriarchy. And I find certain problems with that analysis. And you understood in *The Second Sex* that women are in complicity. But also there are women who are victims of oppression but who also seek power over their children. If a woman, for example, beats her children or burns them with a cigarette. What is she doing? She is dominating.

SB: She is getting revenge for her oppression. It's not a way of getting out of it. In the same way that making a scene in front of her husband is not a way of eliminating oppression.

MS: And the way to eliminate oppression is to. . . .

SB: To be independent. To work.

MS: Yes, especially to work. And what are you doing now in the way of work?

SB: Well, for the moment, I am working a lot on [the journal] *Les Temps Modernes*.

MS: I have heard it said that the feminist movement in France is over.

SB: That's not true, that's not true.

MS: No?

SB: Not at all. It's less loud than before, it's not out in the streets because we have a lot of support from the Ministry of the Rights of Woman. So, we are more organized, we are doing more constructive work now rather than agitation but that doesn't mean that the movement is over. Not at all. That's something that all the anti-feminists say: "It's no longer in fashion, it's no longer in fashion, it's over." But it's not true at all. It's lasting. On the contrary, there are a lot of feminist researchers. There are a lot of feminists in the CNRS [the National Center for Scientific Research]. Well, that is, research, scholarships for doing research on feminism. There is a lot of work, there are a lot of foundations to help feminist or female painters, sculptors. Oh yes, yes, there are a lot of things. It's just that it's all more or less going through the Ministry.

MS: Oh, that will change.

SB: Alas, perhaps. Because Yvette Roudy, who is the Minister of the Rights of Woman [during the early years of Mitterrand's socialist government], is altogether a dedicated feminist. So she helps us enormously, she gives a lot of money to magazines, exhibitions, research, feminist work. For foundations also. Yes, yes. So it is not at all true that the movement is over.

REFERENCES

Beauvoir, Simone de. 1960. *La Force de l'âge*. Paris: Gallimard. My translation.
———. 1974. *Memoirs of a Dutiful Daughter*. New York: Harper & Row, [1958].
Les Chimères. 1975. *Maternité esclave*. Paris: UGE 10/18.
Le Doeuff, Michèle. 1984. Sartre; l'unique sujet parlant. *Esprit—changer la culture et la politique*, 5: 181-191.

Introduction to Kofman's "Rousseau's Phallocratic Ends"

NANCY J. HOLLAND

Sarah Kofman came to Berkeley at a point in my graduate career when I was much in need of role models, and it might provide something of an introduction if I can accurately represent the effect her lectures had on me then. A small, intense woman, she would quietly enter the lecture hall or classroom, wait for the hour to begin, and then explode into an almost overwhelming barrage of rapid-fire French. As she deconstructed both Freud and Nietzsche, she used all those words that I still found so hard to say: "phallus", "penis", "vagina". Listening to her, it became easier to see myself using those words and those methods. In short, Sarah Kofman played a significant role in my becoming comfortable as a woman who did deconstruction.

Part of the problem of introducing Kofman's work to an American audience, however, is exactly how to introduce deconstruction itself, since in this country it is most often seen as a form of literary theory. This perception is understandable insofar as deconstruction is often presented as a way of "reading" texts, not as a way of determining their "truth". When the text that is "read" is Plato, Aristotle, or Kant, however, one calls the reading "literary", and hence irrelevant to the "truth" of the text, only at considerable risk.

Kofman's choice of Rousseau as a subject in the paper that follows only complicates this problem. Since Rousseau is most often considered a minor philosopher or literary figure in the United States, Kofman's argument assumes a familiarity with Rousseau that many American readers may lack. This makes it difficult to evaluate her "reading" of his work, especially since the links between her conclusions and the text are occasionally somewhat obscure. Furthermore, given what we do know about Rousseau and what Kofman has to say about him, one obvious question is why a feminist philosopher would want to "read" Rousseau at all. Kofman tells us why she does: she is interested in supporting a thesis about how references to nature function in various phallocratic (that is, patriarchal) texts to rationalize and naturalize the subordination of women. That this process of rationalization can be shown to rely on very irrational logical "phallacies" provides an excellent example of the use of deconstructive method in the feminist "reading" of a text.

Hypatia vol. 3, no. 3 (Winter 1989) © by Nancy J. Holland

Kofman's "reading" of Rousseau illustrates at least three common techniques of deconstruction which are closely related to Freud's method of psychoanalytic interpretation. First, there is her allusion to "cauldron logic." The expression comes from Freud's work on dreams, although he himself uses this form of "logic" as often as anyone. The cauldron story involves a borrowed cauldron that is returned with holes in it. Asked about the holes, the borrower says: (1) "The holes were in it when I borrowed it"; (2) "There are no holes in the cauldron"; and (3) "I never borrowed your cauldron." This form of "protesting too much" frequently appears when a phallocratic text is confronted with its own internal inconsistencies: as in the psychoanalytic interpretation of a dream, the logical "holes" are denied in a multitude of mutually contradictory ways.

Kofman exposes another form of patriarchal denial in what she calls "sophisms," that is, question-begging arguments that are persuasive because the (male) audience wants to believe them true. One obvious case of this can be found almost every time (patriarchal) metaphysics has proven that the sexes must be separated and one sex secluded to create the restricted sexual economy (scarcity of pleasure) required by our culture. There is never any argument to show why it is *women* who must be cloistered, but simply the claim that someone must be, and surely is cannot be the men. Kofman makes this point with regard to Rousseau in the following essay; elsewhere she makes it with regard to Kant (1982) and Freud (1985) as well.

Kofman also makes use of a third form of argument which should be familiar from John Stuart Mill and Harriet Taylor's *The Subjection of Women*: if the subordination and inferiority of women (or the aversion to incest or to homosexuality, to take two other frequently cited cases) is "natural," then why does (phallocratic) metaphysics insist that people must be *made to* act in the way that it is "natural" for them to act? Why do these treatises always become *prescriptive* as well as descriptive? Kofman finds this slide from the postulation of a natural "feminine reserve" to women's "confinement on a reservation" in Freud, Kant, and others, as well as in Rousseau. The possibility of "reading" such a large range of thinkers as exemplifying this fairly obvious logical "phallacy" (as well as the others mentioned above) is taken by feminist deconstruction to be the sign of a shared denial that marks a deep anxiety in phallocratic metaphysics.

Having situated Kofman's work in the context of deconstruction, it remains necessary to situate it in the context of feminist thought as well. While the success of her paper on Rousseau in exposing at least one facet of the ideology that oppresses women will be clear to all who read it, its relationship to feminism is harder to characterize. One way to approach this problem might be through Kofman's curious comment that Rousseau's compensatory overvaluation of women, his turning women into goddesses, makes his phallocratism a sort of "feminism." Since she makes similar remarks about Kant (1982) and Hegel (1981), it is important to know exactly what kind of "feminism" she has in mind here.

The most obvious meaning of the kind of "feminism" that Kofman attributes to Rousseau derives from the fact that deconstruction rejects any putative "overcoming" of metaphysics that would consist in a simple reversal of a metaphysical hierarchy. This is because a reversal would only produce a new hierarchy and a new version of (phallocratic) metaphysics. Kofman, therefore, is wary of an "essentialist" feminism that would reproduce the phallocratic overvaluation of women, and, so, remain part of the same patriarchal text. Women will have made no advance if their "feminism" follows Rousseau (or Kant or Hegel) in merely changing which side of the goddess/whore duality is to be emphasized in the essential cultural definition of femininity.

At the same time, in her recently translated book on Freud (1985), Kofman also takes issue with a kind of feminism that would simply reject the work of Freud, and of other phallocratic thinkers, without any regard for the use that feminist thought might make of their insights in deconstructing the metaphysical tradition itself. She notes that Freud, like other phallocratic writers, forces women to play the role either of accomplices of the Freudian *logos*, the word of the Father, or of criminals, outside the law created by the Father's word. Kofman rejects the view, which she attributes to Luce Irigaray, that the best response to this dilemma is to accept the role of criminal. Instead, she denies that there are only two options. Kofman points out that we can choose a third course, namely, to use the deconstructive character of Freud's work for our own feminist purposes. Thus, she develops what is really a psychoanalysis of Freud's work on women. Turning one side of Freud against the other, she implies, allows her more independence from the Freudian text than does a simple rebellion against it.

What will American feminists make of Kofman's work? Many of us share her deconstructive reservations about a feminist critique that tries to reject phallocratic metaphysics by appealing to a counter "truth" defined in traditional philosophical terms. Many of us also share her distaste for a new feminist "essentialism," which, in establishing, say, a mother goddess, merely reverses the traditional metaphysical hierarchies, or worse yet, leaves us, barefoot and pregnant again, on Rousseau's pedestal. Beyond that, however, many of us are ambivalent about our relationship to male discourse. Should we continue to teach and use, even if critically, the texts of Plato, Aristotle, Descartes, and Kant, not to mention Nietzsche and Freud? Or should we reject them entirely because of their phallocratic bias? Kofman's deconstruction of Rousseau gives American readers an opportunity to evaluate the usefulness of her strategy of turning phallocratic discourse against itself. It suggests that, in simply rejecting such discourses, we may deprive ourselves of useful methods for doing what we, as feminists and as philosophers, want and need to do.

REFERENCES

Kofman, Sarah. 1981. "Ça cloche" in *Les fins de l'homme: A partir du travail de Jacques Derrida*. (89-112). Paris: Galilée.
——. 1982. "The Economy of respect: Kant and respect for women". Trans. Nicola Fisher, *Social Research*. 49:2. (383-404). (This is an excerpt from *Le Respect des femmes*. 1982. Paris: Galilée.)
——. 1985. *The Enigma of woman*. Trans. Catherine Porter. Ithaca: Cornell University Press.

Rousseau's Phallocratic Ends

SARAH KOFMAN
Translated by MARA DUKATS

Kofman traces Rousseau's argument that women's role as mothers requires the subordination of women to men, and the companion argument that women's lust is a threat to the (male) social order, which also justifies the confinement of women within the home. She then relates the claim that women so confined exert a power of their own to Rousseau's erotic obsession with dominant, but maternal, women. Thus, the "Nature" to which Rousseau appeals is seen to be both a reflection of his own specific nature and representative of all phallocratic discourse in its defense of male domination.

Everybody knows it: Rousseau is very free in calling on Nature, on good Mother Nature. It's always in Her name that he couches his claims. Just as he identifies with his mother who died bringing him into the world;[1] and just as he attempts to supplant that one indispensable woman,[2] to bring her back to life by himself becoming woman and mother;[3] so in the same way he tries to speak in the place of Nature, the mother of us all, the Nature who is not dead even though her cries have been muffled by the philosophy fashionable in the cities, that is, by an artificial and falsifying culture.[4] It appears that Rousseau alone, in this depraved century, has understood her voice, and has rushed to the rescue in order to protect her from the fashionable philosophers, who have joined forces with those citified and denatured women, women in name only, for they have become dolls and puppets, and have decked themselves out as a bastard sex. They are no longer women since they deny their one and only natural destiny: childbearing. Therefore, it is necessary to resuscitate and disseminate nature's suppressed voice, reminding these "women" of their one and only duty: motherhood. "Women have ceased to be mothers; they no longer will be mothers; they no longer want to be mothers."[5] The family and the whole moral order of society depend on this duty. "As soon as women become mothers again men will quickly become fathers and husbands" (*Emile*, p. 48). This single but fundamental duty thus has multiple implications. Rousseau claims to deduce from it the entire temperament, the entire physical and moral constitution of women, as well as an entire educational program. For, in order to conform to nature, the education of women would have to differ radically from that of men.

Hypatia vol. 3, no. 3 (Fall 1988) © by Sarah Kofman

Thus, natural teleology alone would legitimate all the inequalities of development, all the dissymmetries attributed to sexual difference. However, insofar as these dissymmetries favor the masculine sex, as they always do, we might wonder if good Mother Nature doesn't serve as a mere pretext here, if the ends of Nature don't in fact dissimulate the ends of man (*vir*), rationalizing his injustices and violences.

Several of Rousseau's texts come close to acknowledging this. In the "Entretien sur les romans" ("Reflections on the Novel"), which precedes the second edition of *La Nouvelle Héloïse* (The New Héloïse), he writes: "Let us give women their due: the cause of their disorder is less in themselves than in our faulty institutions." In "Sur les femmes" ("On Women"), his unfinished essay on the "Evénements importants dont les femmes ont été la cause secrète" ("Important events of which women were the secret cause"), Rousseau accuses men of having prevented women from governing and thereby, from doing everything that they could have done in politics, morals and literature. In all areas of life, the law of the strongest has enabled men to exercise a veritable tyranny over women, preventing them from evincing their true virtues.

> Relatively speaking, women would have been able to present more and better examples of noble-mindedness and love of virtue than men, had our injustice not deprived them of their liberty, and of the opportunity to manifest these qualities to the world . . . [I]f women had had as large a share as we've had in handling affairs and governing empires, they might have carried heroism and courage to greater heights and more of them might have distinguished themselves in this regard.[6]

Rousseau's story "La Reine fantasque" ("The Capricious Queen") shows, in a comic vein, how men always exclude women from power. They prefer the stupidest man, even an animal, "a monkey or a wolf," to the wisest woman, since they think women should always be subject to men's will.

It is probably not just a coincidence that such writings remained unfinished, are considered "minor" and are usually ignored. Rousseau usually adopts a very different language, a language of Nature which partakes of the most traditional phallocratic discourse.[7] This is especially the case in *Lettre à d'Alembert* and *Emile*, where he is "hardest" on women, as opposed to *La Nouvelle Héloïse* where he adopts a more conciliatory tone.[8] Thus, at the very moment when he claims to speak in the name of Nature, to oppose the "philosophers" and their prejudices, he can only repeat the most hackneyed and symptomatically masculinist philosophical discourse. For example, that of Aristotle, who also claimed, of course, to write neutrally and objectively and to found an intellectual, moral and political hierarchy on a natural ontological hierarchy. At the top of this hierarchy is divinity, followed by the philosopher and men in general. As for woman, she ranks below the child of the masculine sex, for whereas he is male in potentiality, if not yet in actuality, she remains branded throughout her entire life with an "indelible inferiority" because of her sex. She is and always will be a "mutilated male," even a "monster," a flaw of nature, a male manqué.

Rousseau repeats the discourse of Aristotle as well as that of the Bible, which, although it stems from another tradition, is no less phallocentric.

So, in Book V of *Emile*, he purports to provide a rational deduction of the temperament, constitution, duties and education of women. A sophistic argument, actually, in which the pseudo-voice of Nature becomes the vehicle for the expression of Rousseau's prejudices. It is significant that the question of women and their education is not approached until Book V. In the dramatic fiction of *Emile*, women are granted only one act of the play, the last one. This gesture is emblematic of the subordination of woman—the weak sex, the second sex—to the strong sex—the sole referent and prototype for humanity. It reenacts the gesture of divine creation in which the first woman is made from the rib of the first man, in which she is derived from him and is created *for* him.

> It is not good for man to be alone; I shall make for him a companion similar to him [*Genesis* II,8]. It is not good that man be alone. Emile is a man; we promised him a companion; now we must give her to him [*Emile*, p. 465].

As a pedagogical novel, *Emile* sets out to re-create women so as to perfect and improve upon divine creation. An appropriate education, one in conformity with nature, should beget the sort of woman who can now only be found in some mythical natural preserve, untouched by civilization—a wise and perfect woman, Sophie, a woman who knows how to stay within the limits Nature has assigned to her, in the place befitting her sex, subordinate to man, the one and only king of creation. Rousseau takes Sophie, not Eve or Lilith, as this model woman. Certainly not those corrupt and seductive Parisian women who are the source of all of men's woes, those women who have failed to respect the natural hierarchy between the sexes, who have abandoned their place and their reserve, who have aspired to Knowledge, and who have not hesitated to show themselves in public and to mix with the other sex. According to Rousseau, all disorders, abuses and perversions originate in the "scandalous confusion" of the sexes.

Thus, Rousseau, in his divine magnanimity, gives Emile a companion and a helpmeet "made for him" but not "similar to him." No, she must certainly not be "similar to him," and it will be up to education to see to that, on pain of the direst disasters. For if it is true that "in everything not having to do with sex, the woman is a man," and that she contains within herself a divine model just like he does, it is no less true that "in everything that does have to do with sex, . . . man and woman always have both similarities and dissimi-larities" [Emile, p. 465-66]. Thus, if it is to fulfill its natural destiny in the physical and moral order, each sex must be subject to its own sex-specific model. "A perfect man and a perfect woman must no more resemble each other in mind than in face, and there is no such thing as being more or less perfect" [Emile, p. 466].

Although in Genesis, woman's name (icha) derives from that of man (ich), Rousseau is careful not to derive the name of the perfect woman from that of the perfect man. Her name is not Emilie, but Sophie. In his overt discourse, he never claims to establish any derivation or hierarchy, only differences. Neither sex is to be superior to the other, nor even comparable to the other. Each is to be perfect of its own kind, incomparable to the other insofar as they differ, equal to the other insofar as they are similar. If each remained in the place nature assigned to it, perfect harmony and happiness would reign, just like at Clarens. The two sexes would then be like a single person:

> Woman would be the eye and man the arm. They would be so dependent on one another that woman would learn from man what should be seen and man would learn from woman what must be done. . . . Each would follow the impetus of the other; each would obey and both would be masters [Emile, p. 492].

Although, shades of Aristotle, the temperaments, tastes, inclinations, tasks and duties of the two sexes vary as a function of their respective natural destinies, they nonetheless "participate in a common happiness" albeit by different routes [Emile, p. 466]. "This division of labor and of responsibilities is the strongest aspect of their union."[9]

"Common happiness," he says. Yet this alleged equality surely conceals a profound hierarchical inequality, a profound unhappiness which can only be interpreted as happiness if one postulates that women enjoy subordination, subjection and docility. And in fact, Rousseau does not recoil from asserting this. Following Aristotle, he contends that women are made to obey. "Since dependence is women's natural condition, girls feel they are made to obey" [Emile, p. 482].

The rigid segregation of sexes and the sexual division of labor result in the extensive confinement of women. In the name of their natural destiny, they are condemned to a sedentary and reclusive life in the shadows of domestic enclosure. There they are excluded from knowledge and public life. The lat-ter are reserved for men who are destined for the active life, life in the open air and in the sun. Thus Rousseau, as early as Book I of Emile, deems that, if a man were to engage in "a typical stay-at-home and sedentary occupation" like sewing or some other "needle trade," he would be reduced to a cripple or a eunuch because these occupations "feminize and weaken the body." They "dishonor the masculine sex" for "the needle and the sword cannot be wielded by the same hands." (Moreover, in Book V, Hercules, forced to spin near Omphale, is deemed, despite his strength, to be dominated by a woman.)

How, then, does Rousseau justify the domestic lot of women and their confinement? He claims to ground these in the feminine temperament as he deduced it, in the most natural way, in the beginning of Book V:

> In the union of the sexes, each contributes equally to the common goal, but not in the same manner. From this diversity comes the first major difference between our moral relation to the one and to the other. One should be active and strong, the other passive and weak. It follows that the one should be willing and able; that the other should not resist too much [*Emile*, p. 466].

And it seems obvious that it is the woman who must be passive and weak and not the reverse. So obvious, in fact, that only the authority of Aristotle can guarantee it. "Once this principle is established,"—but is it?—it would follow naturally that woman's specific function is to please man and to be subjugated. From that, in turn, it would follow that woman should "resist" his advances in order to be agreeable to man and to arouse his strength. Man, however, turns out not to be that strong since an elaborate feminine strategy is required to actualize his potentiality, to awaken the flames of a rather feeble fire.

Hence the audacity of the masculine sex and the timidity of the other sex, "the modesty and the shame with which Nature armed the weak in order to subjugate the strong" [*Emile*, p. 467].

Timidity, modesty, decency, or again, reserve and a sense of shame (*pudeur*). These are the natural virtues, the cardinal virtues, of women. This premise is essential to Rousseau's argument. From it he infers—not without a certain slippage—the necessity of confining women. From their pseudo-natural reserve he deduces their forcible relocation to a reservation.

Here, a sense of shame is cast as a brake given to the feminine sex in order to make up for the animal instinct it lacks, an instinct which naturally moderates animals' sexual avidity. Once "the cargo is loaded" and "the hold is full," female animals reject their mates. Human women, by contrast, can never get enough, and if it were not for this sense of shame, they would pursue these poor men to their deaths. For although men are held to be the strong and active sex, they have no real sexual need; whereas women, supposedly the weak and passive sex, have a lust which knows no bounds.[10]

> Given the facility women have for exciting men's senses and
> for awakening, deep in their hearts, the remnants of a most

feeble disposition, if there existed some unfortunate climate on earth where philosophy might have introduced a practice [whereby women initiate aggression], especially in hot climates where more women than men are born, men would be women's victims, tyrannized by them, and they would all end up dragged to their death without any means of defense. [*Emile*, 467]

Nature would thus have granted women a supplement of shame not so much to compensate for their weakness as to compel man to "find his strength and use it," that is, in order to give him the illusion that he is the strongest. The point is not so much to prevent the downfall of both sexes and to save the human race, although without this feminine reserve the species would "perish by the means established to preserve it" [*Emile*, 467]. It is rather, above all, to save the male sex. This whole economy of shame is aimed at sparing the male some loss or narcissistic wound.

If it were indeed "Nature" that had "given" women a sense of shame, then the generosity of Nature would be entirely at the service of man. But is this sense of shame really a gift of Nature? Doesn't Nature's generosity rather serve as a pretext and a cover for the phallocratic aim of Rousseau's discourse? The demonstration of the natural character of shame, whether in *Emile* or in *Lettre à d'Alembert*, is highly shaky. In vain does Rousseau multiply his arguments and respond to the *philosophes'* objections; he remains caught in a web of sophisms. Thus, in *Lettre à d'Alembert*, he tries to show that, contrary to the fashionable opinion of the *philosophes*, shame is not a prejudice but a natural virtue. Natural because necessary to the sexual economy of the two sexes! Necessary to preserve feminine charm so that man can be sexually aroused without ever being fully satisfied. The sense of shame, then, would be the natural veil that introduces a beneficial distance into the economy. It would be the shared safeguard that Nature provided for the sake of both sexes in order that they not be subject to indiscriminate advances when in a "state of weakness and self-forgetfulness." It would be the sense of shame that hides the pleasures of love from the eyes of others, just as the shade of night conceals and protects sexual relationships.

But why, if it is a matter of a shared safeguard, is it woman who must have a sense of shame? Why, if it is a matter of natural virtue, is there a difference between human and animal behavior?

Pushed into a corner, Rousseau responds to the first objection with a true *petitio principii*: only Nature, the Maker of the human race, could answer this, since it is She who has endowed woman, and only woman, with this sentiment. Then, taking the place of Nature, identifying himself with Her, as always, Rousseau tries to supply the natural reasons for this difference: both sexes have equal desires, but they don't have equal means to satisfy these. If the order of advance and defense were changed, then chance would rule. Love would no longer be the support of Nature, but its destroyer and its bane.

Equal liberty of the two sexes, by overcoming every obstacle, would suppress amorous desire.

Finally, and above all, shame is reserved for woman because the consequences are not the same for the two sexes: "A child must have *one* father."

Because women's proper destiny is to bear children (even if they don't always do so), because the lot of women is motherhood, Nature and manners must provide for this by general laws such as that of shame. In *Emile* it is this same "lot" of women which justifies the view that the duty of conjugal fidelity, and that of a reputation for fidelity, fall upon women only. It is on women that Nature has conferred exclusive responsibility for protecting natural family ties; it is to women that Nature has confided the sacred trust of children: "when a woman gives a man children who are not his own, she betrays both of them, she combines perfidy with infidelity." All "disorders" and "crimes" are linked with this one. Thus, a woman must be "modest, attentive and reserved"; she must display to the eyes of the world the "evidence of her virtue" so that children can esteem and respect their mothers. "Honor and reputation are no less necessary than chastity."[11]

It is indeed Nature, then, who intended to adorn women with the veil of shame and it is a crime to stifle Her voice. Once this constraint is removed, women will cease to have any reticence whatever. Woman can't attach any importance to honor, she can't respect anything anymore, if she doesn't respect her own honor.[12] Just look, says *Emile*, at Ninon de Lenclos!

Experience would confirm this reasoning: the closer women are to their natural state, the more susceptible they are to shame. Don't think that the nakedness of savage women disproves this, for it is not the sign of an absence of shame. On the contrary, it is clothing that arouses the senses by exciting the imagination. As pointed out in *Emile*, nakedness, that of children, for example, is always a sign of innocence. Lacedaemonian maidens used to dance naked: this is a scandal only for depraved modern man.

> Do we really believe that the skillful finery of our women is less dangerous than an absolute nakedness which, if habitual, would soon turn first impressions into indifference, maybe even into disgust! Don't we know that statues and paintings offend our eyes only when the combination of clothes renders nakedness obscene? The greatest ravages occur when imagination steps in.[13]

Do not assume, however, that Rousseau condemns clothing and finery. On the contrary, they are necessary in order that woman preserve her charm, that she continue to excite man's imagination. In this sense, "clothing" is part of sexual strategy. It is in the service of shame and its ends. The taste for finery, ornament, mirrors and jewels is part of feminine nature. A girl "has more hunger for finery than for food" [*Emile*, p. 479].

In this argument, aimed at demonstrating the natural character of shame, clothing has a complex function and plays a strategic rôle. Rousseau still has to justify the difference between human and animal behavior with respect to shame. At this point, he resorts to a true "cauldron argument."[14]

On the one hand, man is precisely not an ordinary animal like any other; he alone is capable of conceiving of honesty and of beauty. On the other hand, animals are more susceptible to shame than one would think, even though they too, like children, are naked. . . . In any case, even if we grant to d'Alembert and the other *philosophes* that shame is not a natural sentiment but, rather, a conventional virtue, the same essential consequence remains: women ought to cultivate the virtues of shame and timidity. Their lot is to lead a secluded domestic life, a life hidden in a cloister-like retreat. Woman should not be showy nor should she put herself on show. Her home is her ornament; she is its soul. Her place is not in public. For her to appear there is to usurp man's place and to debase him, to degrade both her sex and his.

If you object that Rousseau imprisons women in the home, that he demands from them an excessive reserve, he will respond like Lucrèce to Pauline:

> Do you call the sweetness of a peaceful life in the bosom of one's family a prison? As for me, my happiness needs no other society, my glory needs no other esteem, than that of my husband, my father and my children.[15]

It's no coincidence that, when Rousseau does concede that shame might be a cultural prejudice, there is a slide in his logic. He slides from an insistence on women's reticence to a demand for female seclusion, from feminine reserve to the confinement of the feminine on a reservation. In this slippage Rousseau repeats a familiar social operation of masculine domination. Under the pretext of giving back Nature her suppressed voice and of defending Nature's ends, what is really being advocated, as always, are the phallocratic ends of man. It is the voice of man (*vir*)—stifled by women, those wicked and degenerate women—that Rousseau restores.

These maxims, these natural or conventional maxims which demand the isolation and domestic confinement of women, would be doubly confirmed by experience: wherever women are free, low morals are rampant; conversely, wherever morals are regulated, women are confined and separated from men. This separation of the sexes is necessary for their pleasure and their union. Indeed, there is no union without separation. Every communication, every commerce between the sexes is indiscreet, every familiarity is suspect, every liaison dangerous! Thus, it is in order to insure a lasting bond between them that Emile is separated from Sophie. Thus, the "admirable" order maintained by Julie at Clarens is based on the separation of the sexes. In this well-run domestic economy, there is little commerce between men and women. They live apart from one another like men and women everywhere, be they civilized or savage. The very universality of this practice proves its conformity to nature.

> Even among savages, men and women are never seen indiscriminately mixed. In the evening the family gathers, every man spends the night with his woman; the separation resumes with the light of day and the two sexes have nothing but meals, at the most, in common.[16]

Lettre à d'Alembert privileges the people of Antiquity (for they are the closest to nature): Rome and Sparta would be the best models of this admirable domestic economy where, when men and women do see each other, "it is very briefly and almost secretly."[17]

Thus, nothing justifies the natural character of shame, the slippage from feminine reserve to the confinement of the feminine on a reservation, and the strict segregation of the sexes, unless it is Rousseau's phallocratic aim. But isn't the latter itself based on Rousseau's libidinal economy, on a certain paranoiac structure? Isn't it based on his desire to be confused with women, and at the same time, on his fear of being contaminated by women, the very women to whom he feels himself so very close? Isn't it this very proximity which compels him to erect barriers, to emphasize the differences and the separations? Consider the passage in *Lettre à d'Alembert* where, for once, Rousseau declares that if women are brave enough they should, like Spartan women, imitate the masculine model. This passage is symptomatic of his desire/fear of becoming woman. It shows that this whole discourse is motivated by that desire/fear. Now we see what is really at stake in the segregation of sexes: the point is not so much to avoid the general confusion of the sexes; it is rather to avoid the contamination of the masculine by the feminine and a general effeminization.

> Among barbaric peoples, men did not live like women because women had the courage to live like men. In Sparta, women became robust and man was not enervated. . . . Unable to make themselves men, women make us women, [a frightening perversion, degradation, and denaturation] especially in a Republic where men are needed.

The thesis that Rousseau defends is always already anticipated by his libidinal drives; the voice of Nature is equally the echo of *his* nature. That the singularity of his nature resonates with the universality of traditional philosophic discourse is not an objection to, but rather a proof of, the complicity or, as Freud would say, the secret kinship between philosophic Reason and "paranoiac" madness.[18] On this subject, we must proceed with caution. Let's restrict ourselves here to emphasizing the "kinship" between the apparently non-biographical texts and the *Confessions* or the *Dialogues*.

The "theoretical" insistence on virile mobility and activity is inseparable from Rousseau's fantasies of being suffocated, paralyzed, and imprisoned in the maternal womb. We can read this fantasy when Rousseau describes the doll-woman, the Parisienne, who illegitimately reverses the relation of domination. "[F]ragility, sweetness of voice and delicate features were not given to her in order that she may be offensive, insulting, or disfigure herself with anger."[19] Thus, when she assumes the right to command, woman fails to heed the voice of the master; seeking to usurp his rights, she unleashes disorder, misery, scandal, and dishonor. Far from guaranteeing his freedom, the new empire of women enslaves, deforms, and emasculates man. Henceforth, woman confines him in chains in the darkness of her enclosure. Instead of being a mother, of *bringing him into the world*, into the light of day, she tries to keep him in her cave, to put him back into her womb, to *suffocate* him by denying him air and mobility.

Terms like these abound in *Lettre à d'Alembert*, *Emile*, and *La Nouvelle Héloïse*. So "unnatural" and perverse is this stifling and paralyzing "feminine" operation that, even as it feminizes man, it cannot obliterate every "vestige" of his real nature and destiny. His virility reasserts itself in his desire for mobility, in the involuntary agitation and anxiety he experiences whenever woman, by nature sedentary and indolent, reclines tranquilly on a chaise lounge, suffocating him behind the closed doors of some over-stuffed parlor. This, as Rousseau describes in *Lettre à d'Alembert*, is especially true in Paris, where women harbor in their rooms a true seraglio of men (more feminine than masculine) whose automatic instinct struggles incessantly against the bondage they find themselves in and drives them, despite themselves, to the active and painstaking life that nature imposes upon them.

Likewise in the theaters of Paris,

> men stand in the orchestra stalls as if wanting to relax after having spent the whole day in a sitting room. Finally, overwhelmed by the ennui of this effeminate and sedentary idleness, and in order to temper their disgust, to involve themselves in at least some sort of activity, they give their places to strangers and go looking for the women of other men.[20]

However, these vestiges of man's former nature are laughable. They express only a half-hearted desire to reclaim his nature. They don't prevent him from dribbling away his strength in the idle and lax life of a sex-junkie, nor from keeping to the "abode and repose of women," where he is enervated and loses his vigor.

Such passages from *Lettre à d'Alembert*, *Emile*, or *La Nouvelle Héloïse*, which depict the sadistic spectacle of the male paralyzed, suffocated, and imprisoned, call to mind certain passages of the *Confessions*. How can one not think, for example, of the passage where Jean-Jacques states that for him to remain seated in a room, arms crossed, inactive, chatting with others, "moving only his tongue," is an "unbearable torture"?[21] How, in general, can one fail to recall Rousseau's claustrophobia, his taste for the outdoor life, his hikes, his disgust at traveling in a poste chaise, which he likens to a small, locked cage where one is bound and blinded, an obscure prison which no free man could tolerate?

> One does not acquire a taste for prison by virtue of residing in one. . . . Active life, manual work, exercise, and movement have become so necessary that man couldn't give them up without suffering. To suddenly reduce him to an indolent and sedentary life would be to imprison him, to put him in chains, to keep him in a violent and constrained state. No doubt his disposition and health would be equally altered. He can scarcely breathe in a stuffy room. He needs the open air, movement, and fatigue . . . ; he is disturbed and agitated; he seems to be struggling; he stays because he is in chains. [*Emile*, 567-68]

These are the words of Emile's private tutor. But they betray all the fantasies of Jean-Jacques as endlessly repeated in the *Dialogues*: his fear, his horror of the dark, the belief that his persecutors have surrounded him with a "triple enclosure of darkness," entombed him behind impenetrable walls of darkness; his fantasy of being weighed down with chains, of being unable to say a word, take a step, move a finger without the knowledge and permission of his enemies; of being enclosed in an immense labyrinth where tortuous and subterranean false paths lead him further and further astray; and finally, the fantasy of being buried alive. All of these persecution fantasies express not only horror but also desire: the desire "to be beaten." Caught in the grip of his persecutors, he barely tries to escape. Surrounded by falsity and darkness, he waits, without a murmur of protest, for truth and light. Finally, buried alive in a coffin, he lies still, not even thinking of death. Is this the tranquility of innocence? Or the tranquility of masochistic pleasure at being punished, immobilized, possessed like a woman and by women, the pleasure of being suffocated and humiliated by women, of being made into their thing, their property?

In the *Confessions*, we learn that the episode with Mlle Lambercier determined the shape of the remainder of Jean-Jacques' love life. Her severity was for him a thousand times sweeter than her favors would ever have been. She treated him "as a thing that belonged to her," possessing him as one possesses private property. Their encounter becomes a prototype: to kneel before an imperious mistress, obeying her orders, begging her forgiveness—these always remain very sweet pleasures for him. Mlle Goton, who deigns to act the school mistress, showers him with joy. On his knees before Mme Basile, silent and still, afraid to do or say anything, Jean-Jacques finds this state ludicrous but delightful. "Nothing I ever experienced in possessing a woman could rival the two minutes I spent at her feet without even daring to touch her dress."[22] It's the same with Sophie d'Houdetot who, for six months, floods his heart with a delight he defies any mere sensualist to match. "Am I not your possession? Have you not taken possession?" he writes to her.[23]

Now, all of these captivating women, these castrating women, are also maternal figures, figures of and substitutes for the mother who died bringing him into the light of day. It is perhaps in order to still the reproaches for this death "which cannot be atoned," that Rousseau effects an inversion. Man will no longer be the cause of the death of women or mothers. Rather, women will be responsible for the death of man. By refusing motherhood, refusing to put themselves entirely at his service, to be filled with pity and tenderness for him, women will be responsible for his degeneration, perversion, emasculation, and depropriation. This masterful inversion displaces all aggression onto the "dolls." At the same time, it preserves, or rather constructs and internalizes, the image, intact and pure, of an idealized and divine Mother, a Mother who could only be the best of mothers—even if she nearly suffocated him in her womb, causing him to be born "disabled and sickly."

Thus, there is a split between two mother figures—the whore and the Virgin—between public women unafraid to trespass the domestic enclosure (the comediennes, the Dolls, the prostitutes, the Parisiennes, all "public women" in Rousseau's eyes) and the women who live within the shadow of the enclosure, the respectable Mothers, surrounded by their husbands and children (can there be a more pleasing sight?). This split suggests that the phallocraticism of Rousseau is also, as always, a *feminism*.[24]

The sense of shame, whose corollary is the enclosure of women, is in effect responsible for the "natural" inversion of domination: through it, the strongest become dependent on the weakest, the weakest truly rule over the strongest. The respectable woman, reserved and chaste, the woman who knows her place, incites a love which verges on enthusiasm, on sublime transports of emotion. Admittedly, she does not govern, but she reigns. She is a queen, an idol, a goddess. With a simple sign or word she sends men to the ends of the world, off to combat and to glory, here, there, wherever she pleases. A note in *Emile* cites the case of a woman who, during the reign of François I, imposed a vow of strict silence upon her garrulous lover. For two-and-a-half years he kept it faithfully.

> One thought that he had become mute through illness. She
> cured him with a single word: speak! Isn't there something
> grand and heroic in such love? Doesn't one imagine a divinity

giving the organ of speech to a mortal with a single word?
[*Emile*, p. 515].

The empire of women—these women, the "true" women, the respectable mothers— is not feared by men because it doesn't debase them. On the contrary, it enables them to fulfill their duties, to prove their heroism and their virility. For men, there is "no sweeter" or more respected "empire." If only women really wanted to be women and mothers, their uncontested power would be immense. Mothers, "be all that you should be and you will overcome all obstacles."[25]

Women are thus wrong to demand equal rights and the same education as men. If they aspire to become men, they can only fail. They would surely be inferior men and in the bargain they would lose the essential thing—the empire in which they naturally reign.

Obviously, this reign is conditional upon women's natural qualities, their submission, docility, and gentleness. It is given to them on the condition that, from childhood on, they be schooled in constraints and permanent discomforts, since their "natural state" is to be dependent, to be subjected to man and at the service of man.

Since men are, from the beginning, dependent on women, the education of women must be relative to men. Here in a nutshell is the sophism.

> The formation of children depends on the formation of mothers, the first education of men depends on the care of women; the manners, passions, tastes, pleasures and even happiness of men depends on women. Thus the entire education of women must be relative to men. To please men, to be useful to them, to be loved and honored by them, to raise them when they are young, care for them when they are grown-up, to console them, to make their lives agreeable and gentle—these are the duties of women in all times and this is what they must be taught from childhood. Unless we return to this principle, we will stray from the goal, and all of the precepts we give to women will serve neither their happiness nor our own. [*Emile*, 475]

No confession could be clearer: he who claims always to "follow the directions of Nature," is really following the best of guides. In fulfilling his own "nature" to the maximum, he serves the interests and ends of man (*vir*).

NOTES

1. "I was born disabled and sickly; I cost my mother her life, and my birth was the first of my misfortunes." *Confessions*, éd. Livre de Poche, t. I, p. 8. This and all other translations of Rousseau are my own—M.D.

2. On the death of Julie's mother he writes in La Nouvelle Héloïse, Part III, Letter VI: "a loss which cannot be restored and for which one never finds consolation once one has been able to reproach oneself for it." And in Emile, Book I: "Maternal solicitude cannot be supplied."

3. See S. Kofman, Le Respect des femmes, Galilée, 1980.

4. See, for example, Lettre à d'Alembert, "At this very instant the short-lived philosophy that is born and dies in the corner of a great city, this philosophy that seeks to suppress the cry of Nature and the unanimous voice of humankind is going to rise up against me." ["à l'instant va s'élever contre moi, cette philosophie d'un jour . . . (Garnier-Flammarion p. 168)], and further: "Thus it was willed by nature, it is a crime to suppress her voice" ["Ainsi l'a voulu la Nature, . . . (p. 171)].

5. Emile, éd. Garnier-Flammarion, p. 48. All page numbers given in this text for Emile refer to the Garnier-Flammarion edition. Translations are my own—M.D.

6. "Sur les femmes" in Oeuvres complètes, Pléiade, t. II, p. 1255.

7. One could find this contrast between "major" and "minor" texts, between texts of "youth" and those of "maturity" in other philosophers. This is the case with Auguste Comte, another phallocrat, whose early letter to Valet, dating from Sept. 24, 1819, espouses a position which will later be that of his adversary, John Stuart Mill. See S. Kofman: Aberrations, le devenir-femme d'A. Comte (Aubier-Flammarion p. 230 and following).

8. See Kofman, Le Respect des femmes, Galilée, 1980.

9. La Nouvelle Héloïse, Part IV, Letter X.

10. The Rousseauistic description is the opposite of that of Freud for whom libido is essentially "masculine." See Kofman, The Enigma of Woman, Cornell University Press, 1985. Despite this difference, both appeal to the same "Nature" to justify the sexual subjugation of women, the essential point of the whole argument.

11. Emile, p. 470-71. See also La Nouvelle Héloïse, Part II, Letter XVIII, where Julie writes to Saint-Preux about the married woman: "She not only invested her faith, but alienated her freedom. (. . .) It is not enough to be honest, it is necessary that she be honored; it is not enough to do only what is good, it is necessary that she refrain from doing anything that isn't approved. A virtuous woman must not only merit the esteem of her husband, but obtain it. If he blames her, she is blameful; and if she were to be innocent, she is wrong as soon as she is suspect—for appearance itself counts as one of her duties."

12. Lucrèce, who preferred death to the loss of honor, is quoted by Rousseau as being among the heroines comparable and superior to male heros. (See "Sur les femmes" and La Mort de Lucrèce, O.C., II).

13. Lettre à d'Alembert, éd. Garnier-Flammarion, p. 246.

14. See Nancy Holland's "Introduction," in this volume, for an explanation of this reference to "cauldron" logic (tr.).

15. La Mort de Lucrèce

16. La Nouvelle Héloïse, Part IV, Letter X.

17. It would be interesting and very enlightening to compare Rousseau's discourse on decency with that of Montesquieu in L'Esprit des lois (Books XVI, X, XI, XX). In particular, one would find clarification for the allusion to warm countries where climate renders feminine sexual avidity fearsome. Montesquieu overtly grounds decency and the domestic confinement of women in the sexual danger that these represent for men in warm countries. In contrast, where climate is temperate, it is unnecessary to confine women. Men can "communicate" with them for the pleasure and "entertainment" of both men and women.

18. See De l'intérêt de la psychanalyse; in Aberrations, le devenir-femme d' A. Comte (Aubier-Flammarion, 1978) Kofman offers a detailed analysis of the possible relationships between a philosopher's delirium and his philosophical system.

19. Emile, Book V.

20. La Nouvelle Héloïse, Part IV, Letter X.

21. Confessions, Book XII.

22. for Mlle Lambercier, see Book I and L'Ebauche des Confessions, 13. For Mlle Goton, Book I. For Mme Basile, Book II.

23. Letter of October 15, 1757.

24. For an explanation of Kofman's use of 'feminism' in this passage, see Nancy Holland's "Introduction," in this volume.

25. La Nouvelle Héloïse, Part V, Letter III.

Introduction to "Sorcerer Love," by Luce Irigaray

"Sorcerer Love" is the name that Luce Irigaray gives to the demonic function of love as presented in Plato's Symposium. She argues that Socrates there attributes two incompatible positions to Diotima, who in any case is not present at the banquet. The first is that love is a mid-point or intermediary between lovers which also teaches immortality. The second is that love is a means to the end and duty of procreation, and thus is a mere means to immortality through which the lovers lose one another. Irigaray argues in favor of the first position, a conception of love as demonic intermediary.

Luce Irigaray's "Sorcerer Love" is unique among her presently translated works because it was originally composed as a lecture, to be spoken. As such, it forms a bridge to written language, including the versions of experimental *l'écriture féminine* or feminine writing for which Irigaray is better known to readers of English (1979, 1974, 1977). Irigaray delivered "Sorcerer Love," on Diotima's speech in Plato's Symposium, at Erasmus University, Rotterdam, in 1982, during her appointment to a chair honoring the animal behaviorist Jan Tinbergen. She published it as the second chapter of her book, *Éthique de la différence sexuelle* (Irigaray, 1984). In this work Irigaray also discusses texts by Aristotle, Descartes, Spinoza, Hegel, Merleau-Ponty, and Levinas, primarily, as the title tells us, as a point of departure for her ethics.

In her ethics, Irigaray both presupposes and seeks to disclose a female unconscious, hidden in traditional discourse, including the discourse of philosophers, both male and female. In her ontology, she evokes Nietzsche and Heidegger, for whom being is not fixed but constantly to be won, without, however, subscribing to their assumptions of separation and distance (1980; 1983b). In her method, Irigaray, who began her career as a psycholinguist (Irigaray, 1973), invokes Derridean deconstruction without endorsing what she perceives as Derrida's false presupposition of gender-neutrality in his accounts of language learning and morality (Irigaray, 1983a; 1987).

Irigaray's ontology, ethics, and method have been criticized both for her rendition of Freud's views on femininity (Kofman, 1980: 101-120) and for her supposed dependence on Freud and Lacan (Plaza, 1980; Gallop, 1982: 38-42). But since the 1970's, Irigaray has attempted to develop an alternative feminist account of the unconscious origins of language and morality which differs sharply from Freud and Lacan. For example, in *Speculum of the Other Woman*, (Irigaray, 1974), written in an unorthodox literary style which at times parodies Lacan as well as Plato, Irigaray reverses the direction of the philosopher's journey in Plato's Republic. For Irigaray, the philosopher's journey from Plato's cave to the sun and so from ignorance and delusion to a closer understanding of the Good, prefigures a Freudian and Lacanian ontology: the philosopher's emergence from the cave is the son's rupture of his bond with his mother at the father's behest. In her feminist alternative, Irigaray interprets the cave instead as a source of connection and so, of moral knowledge.

The connection is also magical. The ballet *El Amor Brujo* (1915), composed by Manuel de Falla and presented on the Paris stage as *L'Amour Sorcier* (1925), culminates in a ritual fire dance. Luce Irigaray's "Sorcerer Love," like its namesake, also creates an atmosphere of bewitchment. Published ten years after *Speculum*, "Sorcerer Love" is Irigaray's only other work on Plato. Here, as elsewhere, her effort is deconstructive in that it questions both explicit and covert presuppositions of gender in the text and its presentation. But the analysis in "Sorcerer Love" is also constructive in that it supports an ontology grounded in what Irigaray understands as women's experience, such as maternity, and an ethic honoring connection with or among women, rather than separation. Irigaray argues more explicitly for this ontology and ethic in later chapters of *Éthique de la différence sexuelle* entitled "L'Amour du Même, l'Amour de l'Autre" ["Love of the Same, Love of the Other"] and "Éthique de la différence sexuelle" (1984: 127-141).

In the Symposium, Plato reports Socrates in turn reporting a speech by Diotima in praise of love. This speech, Irigaray suggests in "Sorcerer Love," suffers from an internal contradiction in which love is described in two incompatible ways. On the one hand, it is said to be a constantly moving intermediary, neither lover nor beloved but both; on the other hand, it is said to become stabilized in the form of a third person, for example, a child, thereby separating lover from beloved. Moreover, Irigaray claims that the dramatic setting in which Plato situates the speech undermines its overt content and thesis. Socrates attributes to Diotima a purportedly universal theory of love at a banquet from which she and all other women are absent, a banquet at which a high level of sexual tension develops among the men. Thus, the conception of love presented as universal is not universally practiced, since women cannot participate directly in the discourse at the banquet. Further, both the examples and the very conception of what is said to constitute love—discourse with the divine—exclude women from all but love's initial and least enlightened phase—the physical desire to procreate.

Irigaray's interpretation of Diotima's speech is, of course, controversial. Andrea Nye, for example, in a critical essay that appears in this volume, argues that Irigaray misreads Diotima (or Socrates, or Plato) since, according to less literal translations, Diotima can be interpreted as consistently characterizing love as intermediary or demonic. And although some critics have argued that Diotima's very existence was an invention, the *Symposium* can also be read as acknowledging the existence of an actual historical female person, even though that acknowledgement is somewhat ambivalent since the contribution is a second-hand one (Wider, 1986: 44-48).

Yet Irigaray is not unaware of these issues. She herself points out that the text of the *Symposium* presents Diotima's speech in praise of love as a quotation by Socrates—whose own speech is a quotation by Plato. Historically, Diotima's actual presence at the banquet would have been highly unlikely. The fact that a male philosopher is speaking for an absent woman, a fact which is supposed to be irrelevant to the explicit celebration of love as universal, renders that celebration ironic. Why the all-male dramatic setting of this banquet celebrating love, from which not only Diotima but also all women, even the flute players and dancers, were absent? Why Diotima's identification of love between men as love's highest individual realization, albeit a realization to be transcended? And why, after Diotima's speech, does Plato recount the embarrassing confrontation of a disdainful Socrates by a drunken Alcibiades for whom, it turns out, Socrates hardly provided an adequate ethical model? (Whitbeck,1984:393) These are some of the questions with which the feminist reader of this text must grapple. Irigaray reads them as indications of conflicts of unconscious motives or of speech acts, as would Lacan or Derrida; but she also reads them as indications that the conception of love itself presented in the *Symposium* is deeply masculinist.   At the end of "Sorcerer Love", Irigaray departs from her deconstruction of the speech of Plato's Socrates' Diotima to sketch the beginnings of an ethic of her own, one grounded in an alternative ontology. The transformation that she celebrates here and elsewhere in her work comes from what she takes to be experiences of boundarylessness specific to women, such as maternity. But Irigaray does not intend this as a crude "essentialism" grounded on experiences available only to women. She rather seeks in women's experience an alternative to the ontology of separation and desire posited by Plato through Socrates and Diotima. Irigaray's reading of Plato's *Symposium*, like her readings of philosophers elsewhere, opens a dialogue with Plato, with Socrates, with Diotima, and with Irigaray herself, which we are now challenged to continue.

REFERENCES

Gallop, Jane. 1982. The daughter's seduction: feminism and psychoanalysis. Ithaca: Cornell University Press.

Irigaray, Luce. 1973. *Le langage des déments*. The Hague: Mouton.

———. 1974. *Speculum of the other woman*. Trans. Gillian Gill, 1985. Ithaca: Cornell University Press.

———. 1977. *This sex which is not one*. Trans. Catherine Porter with Carolyn Burke, 1985. Ithaca: Cornell University Press.

———. 1979. And the one doesn't stir without the other. Trans. Helene Vivienne Wenzel. *Signs* 7 (1981): 60-67.

———. 1980. *Amante marine*. Paris: Les Editions de Minuit.

———. 1983a. *La Croyance Même*. Paris: Galilée.

———. 1983b. *L'oubli de l'air*. Paris: Les Editions de Minuit.

———. 1984. *Ethique de la différence sexuelle*. Paris: Les Editions de Minuit.

———. 1985. *Parler n'est jamais neutre*. Paris: Les Editions de Minuit.

———. 1987. *Sexes et parentés*. Paris: Les Editions de Minuit.

Kofman, Sarah. 1980. *The Enigma of Woman*. Trans. Catherine Porter, 1985. Ithaca: Cornell University Press.

Kuykendall, Eleanor H. 1983. Toward an ethic of nurturance: Luce Irigaray on mothering and power. In *Mothering: essays in feminist theory*, ed. Joyce Trebilcot. Totowa, N. J.: Rowman & Allanheld: 263-274.

Nye, Andrea. 1991. The hidden host: Irigaray and Diotima at Plato's Symposium. This volume.

Plaza, Monique. 1980. "Phallomorphic" Power and the Psychology of "Woman." *Feminist Issues*, I: 71-102.

Trebilcot, Joyce, ed. 1983. *Mothering: essays in feminist theory*. Totowa, N. J.: Rowman & Allanheld.

Whitbeck, Caroline. 1984. Love, knowledge, and transformation. *Women's Studies International Forum* 4 (5): 393-405.

Wider, Kathleen. 1986. Women philosophers in the ancient greek world: Donning the mantle. *Hypatia*, 1(1): 21-62.

Sorcerer Love: A Reading of Plato's Symposium, Diotima's Speech

LUCE IRIGARAY

Translated by Eleanor H. Kuykendall

"Sorcerer Love" is the name that Luce Irigaray gives to the demonic function of love as presented in Plato's Symposium.[1] She argues that Socrates there attributes two incompatible positions to Diotima, who in any case is not present at the banquet. The first is that love is a mid-point or intermediary between lovers which also teaches immortality. The second is that love is a means to the end and duty of procreation, and thus is a mere means to immortality through which the lovers lose one another. Irigaray argues in favor of the first position, a conception of love as demonic intermediary. E.K.

In the *Symposium*, the dialogue on love, when Socrates finishes speaking, he gives the floor to a woman: Diotima. She does not participate in these exchanges or in this meal among men. She is not there. She herself does not speak. Socrates reports or recounts her views. He borrows her wisdom and power, declares her his initiator, his pedagogue, on matters of love, but she is not invited to teach or to eat. Unless she did not want to accept an invitation? But Socrates says nothing about that. And Diotima is not the only example of a woman whose wisdom, above all in love, is reported in her absence by a man.

Diotima's teaching will be very dialectical—but different from what we usually call dialectical. Unlike Hegel's, her dialectic does not work by opposition to transform the first term into the second, in order to arrive at a synthesis of the two. At the very outset, she establishes the *intermediary* and she never abandons it as a mere way or means. Her method is not, then, a propaedeutic of the *destruction* or *destructuration* of two terms in order to establish a synthesis which is neither one nor the other. She presents, uncovers, unveils the existence of a third that is already there and that permits progression: from poverty to wealth, from ignorance to wisdom, from mortality to immortality. For her, this progression always leads to a greater perfection of and in love.

Hypatia vol. 3, no. 3 (Winter 1989) © by Luce Irigaray

But, contrary to the usual dialectical methods, love ought not to be abandoned for the sake of becoming wise or learned. It is love that leads to knowledge—both practical and metaphysical. It is love that is both the guide and the way, above all a mediator.

Love is designated as a theme, but love is also perpetually enacted, dramatized, in the exposition of the theme.

So Diotima immediately rebuts the claims that love is a great God and that it is the love of beautiful things. At the risk of offending the Gods, Diotima also asserts that love is neither beautiful nor good. This leads her interlocutor to suppose immediately that love is ugly and bad, incapable as he is of grasping the existence or instance of what is held *between*, what permits the passage between ignorance and knowledge. If we did not, at each moment, have something to learn in the encounter with reality, between reality and already established knowledge, we would not perfect ourselves in wisdom. And not to become wiser means to become more ignorant.

Therefore, between knowledge and reality, there is an intermediary which permits the meeting and transmutation or transvaluation between the two. The dialectic of Diotima is in *four terms*, at least: the here, the two poles of the meeting, the beyond, but a beyond which never abolishes the here. And so on, indefinitely. The mediator is never abolished in an infallible knowledge. Everything is always in movement, in becoming. And the mediator of everything is, among other things, or exemplarily, love. Never completed, always evolving.

And, in response to the protestation of Socrates that love is a great God, that *everyone says so or thinks so*, she *laughs*. Her retort is not at all angry, balancing between contradictories; it is laughter from elsewhere. Laughing, then, she asks Socrates who this *everyone* is. Just as she ceaselessly undoes the assurance or the *closure* of opposing terms, so she rejects every ensemble of unities reduced to a similitude in order to constitute a whole:

> "You mean, by all who do not know?" said she, "or by all who know as well?" "Absolutely all." At that she laughed. (202)[2]

> ("Ce tout le monde dont tu parles, sont-ce, dit-elle, ceux qui savent ou ceux qui ne savent pas?—Tous en général, ma foi!" Elle se mit à rire.)

The tension between opposites thus abated, she shows, demonstrates, that "everyone" does not exist, nor does the position of love as *eternally* a great God. Does she teach nothing that is already defined? A method of becoming wise, learned, more perfect in love and in art [*l'art*]. She ceaselessly questions Socrates on his positions but without, like a master, positing already constituted truths. Instead, she teaches the renunciation of already established truths. And each time that Socrates thinks that he can take something as certain, she undoes his certainty. All entities, substantives, adverbs, sentences are patiently, and joyously, called into question.

For love, the demonstration is not so difficult to establish. For, if love possessed all that he desired, he would desire no more.[3] He must lack, therefore, in order to desire still. But, if love had nothing at all to do with beautiful and good things, he could not desire them either. Thus, he is an *intermediary* in a very specific sense. Does he therefore lose his status as a God? Not necessarily. He is neither mortal nor immortal: he is between the one and the other. Which qualifies him as demonic. Love is a *demon*—his function is to transmit to the gods what comes from men and to men what comes from the gods. Like everything else that is demonic, love is complementary to gods and to men in such a way as to join everything with itself. There must be a being of middling nature in order for men and gods to enter into relations, into conversation, while awake or asleep. Which makes love a kind of divination, priestly knowledge of things connected with sacrifice, initiation, incantation, prediction in general and magic.

The demons who serve as mediators between men and gods are numerous and very diverse. Love is one of them. And Love's parentage is very particular: child of *Plenty* (himself son of *Invention*) and of *Poverty*, conceived the day the birth of Aphrodite was celebrated. Thus love is always poor and

> . . . rough, unkempt, unshod, and homeless, ever couching on the ground uncovered, sleeping beneath the open sky by doors and in the streets, because he has the nature of his mother. . . . But again, in keeping with his father, he has designs upon the beautiful and good, for he is bold, headlong, and intense, a mighty hunter, always weaving some device or other, eager in invention and resourceful, searching after wisdom all through life, terrible as a magician, sorcerer, and sophist. Further, in his nature he is not immortal, nor yet mortal. No, on a given day, now he flourishes and lives, when things go well with him, and again he dies, but through the nature of his sire revives again. Yet his gain for ever slips away from him, so that Eros never is without resources, nor is ever rich.
>
> As for ignorance and knowledge, here again he is midway between them. The case stands thus. No god seeks after wisdom, or wishes to grow wise (for he already is so), no more than anybody else seeks after wisdom if he has it. Nor, again, do ignorant folk seek after wisdom or long to grow wise; for here is just the trouble about ignorance, that what is neither beautiful and good, nor yet intelligent, to itself seems good enough. Accordingly, the man who does not think himself in

need has no desire for what he does not think himself in need of.

[*Socrates.*] The seekers after knowledge, Diotima! If they are not the wise, nor yet the ignorant (said I), who are they, then?

[*Diotima.*] The point (said she) is obvious even to a child, that they are persons intermediate between these two, and that Eros is among them; for wisdom falls within the class of the most beautiful, while Eros is an eros for the beautiful. And hence it follows necessarily that Eros is a seeker after wisdom [a philosopher], and being a philosopher, is midway between wise and ignorant. (203-204)

(rude et malpropre; un va-nu-pieds qui n'a point de domicile, dormant à la belle étoile sur le pas des portes ou dans la rue selon la nature de sa mére. Mais, en revanche, guettant, sans cesse, embusqué les choses belles et bonnes, chasseur habile et ourdissant continûment quelque ruse, curieux de pensée et riche d'expédient, passant toute sa vie à philosopher, habile comme sorcier, comme inventeur de philtres magiques, comme sophiste, selon la nature de son père. De plus, sa nature n'est ni d'un mortel ni d'un immortel, mais, le même jour, tantôt, quand ses expédients ont réussi, il est en fleur, il a de la vie; tantôt au contraire il est mourant; puis, derechef, il revient à la vie grace au naturel de son pere, tandis que, d'autre part, coule de ses mains le fruit de ses expédients! Ainsi, ni jamais Amour n'est indigent, ni jamais il est riche! Entre savoir et ignorance, maintenant, Amour est intermédiaire. Voici ce qui en est. Parmi les Dieux, il n'y en a aucun qui ait envie de devenir sage, car il l'est; ne s'emploie pas non plus à philosopher quiconque d'autre est sage. Mais pas davantage les ignorants ne s'emploient, de leur côté, à philosopher, et ils n'ont pas envie de devenir sages; car, ce qu'il y a precisement de fâcheux dans l'ignorance, c'est que quelqu'un, qui n'est pas un homme accompli et qui n'est pas non plus intelligent, se figure l'être dans la mesure voulue; c'est que celui qui ne croit pas être depourvu n'a point envie de ce dont il ne croit pas avoir besoin d'etre pourvu. —Quels sont donc alors, Diotime, m'écriai-je, ceux qui s'emploient à philosopher si ce ne sont ni les sages ni les ignorants? —La chose est claire, dit-elle, et même déjà pour un enfant! Ce sont ceux qui sont intermediares entre ces deux extrêmes, et au nombre desquels doit aussi se trouver Amour. La sagesse, en effet, est évidemment parmi les plus belles choses, et c'est au beau

qu'Amour rapporte son amour; d'où il suit que, forcément,
Amour est philosophe, et, étant philosophe, qu'il est intermé-
diare entre le savant et l'ignorant.)

Eros is therefore *intermediary* between couples of opposites: poverty-plenty,
ignorance-wisdom, ugliness-beauty, dirtiness-cleanliness, death-life, etc.
And that would be inscribed in love's nature as a result of his genealogy and
date of conception. And love is a philosopher, love is philosophy. Philosophy
is not formal knowledge, fixed, abstracted from all feeling. It is the search for
love, love of beauty, love of wisdom, which is one of the most beautiful
things. Like love, the philosopher would be someone poor, dirty, a bit of a
bum, always an outsider, sleeping under the stars but very curious, adept in
ruses and devices of all kinds, reflecting ceaselessly, a sorcerer, a sophist,
sometimes flourishing, sometimes expiring. Nothing like the representation
of the philosopher we generally give: learned, correctly dressed, with good
manners, understanding everything, pedantically instructing us in a corpus of
already codified doctrine. The philosopher is nothing like that. He is barefoot, going out under the stars in search of an encounter with reality, seeking
the embrace, the acquaintance [connaissance] (co-birthing) [(co-naissance)]
of whatever gentleness of soul, beauty, wisdom might be found there. This
incessant quest he inherits from his mother. He is a philosopher through his
mother, an adept in invention through his father. But his passion for love, for
beauty, for wisdom, comes to him from his mother, and from the date when
he was conceived. Desired and wanted, besides, by his mother.

   How is it that love and the philosopher are generally represented otherwise? Because they are imagined as *beloved* and not as *lovers*. As beloved
Love, both like and unlike the philosopher, is imagined to be of unparalled
beauty, delicate, perfect, happy. Yet the lover has an entirely different nature. He goes toward what is kind, beautiful, perfect, etc. He does not possess
these. He is poor, unhappy, always in search of . . . But what does he seek or
love? That beautiful things become his—this is Socrates' answer. But what
will happen to him if these things become his? To this question of Diotima's,
Socrates has no answer. Switching "good" for "beautiful", she asks her question again. "That the good may be his," ("Qu'elles devienne siennes")
Socrates repeats.

> "And what happens to the man when the good things become
> his?" "On this," said [Socrates], "I am more than ready with
> an answer: that he will be happy." (204-205)

> ("Et qu'en sera-t-il pour celui a qui il arrivera que les choses
> bonnes soient devenues siennes?" "Voilà, dit Socrate, à quoi
> je serai plus à mon aise pour répondre! Il sera heureux")

And happiness seems to put an ultimate end to this dialogical repetition between Diotima and Socrates.

Socrates asks: what should we call what pertains to lovers? "By what manner of pursuit and in what activity does the eagerness and straining for the object get the name of Eros? And what may this action really be?" ("Quel est le genre d'existence, le mode d'activité pour lesquels à leur zèle, à leur effort soutenu conviendrait le nom d'amour, dis-moi? En quoi peu bien consister cet acte?") And Diotima replies: "This action is engendering in beauty, with relation both to body and to soul." (205, 206) ("C'est un enfantement dans la beauté et selon le corps et selon l'âme.") But Socrates understands nothing of another, equally clear, revelation . . . He understands nothing about fecundity in relation both to body and to soul:

> The union of a man and woman is, in fact, a generation; this is
> a thing divine; in a living creature that is mortal, it is an ele-
> ment of immortality, this fecundity and generation. (206)

> (L'union de l'homme et de la femme est en effet un enfante-
> ment et c'est une affaire divine, c'est, dans le vivant mortel, la
> présence de ce qui est immortel: la fécondité et la procréa-
> tion.)

This statement of Diotima's never seems to have been understood. Besides, she herself will go on to emphasize the procreative aspect of love. But first she stresses the character of *divine generation in every union between man and woman*, the presence of the immortal in the living mortal. All love would be creation, potentially divine, a path between the condition of the mortal and that of the immortal. Love is fecund before all procreation. And it has a *mediumlike, demonic* fecundity. Assuring everyone, male and female, the immortal becoming of the living. But there cannot be procreation of a divine nature in what is not in harmony. And harmony with the divine is not possible for the ugly, but only for the beautiful. Thus, according to Diotima, love between man and woman is beautiful, harmonious, divine. It must be in order for procreation to take place. It is not procreation that is beautiful and that constitutes the aim of love. The aim of love is to realize the immortality in the mortality between lovers. And the expansion which produces the child follows the joy at the approach of a beautiful object. But an ugly object leads to a turning back, the shriveling up of fecundity, the painfully borne weight of the desire to procreate. Procreation and generation in beauty—these are the aim of love, because it is thus that the eternity and imperishability of a mortal being manifest themselves.

Fecundity of love between lovers, regeneration of one by the other, passage to immortality in one another, through one another—these seem to become the condition, not the cause, of procreation. Certainly, Diotima tells

Socrates that the creation of beauty, of a work of art [*l'oeuvre*] (solitary creation this time?) is insufficient, that it is necessary to give birth together to a
child, that this wisdom is inscribed in the animal world itself. She continues
to laugh at the way he goes looking for his truths beyond the most obvious everyday reality, which he does not see or even perceive. She mocks the way his
dialectical or dialogical method forgets the most elementary truths. The way
his discourse on love neglects to look at, to inform itself about, the amorous
state and to inquire about its cause.

Diotima speaks of *cause* in a surprising way. We could note that her
method does not enter into a chain of causalities, a chain that skips over or
often forgets the intermediary as generative milieu. Usually, causality is not
part of her reasoning. She borrows it from the animal world and evokes it, or
invokes it, with respect to procreation. Instead of allowing the child to ger-
minate or develop in the milieu of love and fecundity between man and
woman, she seeks a cause of love in the animal world: procreation.

Diotima's method miscarries here. From here on, she leads love into a
schism between mortal and immortal. Love loses its demonic character. Is
this the founding act of the meta-physical? There will be lovers in body and
lovers in soul. But the perpetual passage from mortal to immortal that lovers
confer on one another is put aside. Love loses its divinity, its mediumlike,
alchemical qualities between couples of opposites. The intermediary becomes
the child, and no longer love. Occupying the place of love, the child can no
longer be a lover. It is put in the place of the incessant movement of love. Beloved, no doubt; but how be beloved without being a lover? And is not love
trapped in the beloved, contrary to what Diotima wanted in the first place? A
beloved who is an end is substituted for love between men and women. A beloved who is a *will*, even a *duty*, and a *means* of attaining immortality. Lovers
can neither attain nor advance that between themselves. That is the weakness of love, for the child as well. If the couple of lovers cannot care for the
place of love like a third term between them, then they will not remain lovers
and they cannot give birth to lovers. Something gets solidified in space-time
with the loss of a vital intermediary milieu and of an accessible, loving, transcendental. A sort of teleological triangle replaces a perpetual movement, a
perpetual transvaluation, a permanent becoming. Love was the vehicle of
this. But, if procreation becomes its goal, it risks losing its internal motivation, its fecundity "in itself", its slow and constant regeneration.

This error in method, in the originality of Diotima's method, is corrected
shortly afterward only to be confirmed later on. Surely, once again, *she is not
there. Socrates reports her views.* Perhaps he distorts them unwittingly and un-
knowingly.

The following paragraph takes up what was just asserted. It explains how it
is that there is permanent renewal in us. How there is, in us, a ceaseless loss
of the old, of the already dead, both in our most physical part—hair, bones,

blood, our whole body—and in our most spiritual part: our character, our opinions, our desires, joys and pains, our fears. None of these elements is ever identical to what they were; some come into existence while others perish. The same is true for knowledges, which are acquired and forgotten—thus constantly renewed:

> ". . . . This is the fashion in which everything mortal is pre-
> served, not in being always perfectly identical, as is divinity,
> but in that the disappearing and decaying object leaves behind
> it another new one such as it was. By this arrangement,
> Socrates," said she, "the mortal partakes of immortality, both
> in body and all else; the immortal does so in another way. So
> do not marvel if everything by nature prizes its own offspring;
> it is for the sake of immortality that every being has this ur-
> gency and love." . . . (208)

> ([C'est] de cette façon qu'est sauvegardé ce qui est mortel, non
> point comme ce qui est divin par l'identite absolue d'une exist-
> ence eternelle, mais par le fait que ce qui s'en va, mine par son
> ancienneté, laisse après lui autre chose, du nouveau qui est
> pareil à ce qu'il était. C'est par ce moyen, dit-elle, qui ce qui
> est mortel participe à l'immortalité, dans son corps et en tout
> le reste . . . Donc, ne t'émerveille pas que, ce qui est une
> repousse de lui-même, chaque être ait pour lui tant de sollici-
> tude naturelle, car c'est en vue de l'immortalité que font cor-
> tège à chacun d'eux ce zèle et cet amour!)

Here, Diotima returns to her type of argumentation, including her mocking of those who suspend the present in order to search "for an eternity of time an immortal glory" ("pour l'eternité du temps une gloire immortelle"). She speaks—in a style that is loosely *woven* but never definitively *knotted*—of be-coming in time, of permanent generation and regeneration here and now in each (wo)man [chacun(e)] of what is more corporeally and spiritually real. Without saying that one is the fruit of the other. But that, at each moment, we are a "regrowth" of ourselves, in perpetual increase. No more quest for im-mortality through the child. But in us, ceaselessly. Diotima has returned to a path which admits love as it was defined before she evoked procreation: an intermediate terrain, a mediator, a space-time of permanent *passage* between mortal and immortal.

Next, returning to an example of the quest for immortality through fame, she re-situates (the) object (of) love outside of the subject: reknown, immor-tal glory, etc. No more perpetual becoming-immortal in us, but rather a race toward some thing that would confer immortality. Like and unlike procrea-tion of a child, the stake of love is placed outside the self. In the beloved and

not in the lover? The lovers cited—Alcestis, Admetus, Achilles, Codros—
would not have been cited unless we always remembered them. It was with
the goal of eternal reknown that they loved unto death. Immortality is the
object of their love. Not love itself.

> Well then (said she), when men's fecundity is of the body,
> they turn rather to the women, and the fashion of their love is
> this: through begetting children to provide themselves with
> immortality, reknown and happiness, as they imagine—
>   Securing them for all time to come.
> But when fecundity is of the soul—for indeed there are (said
> she) those persons who are fecund in their souls, even more
> than in their bodies, fecund in what is the function of the soul
> to conceive and also to bring forth—what is this proper off-
> spring? It is wisdom, along with every other spiritual value.
> . . . (208-209)

> (Cela étant, dit-elle, ceux qui sont féconds selon le corps se
> tournent plutôt vers les femmes, et leur façon d'etre amoureux
> c'est, en engendrant des enfants, de se procurer à eux-mêmes,
> pensent-ils, pour toute la suite du temps, le bonheur d'avoir un
> nom dont le souvenir ne périsse pas. Quant à ceux qui sont
> féconds selon l'âme, car en fait il en existe, dit-elle, dont la
> fécondité réside dans l'âme, à un plus haut degré encore que
> dans le corps, pour tout ce qui appartient à une âme d'être fé-
> conde et qu'il lui appartient d'enfanter. Or, qu'est-ce cela qui lui
> appartient? C'est la pensée, et c'est toute autre excellence)

What seemed to me most original in Diotima's method has disappeared
once again. That irreducible intermediary milieu of love is cancelled between
"subject" (an inadequate word in Plato) and "beloved reality." Amorous becoming no longer constitutes a becoming of the lover himself, of love in the
(male or female) lover, between the lovers [un devenir de l'amant lui-même,
de l'amour en l'amante(e), entre amants].[4] Instead it is now a teleological
quest for what is deemed the highest reality and often situated in a transcendence inaccessible to our condition as mortals. Immortality is put off until
death and is not counted as one of our constant tasks as mortals, as a transmutation that is endlessly incumbent on us here and now, as a possibility inscribed in a body capable of divine becoming. Beauty of body and beauty of
soul become hierarchized, and the love of women becomes the lot of those
who, incapable of being creators in soul, are fecund in body and seek the immortality of their name perpetuated by their offspring.

>   . . . By far the greatest and most beautiful form of wisdom
> (said she) is that which has to do with regulating states and

households, and has the name, no doubt, of "temperance" and
"justice." (209)

(. . . de beaucoup la plus considérable et la plus belle manifestation de la pensée etant celle qui concerne l'ordonnance des
Etats comme de tout établissement, et dont le nom, on le sait,
est tempérance aussi bien que justice.)

Amorous becomings, divine, immortal, are no longer left to their intermediary current. They are qualified, hierarchized. And, in the extreme case,
love dies. In the universe of determinations, there will be contests, competi-
tions, amorous duties—the beloved or love being the prize. The lovers disappear. Our subsequent tradition has even taught us the interdiction or the fu-
tility of being lovers outside of procreation.

Yet Diotima had begun by asserting that the most divine act is "the union
of man and woman, a divine affair." What she asserted then accorded with
what she said about the function of love as an intermediary remaining intermediary, a demon. It seems that in the course of her speech she reduces a bit
this demonic, mediumlike function of love; so that it is no longer really a demon, but an intention, a reduction to intention, to the teleology of human
will. Already subjected to a doctrine with fixed goals and not to an immanent
flourishing of the divine in the flesh. Irreducible mediator, at once physical
and spiritual, between lovers; and not already codified duty, will, desire.
Love invoked as a demon in a method toward the beautiful and good often
disappears from the speech, reappearing only in art, "painting", in the
form(s) of love inciting to eroticism and, perhaps, in the shape of angels. Is
love itself split between eros and agape? Yet, in order for lovers to be able to
love each other, there must be, between them, Love.

There remains what has been said about the philosopher-love. But why
would not philosopher Love be a lover of the other? Only of the Other? Of an
inaccessible transcendent? In any case, this would already be an ideal that
suppresses love qua demonic. Love becomes political wisdom, wisdom in regulating the city, not the intermediary state that inhabits lovers and transports
them from the condition of mortals to that of immortals. Love becomes a sort
of raison d'état. Love founds a family, takes care of children, including the
children which citizens are. The more its objective is distanced from an individual becoming, the more valuable it is. Its stake is lost in immortal good
and beauty as collective goods. The family is preferable to the generation of
lovers, between lovers. Adopted children are preferable to others. This,
moreover, is how it comes to pass that love between men is superior to love between man and woman. Carnal procreation is suspended in favor of the
engendering of beautiful and good things. Immortal things. That, surpris-
ingly, is the view of Diotima. At least as translated through the words uttered
by Socrates.

The beings most gifted in wisdom go directly to that end. Most begin with physical beauty and " . . . must love one single object [physical form of beauty], and thereof must engender fair discourses . . . ." (210) (par n'aimer qu'un unique beau corps et par engendrer à cette occasion de beaux discours.") If the teaching is right, that must be so. But whoever becomes attached to one body must learn that beauty is in many bodies. After having pursued beauty in one perceptible form, he must learn that the same beauty resides in all bodies; he will

> . . . abate his violent love of one, disdaining this and deeming it a trifle, and will become a lover of all fair objects. . . . (210)

> ("[devenir] un amant de tous les beaux corps et détendra l'impétuosité de son amour à l'égard d'un seul individu; car, un tel amour, il en est venu à le dédaigner et à en faire peu de cas.")

From the attraction to a single beautiful body he passes, then, to many; and thence to the beauty residing in souls. Thus he learns that beauty is not found univocally in the body and that someone of an ugly bodily appearance can be beautiful and gentle of soul; that to be just is to know how to care for that person and to engender beautiful discourses for him. Love thus passes insensibly into love of works [oeuvres]. The passion for beautiful bodies is transmuted into the discovery of beauty in knowledges. That which liberates from the attachment to only one master opens onto the immense ocean of the beautiful, and leads to the birth of numerous and sublime discourses, as well as to thoughts inspired by a boundless love of wisdom. Until the resulting force and development permit the lover to envision a certain *unique* knowledge (210). This marvelous beauty is perceptible, perhaps, by whoever has followed the road just described, by whoever has passed through the different stages step by step. He will have, then, the vision of a beauty whose existence is " . . . eternal, not growing up or perishing, increasing or decreasing" ([dont] l'existence est éternelle, étrangère à la génération comme à la corruption, à l'accroissement comme au décroissement") and which, besides, is *absolutely* beautiful:

> not beautiful in one point and ugly in another, nor beautiful in this place and ugly in that, as if beautiful to some, to others ugly; again, this beauty will not be revealed to him in the semblance of a face, or hands, or any other element of the body, nor in any form of speech or knowledge, nor yet as if it appertained to any other being, or creature, for example, upon earth, or in the sky, or elsewhere; no, it will be seen as beauty in and for itself, consistent with itself in uniformity for ever, whereas all other beauties share it in such fashion that, while

they are ever born and perish, that eternal beauty, never wax-
ing, never waning, never is impaired. . . . (210-211)

(pas belle à ce point de vue et laide à cet autre, pas davantage
à tel moment et non à tel autre, ni non plus belle en comparaison avec ceci, laide en comparaison avec cela, ni non plus
belle en tel lieu, laide en tel autre, en tant que belle pour certains hommes, laide pour certains autres; pas davantage encore
cette beauté ne se montrera à lui pourvue par exemple d'un
visage, ni de mains, ni de quoi que ce soit d'autre qui soit une
partie du corps; ni non plus sous l'aspect de quelque raison-
nement ou encore quelque connaissance; pas davantage
comme ayant en quelque être distinct quelque part son existence, en un vivant par exemple, qu'il soit de la terre ou du
ciel, ou bien en quoi que ce soit d'autre; mais bien plutôt elle
se montrera à lui en elle-même, et par elle-même, éternel-
lement unie à elle-même dans l'unicité de la nature formelle,
tandis que les autres beaux objets participent tous de la nature
dont il s'agit en une telle façon que, ces autres objets venant à
l'existence ou cessant d'exister, il n'en résulte dans la réalité
dont il s'agit aucune augmentation, aucune diminution, ni
non plus aucune sorte d'altération.)

To attain this sublime beauty, one must begin with the love of young men.
Starting with their natural beauty, one must, step by step, raise oneself to su-
pernatural beauty: from beautiful bodies one must pass to beautiful pursuits;
then to beautiful sciences, and finally to that sublime science that is super-
natural beauty alone, and that allows knowledge of the essence of beauty in
isolation (211). This contemplation is what gives direction and taste to life.
". . . It will not appear to you to be according to the measure of gold and rai-
ment, or of lovely boys and striplings. . . ." (211) ("Ni l'or ou la toilette, ni la
beauté des jeunes garcons ou des jeunes hommes ne peuvent entrer en paral-
lèle avec cette découverte.") And whoever has perceived "beauty divine in
its own single nature" (211) ("le beau divin dans l'unicité de sa nature
formelle"), what can he still look at? Having contemplated "the beautiful
with that by which it can be seen" (211) (le beau au moyen de ce par quoi il
est visible"), beyond all simulacra, he is united with it and is *really* virtuous;
since he has perceived "authentic reality" ("réel authentique") he becomes
dear to the divine and immortal.

   This person would, then, have perceived what I shall call a *sensible transcendental*, the material texture of beauty. He would have "seen" the very spa-
tiality of the visible, the real before all reality, all forms, all truth of particular
sensations or of constructed idealities. Would he have contemplated the "nature" ("nature") of the divine? This is the support of the fabrication of the

transcendent in its different modes, all of which, according to Diotima, are reached by the same propaedeutic: *the love of beauty*. Neither the good nor the true nor justice nor the government of the city would occur without beauty. And its strongest ally is love. Love therefore deserves to be venerated. And Diotima asks that her words be considered as a celebration and praise of Love.

In the second part of her speech, she used Love itself as a *means*. She cancelled out its intermediary function and subjected it to a *telos*. The power [puissance] of her method seems less evident to me here than at the beginning of her speech, when she made love the mediator of a becoming with no objective other than becoming. Perhaps Diotima is still saying the same thing. But her method, in the second part, risks losing its irreducible character and being replaced by a meta-physics. Unless what she proposes to contemplate, beauty itself, is understood as that which confuses the opposition between immanence and transcendence. An always already sensible horizon at the depths of which everything would appear. But it would be necessary to go back over the whole speech again to discover it in its enchantment.

NOTES

1. Luce Irigaray, "L'amour Sorcier: Lecture de Platon, *Le Banquet*, Discours de Diotime" In: Luce Irigaray, 1984, pp. 27-39. Translation published by kind permission of Les Éditions de Minuit.
2. This and subsequent quotations from *The Symposium* are rendered in the English translation of Lane Cooper in Plato (1938) pp. 252-263. References in French, which follow in parentheses, are Irigaray's citations from the French translation of Léon Robin in Platon (1950).
3. In this and subsquent passages "Love" or "love" is rendered in English with the masculine pronoun—a translation required by French grammar. "L'Amour," capitalized, means "the God of Love"—Cupid or Eros, and is always masculine in French. "L'amour" uncapitalized, means "love" and is also standardly masculine in French. "Eros" and "Love" are interchangeable in English translations of most of Diotima's speech; a similar interchangeability exists in French. Historically, "l'amour" was feminine in French until it was made conventionally masculine to accord with Latin use. In poetry, uses of "l'amour" in the feminine persist to this day; but "l'amour" was not grammatically feminine in the passages from Plato that Irigaray was citing. Irigaray's argument in this essay can be read as an exploration of the ethical implications of these grammatical points. Cf. Grévisse (1964): 190-192. [Translator's note]
4. Irigaray is here exploiting the very characteristics of French grammar which exemplify her argument. "L'amant" must be masculine when any of the lovers is male; but it is also possible to specify that the lover is female, as in the title of her *Amante Marine ([Female] Lover from the Seas)*, 1980. [Translator's note]

REFERENCES

Grévisse, Maurice. 1964. *Le bon usage*. Gambloux: Éditions J. Duculot, S.A., 8th edition.
Irigaray, Luce. 1980. *Amante Marine*. Paris: Les Éditions de Minuit.
———. 1984. *Éthique de la différence sexuelle*. Paris: Les Éditions de Minuit.
Plato. 1938. Phaedrus, Ion, Gorgias, and Symposium, with passages from the Republic and Laws. Trans. Lane Cooper. New York: Oxford University Press.
Platon. 1950. Oeuvres Completes. Trans. Léon Robin. Paris: Gallimard (Bibliothèque de la Pléiade 58), I.

The Hidden Host: Irigaray and Diotima at Plato's Symposium

ANDREA NYE

Irigaray's reading of Plato's Symposium in Ethique de la différence sexuelle illustrates both the advantages and the limits of her textual practise. Irigaray's attentive listening to the text allows Diotima's voice to emerge from an overlay of Platonic scholarship. But both the ahistorical nature of that listening and Irigaray's assumption of feminine marginality also make her a party to Plato's sabotage of Diotima's philosophy. Understood in historical context, Diotima is not an anomaly in Platonic discourse, but the hidden host of Plato's banquet, speaking for a pre-Socratic world view against which classical Greek thought is asserted. Understood in historical context, Plato is not the authoritative founder of Western though against whom only marginal skirmishes can be mounted, but a rebellious student who manages to transform Diotima's complex teaching on personal identity, immortality, and love into the sterile simplicities of logical form.

Who is the "host" of that famous philosophical party described in Plato's *Symposium*? Who decided that no woman would be invited so that twenty centuries later, when Luce Irigaray decides to impose her feminine presence in her essay "L'amour sorcier" (this volume), she can only intervene as interloper and eavesdropper? Is the host Agathon, in whose house the Symposium takes place? Is it Socrates, in whose honor the feast is held? Is it Plato, who evokes the scene for us?

The root meaning of "host" is a physical body on whose flesh parasites feed. The host is the nourishment they steal and convert to prolong their own independent existences. The host is a sacrificed animal body offered up to placate heaven. The host is the physical bread the faithful eat at communion to become one with an insubstantial god. If we take "host" in these root senses, then, as I hope to show, it is Diotima and not Agathon, Socrates, or Plato who is the real host of the *Symposium*. And if this is true Irigaray's presence is no intrusion. She, or any woman, enters into the discussion of love with perfect right.

Hypatia vol 3, no. 3 (Winter 1989) © by Andrea Nye

Irigaray, however, feels none of the confidence of an invited guest, nor does she recognize Diotima's authority. Irigaray's Diotima is not the mistress of her own house, but an alienated troubler of dichotomous categories whose success depends on being clever enough to subvert Platonic logic. Irigaray's own commitment to this "feminine operation" prevents her from understanding Diotima's teaching and its relation to Platonism.

Diotima's discourse, as reported by Socrates as reported by Plato, has always been the locus of scholarly skirmishing. In the *Symposium*, when it is his turn to speak on love, Socrates does not speak in his own voice. He repeats the teaching of his mentor, Diotima. Most scholars have found this puzzling and embarrassing. How can the great Socrates, founder of philosophy, be saying that he learned everything he knows from a woman? In a rhetorical competition between Athenian men, what is a woman doing correcting the mistakes of previous male speakers? And what is Plato doing, letting Socrates repeat respectfully the teachings of a woman, teachings not always in keeping with Plato's own?

These anomalies have been handled in a variety of ways. Some scholars have argued that Diotima is a fictional priestess invented by Plato to give divine authority to Socrates, even though this explanation must ignore the many elements in Diotima's teaching inconsistent with Platonic philosophy as well as the fact that Diotima would be the only fictional character in all of the Platonic dialogues. Others have explained her appearance by referring to the romantic subplots of the *Symposium*: Socrates wishes to correct Agathon whom he wants to seduce, but without antagonizing; therefore Socrates puts his correction in Diotima's mouth so that he may imply ingratiatingly that he too once needed instruction and had to be put right. Still others have argued that Plato includes Diotima's discourse in order to ridicule its simplistic naturalism, ignoring the fact that Socrates praises Diotima and reports *her* ridicule of his naivete and excessive abstraction. Almost universally, it is asserted without argument that Diotima is fictional. In translation and commentaries, her teachings are interpreted so as to be compatible with Platonic philosophy.[1]

In fact, Diotima's philosophy of love differs both from the theory of Forms in Plato's *Republic*, and from the mystical Pythagoreanism developed in the *Phaedrus*. Far from suggesting that the body is a degraded prison, Diotima sees bodily love as the metaphor and concrete training ground for all creative and knowledge-producing activities.[2] She argues that sexual love for one person must be outgrown, but not because it is physical and hence imperfect. Rather, the lover must progress to friendship, knowledge, and politics because exclusive sexual love for one person is obsessional, narrow, and makes one servile (Symposium 210c-d).[3] Diotima does not argue that heterosexual intercourse is inferior but urges an expansion of loving intercourse that will bear fruit in new thoughts, new knowledge, and new ways of living with others, as well as in physical children (209a). The beauty-in-itself that the initiate in

Diotima's philosophy may experience as the culmination of her training is not a transcendent Platonic Form. The initiate glimpses no universal, abstracted from imperfect particulars, but an indwelling immortal divine beauty, an attracting center that foments fruitful creation in all areas of existence.[4] Diotima identifies this center with the pre-Hellenic Cretan goddess, Eilethia, goddess of childbirth, and with her attendant spinner of fate, Moira (206d). To be in touch with this divinity, she says, is to live a new enlightened existence and to be a lover of the divine. Only in this way, Diotima concludes, will we be able to avoid false images of virtue and achieve real virtue (212a 1-5). The initiate in Diotima's philosophy cannot dwell in the world of absolute beauty as the philosopher of Plato's Republic aspires to dwell in the upper sunlit world of the Forms. To cut oneself off from the natural generative center of human life, is to be content with only abstract, unreal ideas of virtue and to fail to achieve real virtue which must be lived and generated in the visible, physical world.

At first, there is much in Diotima's teaching that Irigaray approves. She applauds Diotima's mocking of Socrates' simplistic dichotomous thinking: love is either ugly or beautiful, rich or poor, etc. She accepts Diotima's view of love as an intermediary or third term that moves between two opposing terms whose logic is deconstructed. She endorses Diotima's theory of personal identity based on the realization that the self is not unitary but constantly in a process of renewal and destruction.

But then Irigaray withdraws her approval. After such a promising beginning, she charges, Diotima's method "fails" (1984, 33). Diotima searches for a "cause" for love in a natural impulse toward procreation. She sees an "issue" and not sexual pleasure as the end of sexual intercourse. She sees non-procreative sex as only a means to the end of certain "collective goods." She sacrifices sexual pleasure to a teleological goal. She sets up a hierarchy of goods in which an abstract philosophical love of beauty is "higher" than physical love, undermining the plurality of her original deconstruction. In other words, Irigaray judges Diotima as a lapsed French feminist struggling to maintain the "correct method" against philosophical orthodoxy. Although Diotima begins well with an ironic onslaught on dualistic, hierarchical categories, she soon reverts to an orthodoxy of her own. Instead of continuing to derail Socratic logic, Diotima becomes a Platonist.

But has Irigaray listened to what Diotima says? Does she hear Diotima or the voices of Platonic scholars and commentators determined to show that Diotima is a Platonist? Irigaray works from a text glossed by many readings that shape and distort Diotima's teaching to make it compatible with Platonic dogma. For example, Irigaray complains that Diotima thinks some external acquisition such as immortality or collective happiness is the end for which love is only a means. But this popular criticism of Platonic love depends on a misleading translation and interpretation of the expression "γενέσθαι αὐτῶ," literally "to come to be for someone", or "to happen to someone" (204d). Why do we love? asks Diotima. What is it that we want? We want, the Greek reads, "the beautiful to come into being for us." Irigaray, however, accepts the misleading but common translation, "We want the good to be ours" (1984, 31). Possession, however, in the sense of acquiring a property, is not what lovers crave, according to Diotima. Instead, they long for the quickening, fertilizing contact with someone beautiful in body and soul that is necessary if, together, lovers are to generate new ways of thinking and living. Diotima's lover is not the heaven-crazed lover of the *Phaedrus* who glimpses in his idol the dim reflection of an otherworldly vision *he* would like to reclaim.[5] Nor is she the Platonic teacher seeking a suitable receptacle for the "*déssemination*" of his own ideas.[6] Instead, according to Diotima, what we seek in love is the fruitfulness of interaction, the fecundity of dialogue. The "goods" that result are collective, not the possession of any individual.[7]

In another and even more serious misinterpretation of Diotima's teaching, Irigaray accepts a Platonic reading of Diotima's theory of beauty-in-itself. Here, she follows traditional scholarship in taking Diotima's final revelation of unchanging beauty as a less sophisticated version of Plato's theory of hierarchical Forms. In fact, the progress of Diotima's initiate is not vertical, from lower to higher, but lateral, from narrow sexual relations and an exclusive concern with one's own family, to "better" (not "higher"), more inclusive relationships.[8] The lover comes to love souls *as well as* bodies, many *as well as* one. When she finally begins to sense the creative process in all of life, she is "embarked on the wide sea of beauty", and can bear "magnificent thoughts in philosophical abundance" (201d). The final vision of a Beauty that does not change is not of a transcendent Form, seen as a rigid confining model for human excellence. It is the very opposite. The initiate senses an inner generative impulse at the heart of life, an impulse that continually foments change and decay and so prevents the settling in of rigid form. Only when she has this insight, Diotima warns, will the lover be able to give birth to true virtue and not to false images of virtue (212a, 1-5).[9]

Diotima does not proscribe "lower" forms of love or of thought. She does not say what Irigaray has her say: "*de beaucoup la plus considerable et la plus belle manifestation de la pensée etant celle qui concerne l'ordonnonce des États comme de tout établissement*" (by far the most important and the most beautiful expression of thought being that which concerns the government of states as of any establishment) (1984, p. 35). Diotima is more subtle. She says: "Much that is most important and best comes from this sort of thinking (ie. practical wisdom), both for the city and for the management of the household" (209a). The progress of Diotima's initiate, unlike that of Plato's student, never requires the renunciation of "lower" forms of engendering, only a widening circle of those with whom we have loving intercourse, and a widening of the benefits of that intercourse.

Diotima does argue that the point of love is the "goods" that come from harmonious intercourse. She does not say, however, what Plato seems to imply in the *Phaedrus*: that we use the loved one, finding in him an ideal that will assist our reascent to a Platonic heaven inhabited by ideal essences. There is no equivocation in Diotima's naturalistic view of immortality as the good we leave after us. Her goods are not pre-existing eternal essences which the lover wishes to acquire or reach. Instead, loving intercourse *is* creativity: it *is* the process by which we create new forms. When these forms—a child, an idea, a new way of life, a new theory or administrative technique—are identified with a pre-existing ideal, then Diotima's love disappears. The child becomes the false image of the parents' imagination, the idea a spurious abstraction, the theory an alienated intellectualism, the administrative technique a strategy of domination. For Diotima, the issue or outcome of loving harmonious relations are goods, not "The Good." Goods are simply the plurality of things that make us happy. This is so obvious, Diotima says, that no more need be said about it (205a).

According to some of the criteria used in recent works by feminist writers, Diotima's philosophy, with its denial of autonomous alienated consciousness, its recognition of the affective and collective nature of knowledge, its unwillingness to separate the practical from the theoretical, might seem to be deeply feminist. Irigaray, however, sees Diotima as capitulating to Platonic metaphysics. It is not hard to understand why classical scholars choose to interpret Diotima as a Platonist: this is one way to explain the anomaly of her appearance at the *Symposium* and to perpetuate the illusion that the foundations of culture are irrevocably male. But why Irigaray would make such a mistake needs further explanation. The source of the misunderstanding, I believe, is to be found not just in a misleading translation, but in the conceptual infrastructure of Irigaray's feminist strategy: in deconstructive method and textual practise, in "*écriture féminine*", and in the concept of feminine "*jouissance*".

Irigaray, as feminist critic of Western philosophy, adopts a textual practise, a "*travail du langage*." She has no naive notion of refuting male philosophers in their own terms. Instead, she approaches them as texts, that is, as internally generated, more or less ordered systems of meaning whose logical order and pretended truth must be deconstructed. The reader of a text must avoid being taken in both by an establishment of authoritative truth and by the temptation to establish a rival thesis.

> *Autrement dit, l'enjeu . . . est d'enrayer la machinerie théorique elle-même, de suspendre sa prétension à la production d'un vérité et d'un sens par trop univoques.* (In other words, what is at stake is to jam the theoretical machinery itself, to suspend its pretension to the production of a too unitary truth and meaning) (1977, 75).

The source of this strategy is, of course, Jacques Derrida. For Derrida, the pretension to truth and unitary meaning is theological. Logic's claim to self-evidence, the representation of physical fact, even the presence of a human voice in spoken words, all rest on an implicit appeal to a transcendent presence. Once such a "god" is rejected, it becomes clear that speech is not revelatory of any transcendent truth but is an internally ordered phonemic graphism neither prior to nor essentially different from writing. This is not to say that we can do away with a "unitary" meaning ordered in hierarchical oppositions. These must continue, Derrida argues, to form the semantic matrix of thought. However, if, as in traditional philosophical refutation, the premises of a supposed truth are rejected as false and an alternative semantic ordering is asserted which is to be more consistent with the "facts", then the theological presence of truth is reasserted.[10]

Instead, Derrida proposes a variety of deconstructive strategies, many of them adopted by Irigaray. Hierarchical oppositions can be turned on their heads and the supposed presence exposed as a lack against which the opposing term is defined. Or, the deconstructor may read between the lines and discover ways in which the author unwittingly subverts her or his own text. Or she may discover in seemingly unimportant asides and "supplements" the core problem or issue that motivates the text. In all of these cases, deconstructive readings must not claim to find *the* meaning, *the* truth of a text, or even the author's *intended* meaning. Released from such logocentric projects, the reader may proceed to explore an infinite chain of deferrals and differences in which any supposed authoritative order is always compromised.

In *Spurs: Nietzsche's Styles*, a deconstruction of Nietzsche's misogyny, Derrida specifically identifies this subversion of the text as "feminine." For the "woman," outside masculine appropriation, there can be no truth. As feminine, she keeps an ambiguous distance, leaves open a seductive plurality of meanings, and so can play irreverently with the text, taking pleasure in overturning whatever order misogynist, truth-asserting, phallic society tries to establish.[11] Like other French feminists, Irigaray found in these strategies both a possible antidote for the paralyzing realization that sexism can be built into semantic structure, and a flattering reversal of the proverbial sexist claim that women are inferior because they are illogical and incapable of consistency. Derrida seems to suggest a way in which women, excluded from and degraded in male culture, can still undermine, if not overcome, that culture.

This method, however, so brilliantly deployed by Irigaray in her readings of Aristotle, Plato, Kant, and other male philosophers, falters when applied to Diotima.[12] In Diotima's thought, there is no hierarchical logic to expose, no masculine/presence, feminine/absence to deconstruct. Diotima's lovers are humans who must die and the motivation for their interaction does not depend on their sex. But neither can Irigaray successfully claim Diotima as a fellow deconstructionist. Diotima is not concerned with undermining an authoritative logic. Her tone with Socrates does not need to be bolstered by the defiant irony with which Irigaray faces down her philosophical forebears.

Instead, she treats him with the playful condescension due a youth who has not yet grasped the simplest of natural facts. Not only does Diotima not need to deconstruct a Platonic theory of the Forms, she has doubts that Socrates is even capable of following her discussion of the "erotica" or mysteries of love. To her exposure of his ignorance, Socrates responds humbly. Irigaray, however, does not approve the masterful way in which Diotima directs the discussion.

The reason for her disapproval can be found in the theory of language on which Irigaray's textual practice depends. That theory, derived from Derrida and from Irigaray's other mentor, Lacan, depends on a Saussurian view of language as a system of signs internally related.[13] In the Lacanian version, we do not use words to communicate; instead we "enter into" language, a fixed system of meanings structured around the master signifier, the Phallus, and its corollary, the Name of the Father. Once this view of language is accepted, Derridean deconstruction becomes the only liberatory tactic.[14] Fixed configurations of meaning must be broken up or subverted in order to insure a degree of anarchic freedom. On this view, Diotima, as speaker of a language, must enter into the hierarchical system of meaning that structures any semantics. Like Plato, or any philosopher, she must find herself trapped in a system of signifiers with phallic presence at the center. If she is not to lapse into unintelligibility, she must revert to the founding oppositions of Western metaphysics: subordination of the body to the mind, of physical appetite to rationality, of natural existence to spiritual heaven. Her only alternative would be to subvert their authority in a "feminine operation" of deconstruction. Because Irigaray accepts the Lacanian view of language as a system of signs into which we enter, whether to obey or subvert, she can only understand Diotima in the same terms. Not only must Irigaray perform a "feminine operation" in her reading of Diotima, she must evaluate Diotima's own method according to its success as an "*écriture féminine.*"

"*Écriture de la femme*" is Irigaray's version of Derrida's "feminine operation." The subversion of the text of patriarchy, she claims, requires a new kind of feminine style. This style will be always fluid, never allowing itself to be defined or restricted, never taking a fixed position. A woman writer must:

> met . . . feu aux mots fetiches, aux terms propres, aux formes bien
> construites. . et fait exploser toute forme, figure, idée, concept,
> solidement établis. (put fire to fetish words, correct terms, well-
> constructed forms, and explode every solidly built form, fig-
> ure, idea, concept.) (1977, 76).

This advice may be pragmatically sound for a woman struggling in a predominately male establishment who must negotiate concepts and rules of thought devised by men which leaves her little room for intelligible self-expression. Diotima, however, in a different situation, has no interest in sustaining such a style. On the contrary, although she begins with a tertiary logic that Irigaray finds promisingly elusive, Diotima proceeds to refute the views of Aristophanes and Pausanias and to expound a thesis of her own.[15] She speaks with authority, as someone who has come to knowledge through a difficult process and who can pass on that knowledge only by urging an initiate to travel the same road. Irigaray, however, judges Diotima within the context that gives meaning to her own deconstructive practice as if Diotima were a twentieth-century Parisian *"intellectuelle"* struggling against the authority of a male academic establishment to produce an *"écriture féminine"*. But the institutional setting for Diotima's philosophy is not the *École Normale Supérieure*. The ahistorical character of Irigaray's intellectual inheritance prevents her from seeing the difference.[16]

In Lacanian and Derridean metaphysics, the distinction between natural and/or historical reality and the linguistic terms we use to interpret, represent, or criticize that reality is dissolved. For Lacan, the world outside of language is not a human world. It is the world of animal intersubjectivity and unreflective sensation. To learn to speak is not to learn to express sensations or articulate intersubjectively constituted experience, but to enter the world of the symbolic. A split in the self between watching subject and mirrored object, foundational both in the development of an individual and of human culture, allows the construction of an alienated linguistic identity. This identity is then articulated within the context of a social language, a transpersonal symbolic nexus whose central and primal signifier is the phallus. According to Lacan, our identities, as well as our understanding of any situation, are fixed only within this patrifocal symbolic order.

Although for Derrida the meanings in which we find ourselves are more ambiguous, disordered, "frayed", he also sees language as radically discontinuous with physical existence. A cry or a moan may be a natural sign, but words can never express an affective experience. History, literature, culture, everything human, is a text. There are no facts outside of language that language may express, or correctly or incorrectly represent. There is no non-textual situation out of which one may speak. The transition from physical existence to symbolic meaning is absolute and occurs outside of historical time as the precondition of culture itself.

This is not simply to say that language, as socially constructed meaning, mediates an individual's expression of her experience. If our words are never wholly our own but are taken from the mouths of others, we and they still speak from particular material situations. The Saussurian premise is more radical. Language has meaning not from its use in human expression, but from formal syntactical relations. Even when, as for Derrida, these relations are not rigidly ordered, meaning does not depend on who is speaking or where and why she says what she does. This is true because for Derrida the hierarchical oppositions against which deconstruction operates are necessary. More importantly, it is true because even Derridean metaphor, ambiguity, and paradox depend on formal patterning: configurations of differences and deferrals, reversals and spacings. However, to read a text in this way is to refuse to consider the institutional conditions of its production or the identity of its author. Therefore, Irigaray cannot place Diotima's thought within a particular material historical context. Whatever her circumstances or her identity, Diotima, as speaker, has entered the world of the text and has left material existence behind. But this is to erase the specific historical/social setting of the Platonic dialogues.

Much has been written about the sequestered and inferior status of women in classical Greece. There has also been much feminist criticism of the misogynist thought that ratified that inferiority.[17] However, the subjugation of Greek women was not only textual, nor was it a necessary effect of the alienated origins of symbolic thought. Instead, it was the outcome of more than a millenium of social change in the Aegean and Mediterranean areas. Beginning about 2000 B.C., Greek-speaking invaders and emigrants began to arrive in mainland Greece. These invaders brought with them the male-dominated social structures of a nomadic, illiterate, warrior society: political hierarchy, the worship of a supreme sky and thunder god, the restriction of women to the domestic sphere. In Greece they found no primitive animal subsistence, but a civilization focused on a sophisticated Minoan culture. Minoan frescoes and seals document a way of life very different from that of the invaders. Women are depicted in positions of prominence, presiding at religious ceremonies, worshipping a female deity, attending festivals and entertainments, participating in the important ceremony of bull dancing.[18] In the intervening centuries—from the fall of Crete to Mycenaean dominance, through the dark ages, up to classical times—the clash continued between a theology focused on a central female divinity and natural cycles of generation on the one hand, and one focused on a supreme warrior-father-god on the other.[19] By classical times, although subjected to increasing segregation and domestic isolation, as well as to complete political disenfranchisement, women still retained some of their old power in religion. They continued to fill important sacerdotal roles as priestesses of Athena or Demeter; they participated publically in religious festivals and initiations; they celebrated women's rituals such as the Dionysian or the Thesmophorian; they performed as prophetesses at oracular shrines such as Delphi.

In historical context, then, it is neither surprising nor anomalous that Diotima would appear in an authoritative role as the teacher of Socrates.[20] As prophetess/priestess she was part of a religious order that had maintained its authority from Minoan/Mycenaean times. At Delphi, the sibyl still presided as the most respected oracle in Greece. Thousands proclaimed the benefits of initiation into the wisdom of Demeter at Eleusis. Socrates himself points out the respect due Diotima for preparing the sacrifice that rescued

Athens from the plague (201d). As Mantinean prophetess, Diotima does not speak as a lone woman who has painfully managed to gain entrance to a male party. She speaks out of a tradition of female power and female thought still alive in Greek culture. When Socrates refers to the prophetic power of the sibyl or the inspired voices of the Muses in the *Phaedrus*, he taps sources that may not be available in Irigaray's Christianized late twentieth century Paris, where the connection between divinity and masculinity is axiomatic, and the "absence" of the feminine a necessary truth.

Historically locatable psychoanalytic formulations of that necessary truth are part of the conceptual underpinning of Irigaray's feminist method. Women's sexuality, Irigaray argues, is absent from Freudian theory. In her view, women's liberation is intimately connected with the recognition of and indulgence in a specifically feminine sexual pleasure. This feminine "*jouissance*" is defined in contrast with a dominant masculine sexuality.[21] Masculine sexuality is phallic, that is, active, penetrative, aggressive, focused on orgasm. Women's pleasure, on the other hand, is self-touching, interactive, heterogeneous, plural, and flowing rather than gathering to a climax.

This view of feminine sexuality also has at its source the ideas of Lacan. Lacan corrected any lingering biologism still inherent in Freud's account of women's supposed sexual disabilities only to make those disabilities even more inaccessible to feminist reform.[22] In principle, biology can be circumvented by contraception or artifical methods of reproduction. But when Lacan locates women's disability in universal structures of linguistic meaning, he writes women's inferiority into culture itself. For Lacan, that inferiority is inscribed as a kind of nonentity, as what cannot be expressed. Lacan complained with some satisfaction that when women (including women analysts) are asked about their sexuality, "they know nothing about this pleasure" (Lacan 1975, 68).

Irigaray, like Lacan, does not question the contrast between masculine and feminine sexuality. Instead, she attempts to answer Freud's and Lacan's unanswered question (What do women want?), and to make articulate that feminine "*jouissance*" which escapes masculine logic. She supplies Lacan's "Woman", the "*pas-toute*" (not all there), with a specific presence. Women's sexuality will no longer be the simple negative, or lack of masculine phallic presence; nor will it be the ineffable ecstasy-beyond-words of Lacan's appropriation of Bernini's *St. Thérèse*.[23] Instead, it will be an alternative kind of pleasure—describable, recoverable, and connected with a woman's different "self-touching" sexual economy.

Irigaray's neo-Lacanian account of sexuality is in sharp dissonance with Diotima's. Diotima grounds love and sexual desire in natural existence rather than in semantic configurations of meaning. Diotimean love is the same for all, women and men, and makes no distinction between feminine and masculine desire. Diotima's theory of love does not focus on pleasure; genital pleasure in the sense of a private sensation is not mentioned in her philosophy. It is not surprising, therefore, that, given Irigaray's commitment to the explanatory and liberatory power of feminine sexual pleasure, she can make no sense of Diotima's positive view. After a promising beginning, Irigaray charges, Diotima makes no distinction between our human (textual) identity and nature. She looks for a cause in natural phenomena; she leaves intact a hierarchy in which spiritual love is better than physical.

These formulations, however, do not do justice to Diotimean positions which do not share Irigaray's presuppositions. Although Diotima grounds sexual desire in a principle of nature, that principle involves neither women's reproductive organs nor men's penises. Instead, it has to do with the fact of mortality and the impulse of living things to perpetuate themselves. Our desire to transcend our mortality by leaving good after us is not limited to the engendering of children. In fact, our immortality is more secure when we produce new ways of living and thinking. Diotima makes no distinction between men and women in this respect. Both men and women come together to bring up children; in her account this is not an exclusively female activity. Both men and women enter into other kinds of loving relationship to produce virtues, ideas, new ways of management. These relationships can be between any sex, heterosexual or homosexual.[24] In every case, the impulse of desire is the same—cooperative generation of good things both for the couple and for others, both for the household and the community. The pursuit of pleasurable sensation could not be the motive for Diotima's desire; a privatized sensation of pleasure could never account for the universality and urgency of love as she sees it. For Diotima, love is not a recreation but permeates the whole of human activity.

Irigaray, however, sees in Diotima's philosophy another attempt to deprive women of their specific sexual pleasure. Although Irigaray would agree that desire motivates our activities and our thought, this is for her a textual and not a natural fact. Therefore, for her, the key to the subversion of the patriarchal order is non-textual sexual pleasure, a force outside conceptual structures, especially those generative and familial structures that have made women the container/envelope that protects and shelters the male. The maternity so important for Diotima in the lives of both men and women is, for Irigaray, only a trap from which sexual pleasure, or "jouissance", must deliver us. Diotimean love, which has issue in human goodness, knowledge, familial and institutional relationships, is anathema to Irigaray. It makes love, she says, into a "*devoir*" or "*moyen*" (a duty or means) (1984, 33). Love becomes "*sagesse politique, sagesse ordre de la cite*" (political wisdom, wisdom ordering the city) (1984, 36). In contrast, Irigaray's feminine pleasure involves a free, sensuous play of bodies and texts, engaged in for its own sake, opposed to the establishment of any doctrine, politics, or commitment. For Irigaray, to allow stakes in love is to cease to be feminine. It is to found an alienated masculine order. The feminine can never be foundational because its very essence is marginality, a marginality that is liberating because it provokes a constant questioning and mocking of the masculine order that restricts the free circulation of feminine desire.[25]

Diotima, on the other hand, speaks from a different perspective. As priestess, prophetess, member of a theological tradition, she finds nothing inconsistent in the idea of feminine institutions and social forms. She is not the marginalized and repressed female student of an all-powerful male philosophical and psychoanalytic establishment. She has not been painfully rejected by her master. Instead, she speaks to an audience which takes feminine divinity for granted and for which feminine religious leaders continue to command respect. As a result, she has a different sense of herself as feminine than a woman struggling for a foothold, or refusing to find a foothold, within the paranoid closed circle of Lacanian authority.[26]

Irigaray's rejection of Diotima's method is also linked to a view of the subject inherited from post-structuralist theory. In Diotima's philosophy, the self is in a constant process of change, both in mind and body (207d-208e). Therefore, it is clear that she cannot be accused of the Cartesianism that contemporary feminists have found so useful as an objection to masculinist theory (eg. Flax 1980, Irigaray 1974). At the same time, Diotima's view of the loving self, constantly open to mutilations that occur in any relationship and constantly in the process of generating new social forms, has little in common with the split subject of Lacan. Lacan understood that there could be no unitary self. Always in the self is the Other, but this Other of Lacan is not another person. It is the Other of language ruled by the Law of the Father. We are split between the polymorphous feeling "me" and a linguistic order in which we must live out our social lives as human and not animal. This "Other" we have no choice but to accept. Irigaray, like Lacan, sees institutionalization as a return to the Other, to the Law of the Father, and so must posit, as the only escape, a libidinous sensuality that language must leave behind.

Diotima, however, does not see in language a built-in normative order. For her, discourses are interchanges that initiate social orders. Talk between lovers is not a free expression of pure sensuous pleasure, nor is it a programmed lesson resulting in a predetermined definition of good. Neither of these possibilities would lead to the new ideas that Diotima claims are the fruits of love. Irigaray charges Diotima with moving away from an "individualized becoming" to "collective" goods. Indeed, Diotimean talk between lovers "never contemplates an individual becoming"; sexual desire, for Diotima is not an impulse toward self-realization. Instead, in love the mortal subject moves beyond her own individual life into the lives of others. Pregnancy and birth, whether of body or mind, occur only when there is an "engagement" (ἁρμόττον) and a "being together" (συνουσίᾳ) (206c4-d1).

Irigaray, on the other hand, trapped in the metaphysics of Lacan's split self, cannot accept an interactional view of discourse. She sees feminist struggle as an internalized rebellion against the Law of the Father in one's own speech and thought. The goal of this struggle must be free expression of diffuse emotions and sensations, and a feminine speech that has affinites with the "illogic" of hysterics and dreamers:

> Échanges sans termes identifiables, sans comptes, sans fin . . .
> Sans un(e) plus un(e), sans série, san nombre. (Exchanges without identifiable terms, without accounts, without end . . .
> without one plus one, without series, without number. (1977, 193)

This is a language that women may "parler entre-elles", but the revolutionary result is not the development of new forms of social life. It is a personal liberation that frees the subject from the symbolic Law of the Father.

For Diotima, on the other hand, there is no "subject," split or other. There are only selves in constant dissolution and renewal as they relate to each other. The enemy of the self is not an internalized conceptual order, but "ugliness", an ugliness not identified as the opposite of an ideal of perfect beauty but as that which one cannot love. Ugliness can have no issue, because it is rigid, sterile, impotent, arid. (206d) Although Irigaray may be right in thinking that we have finally internalized such an ugliness, she is wrong to ignore the historical specificity of that process.

I, too, read Plato years ago with no interest in Greek geography, religion, or politics, sexual or other, I read Plato as if he were John Austin. Others read him as if we were Frege, or more recently Kripke. We all read him as if he were the practitioner of our own particular brand of rationality. Although we might have disagreed about what rationality consisted in, we were sure that it existed and that it allowed us to read Plato on our own terms. Deconstructive reading and écriture féminine have been a refreshing antidote. They have made us see the veneer of rationalism and the destructive misogyny of those we were taught to respect. Irigaray, performing her "feminine operation" has interrupted academic discourse, disrupted sacred Aristotelian, Platonic and Kantian categories. She has made us see how the Law of the Father operates masked as metaphysical truth.

If, with Diotima, her usual sure touch falters, it is because Diotima does not play the feminine role as deconstruction or Lacanian psychoanalytic theory has conceived it. She is not the uninvited gatecrasher, but the host of the Symposium. She is the spokesperson for ways of life and thought that Greek philosophy feeds on, ways of thought whose authority Plato neutralized and converted to his own purposes.

In Plato's hands, Diotima's loving conversation becomes the Socratic elenchus: a programmed course of study in which pupil is guided toward a "correct" conclusion determined in advance. The generative, divine source of Beauty becomes the Form of the Good, an abstract transcendent object re-

moved from the processes of the natural world. Diotima's concern that, unless we see and involve ourselves with real generative beauty, we may rely on
false "images" of virtue is rejected and a sterile Socratic division manufactures
villains and heroes. Diotima's celebration of erotic union as the divine mode
for all creative activity becomes contempt for the body and for heterosexual
intercourse.

Platonic philosophy is not the primal opening of metaphysical space, as
Irigaray argued in *Speculum*. It is parasitic on an earlier metaphysics, whose
characteristic idioms Plato borrows to build a phantasmic world of images. If
Irigaray showed us the necessary flimsiness of the Platonic "symbolic", her
Derridean and Lacanian heritage withheld from us the actual history of its
fraudulent construction. To reduce Diotima to co-opted feminine marginality
is to perpetuate this deception. To reinstate her is to carry out that necessary
restructuring of our perspective that Irigaray herself described so inspiringly in
Speculum de l'autre femme.

NOTES

1. K.J. Dover (1978) states the typical reasoning. It is unlikely that a woman could have
taught Socrates (p. 161, footnote 11). A more recent example is Martha Nussbaum (1986) who
asserts Diotima's fictionality without argument and further reduces her status by labeling her as
Plato's intellectual "mistress", a woman with whom he has mental intercourse. (p. 177)
2. At 210a, Diotima explains that to reach the first revelation one must begin while young by
falling in love with beautiful bodies. At 206c, she describes the coming together of men and
women to produce children as a "divinity and an immortality in the midst of human life." (Cf.
Phaedrus 250c, where those who have forgotten the vision of beauty from their pre-earth
existences go off like "beasts" and "beget offspring of the flesh.")
3. Line citations are to Bury's (1932) text of the *Symposium*. Translations are my own.
4. Most commentators have assumed the identity of Diotima's pure beauty-in-itself and the
Platonic Form of Beauty as described in the *Phaedrus*. In the *Phaedrus*, the winged soul in its
Pythagorean preexistence climbs a heavenly summit to glimpse the "true being" of Justice, Temperance, Beauty, etc. Once imprisoned in the body, the soul can only dimly discern vestiges of
this heavenly Beauty in actual beautiful objects. For Diotima, the process is reversed. The lover
begins by loving individuals and via a widening loving practise begins to discern the generative
power in all the beautiful things to which she is attracted. Although Diotima's final vision is of a
divine beauty not instantiated in any individual physical thing ("pure, mixed, not filled in with
flesh or with the human, or with color") (211d), there is no suggestion that it has any ghostly
residence in a heaven of Forms. Instead, it is grasped as an immortal life force, independent of
any individual being. The vision of absolute beauty is not an end in itself for Diotima. The goal
continues to be "to bear" (τίκειν) true virtue. (212a3) (There is no good translation for
"τίκτω" which can be used both of the father's and the mother's part in reproduction.)
5. Diotima refers to lovers as "he's" when generic terms are not available. Since Plato's audience and also the audience of the *Symposium* are male, it is to be expected that Plato and perhaps
even Diotima herself would have adapted their presentations for that audience. There is,
however, no reason to think that Diotima's teaching would have been meant only for men. The
content of that teaching clearly refers to both women and men.
6. Cf. Derrida's (1981) deconstructive reading of the *Phaedrus* in which he traces the patriarchal motifs of succession from father to son.
7. Cf. 209b-c. When the "pregnant" lover comes into contact with someone beautiful, she
not only embraces the loved one's body but also they converse. The new insights which are the

"offspring" of this union are "brought up" by the couple together and this "common project" makes their love even stronger. There is no suggestion that only one of the couple profits from or possesses the "goods" that are generated in their relationship.

8. The one passage that seems to suggest a hierarchical progression is 211c, where Diotima says that "in order to approach the philosophy of love correctly one must, beginning from beautiful things, progress for the sake of what is eternally beautiful, like climbing stairs." In what follows, however, she explains what she means, again in nonhierarchical terms. The lover is go to "from one (beautiful body) to two, from two to many . . . "

9. Commentators have had considerable difficulty in giving a Platonic interpretation of the conclusion of Diotima's discourse. She has been describing the final vision of beauty-in-itself, the eternal generative center inherent in everything and everyone we love. Then she adds: "But don't you think that only this person, this seeing person for whom the good is visible, will be able to "give birth" not to images of virtue because she fastens on images, but true virtue because she fastens on true virtues?" (212a, 1-5). In fact, Diotima's conclusion can be read as an implicit warning against Platonism: if we detach ourselves from real concrete beauty, we may manufacture only empty ideas of virtue and not real virtue.

10. This is the argument of Derrida's foundational text, *Of Grammatology* (1976).

11. When Nietzsche's various pronouncements on women are examined, Derrida argues, there are several attitudes revealed. First, the woman is condemned by Nietzsche as a "figure" of falsehood. Second, she is "censured, debased and despised" as a figure of truth. But in a third kind of statement, beyond this double negation, the woman is affirmed as having moved beyond the opposition between truth and falsity. (Derrida 1978, 97).

12. This project is carried out in Irigaray's *Speculum de l'autre femme* where she reads the founding fathers of philosophy, Plato, Aristotle, Kant, Descartes, in order to exhibit and derail their sexist logic.

13. The relations between the master Lacan and Irigaray were troubled. As a Lacanian analyst on the faculty of Lacan's department at Vincennes, Irigaray's seminar was abruptly cancelled as unsuitable after the publication of *Speculum*.

14. Lacan, himself, believing that the symbolic order of the phallus was constitutive of linguistic meaning, promised no escape from the signifier. Psychoanalysis could only bring the subject back to the alienating moment of entering language and make him alive to the fragility of his symbolic existence.

15. When Diotima chides Socrates for employing a simplistic dichotomous logic (love must be ugly or beautiful), Irigaray approves her "non-Hegelian" dialectic, a *"jeu l'intermediare"* which does not destroy two terms to establish a synthesis but that inserts a "third" that allows a progression from one state to another. (1984, 27) Her analysis, however, does not recognize the connection Diotima makes between the textual progression from term to term and the natural urge that aspires to beauty and goodness.

16. Other feminist deconstructive readings of Plato suffer from the same ahistorical assumptions. See eg. du Bois' (1985) deconstruction of Derrida's deconstruction of the *Phaedrus*. Derrida missed, du Bois argues, the submerged femininity in the *Phaedrus*, where Plato has Socrates turn into a king of "transvestite", speaking in the voices of priestesses and female poets. This analysis assumes the eternally degraded, libidinal feminine, excluded from, but erupting into, the eternally dominant masculine.

17. Irigaray herself is at the forefront with her brilliant deconstructive readings of Aristotle and Plato in *Speculum*.

18. Revisions of unfounded assumptions of male superiority by Sir Arthur Evans and others have been necessary. Cf. eg. Willetts (1977) who reviews the literature and describes the now overwhelming evidence that women had a pre-eminent position in Minoan Crete, and also Thomas (1973) for a more ideological, but still persuasive, argument.

19. The degree of survival of Minoan-Mycenean "matriarchal" traditions in Homer and the Archaic age has been controversial. Cf. Pomeroy (1973) for a discussion of the evidence and some speculation as to the causes of the virulence with which scholars have attacked the idea of a surviving matriarchy. There is, however, massive evidence for the continuation of Minoan religious traditions throughout the Archaic age and into classical times. Cf. Dietrich (1974).

20. Cf. also Aristoxenus fr. 15 (Kirk, Raven, and Schofield (1984) frg. 278, 233): "and Aristoxenus says that Pythagoras got most of his ethical doctrine from the Delphic priestess, Themistocleia."

21. Difficult to translate into English, *"jouissance"* implies sensuous pleasure in general, the use or possession of an object for one's own pleasure, and, in colloquial use, the specific pleasure of sexual orgasm.

22. Cf. Freud's essay on "Femininity" (1953) in which Freud argues that, even in "normal" development, the girl's sexuality will be to some extent repressed, resulting in a necessary degree of frigidity, narcissism, and failure to sublimate desire in great works.

23. Bernini's statue of Saint Thérèse, pierced by the love of Christ, is the frontspiece for Lacan's seminar on love, *Encore* (1975).

24. Although Diotima's language has been adapted by Plato for a Greek male homosexual audience, and therefore sometimes seems to apply only to male lovers, the actual content of her teaching shows that it is meant to apply to any combination of sexes. Her teaching was particularly useful for Plato who could adapt it to male homosexual love, or distort it to argue that pederasty between men was superior to heterosexual love.

25. At one place, Irigaray seems to suggest that this marginality is, to some degree, situational (cf. 1977, 125-126), the *"mode d'action aujourd'hui possible pour les femmes"* (the kind of action *today* possible for women). But in the previous paragraph Irigaray makes it clear that an unprecedented revolution in thought must occur before a woman could develop a *"discours de la femme"* or a *"pratique politique."*

26. See Catherine Clément (1981) for a sensitive description of some of the contradictions and compromises such a position could entail.

BIBLIOGRAPHY

Bois, Page du. 1985. Phallocentrism and its Subversion in Plato's *Phaedrus*. *Arethusa* 18: 91-103.

Bury, R.G. 1932. *The Symposium of Plato*. Cambridge: W. Heffer and Sons.

Clément, Catherine. 1981. *Vies et légendes de Jacques Lacon*. Paris: B. Grasset.

Derrida, Jacques. 1976. *Of Grammatology*, Trans. G.C. Spivak. Baltimore: John Hopkins University Press.

——. 1978. *Spurs: Nietzsche's Styles*. Trans, Barbara Harlow. Chicago: University of Chicago Press.

——. 1981. *Dissémination*. Trans. Barbara Johnson. Chicago: University of Chicago Press.

Dietrich, B.C. 1974. *The Origins of Greek Religion*. Berlin: Walter de Gruyter.

Dover, K.J. 1978. *Greek Homosexuality*. Cambridge, Mass: Harvard University Press.

Flax, Jane. 1980. Mother-Daughter Relationships: Psychodynamics, Politics and Philosophy, in *The Future of Difference*, ed. Hester Eisenstein and Alice Jardine. Boston: G. K. Hall.

Freud, Sigmund. 1953. Femininity. *The Standard Edition of the Complete Psychological Works*. XXI. London: Hogarth.

Irigaray, Luce. 1974. *Speculum de l'autre femme*. Paris: Minuit.

——. 1977. *Ce sexe qui n'est pas un*. Paris: Minuit.

——. 1984. *Éthique de la différence sexuale*. Paris: Minuit.

Lacan, Jacques. 1966. *Écrits I and II*. Paris: du Seuil.

——. 1975. *Encore, Le Séminaire de Jacques Lacan, Livre XX*. Paris: du Seuil.

Nussbaum, Martha. 1986. *The Fragility of Goodness: Luck and Ethics in Greek Tragedy and Philosophy*. Cambridge: Cambridge University Press.

Plato, 1932. *The Symposium*. ed: R. G. Bury. Cambridge: W. Heffer and Sons.

Pomeroy, Sarah. 1973. Selected bibliography on women. *Arethusa*. 6:2.

——. 1975. Andromache and the Question of Matriarchy. *Révue des études Greques*. LXXXVIII, 16-19.

Thomas, C.G. 1973. Matriarchy in Early Greece: The Bronze and Dark Ages. *Arethusa*. 6: 2.

Thomson, George. 1949. *The Prehistoric Aegean*. London: Laurence and Wishart.

Willets, R.F. 1977. *The Civilization of Ancient Crete*. London: Batsford.

"Essentially Speaking":
Luce Irigaray's Language of Essence

DIANA J. FUSS

Luce Irigaray's fearlessness towards speaking the body has earned for her work the dismissive label "essentialist." But Irigaray's Speculum de l'autre femme *and* Ce Sexe qui n'en est pas un *suggest that essence may not be the unitary, monolithic, in short, essentialist category that anti-essentialists so often presume it to be. Irigaray strategically deploys essentialism for at least two reasons: first, to reverse and to displace Jacques Lacan's phallomorphism; and second, to expose the contradiction at the heart of Aristotelian metaphysics which denies women access to "Essence" while at the same time positing the essence of "Woman" precisely as non-essential (as matter).*

Perhaps more than any other notion in the vocabulary of recent feminist poststructuralist theory, "essentialism" has come to represent both our greatest fear and our greatest temptation. The idea that men and women, for example, are identified as such on the basis of transhistorical, eternal, immutable "essences" has been unequivocally rejected by many anti-essentialist poststructuralist feminists concerned with resisting any attempts to naturalize "human nature." And yet, one can hear echoing from the corners of the debates on essentialism renewed interest in its possibilities and potential usages, sounds which articulate themselves in the form of calls to "risk" or to "dare" essentialism.[1] Essentialism has been given new life by these invitations to consider a possible strategic deployment of essence; we could even say that, in feminist theory, essentialism is the issue which simply refuses to die. Certainly essentialism is the charge most frequently heard in critiques of Luce Irigaray's "psychophilosophy."[2] The present essay participates in the general calls for a reconsideration of essentialism in order to pose the question of how essentialism might operate *in the service of* Luce Irigaray's feminist theory and politics. Why and when is essentialism invoked in her work? What might be at stake in the deployment of essentialism for strategic purposes? In short, are there ways to think and to talk about essence that might not, necessarily, "always already," ipso facto, be reactionary?

In what follows it will become clear that I do believe that there are such ways to elaborate and to work with a notion of essence that is not, in essence,

Hypatia vol. 3, no. 3 (Winter 1989) © by Diana J. Fuss

ahistorical, apolitical, empiricist, or simply reductive. But before turning to a consideration of Irigaray's strategic use of essentialism, it bears emphasizing that most of the criticisms levelled against Irigaray's work since the publication of *Speculum de l'autre femme* in 1974 are inevitably based upon or in some way linked to this fear of essentialism. A summary sample of the most important and oft-cited of these criticisms is enough to demonstrate how impassioned and genuine the resistance to essentialism is for many feminists, and how problematic the reassessment of essentialism's theoretical or political usefulness is likely to be.

IRIGARAY AND HER CRITICS

In 1981, two critical essays on Luce Irigaray's work were published in the U.S., each in a well-known feminist academic journal: Christine Fauré's "The Twilight of the Goddesses, or the Intellectual Crisis of French Feminism" appeared in *Signs*, and Carolyn Burke's "Irigaray Through the Looking Glass" appeared in *Feminist Studies*. Fauré's critique, a translation from the French, is unquestionably the more severe. She objects to a general trend in French feminist theory, epitomized by Irigaray's search for a female imaginary, which marks "a retreat into aesthetics where the thrust of feminist struggle is masked by the old naturalistic ideal draped in the trappings of supposedly 'feminine' lyricism" (1981, 81).[3] Carolyn Burke also wonders whether Irigaray's work escapes the very idealism which her deconstruction of selected philosophical and psychoanalytic texts so rigorously and persistently seeks to displace:

> Does her writing manage to avoid construction of another idealism to replace the 'phallogocentric' systems that she dismantles? Do her representations of a *parler femme*, in analogy with female sexuality, avoid the centralizing idealism with which she taxes Western conceptual systems? (1981, 302)

Metaphysical idealism is probably the most damaging of the many criticisms charged against Irigaray; it finds its most recent and perhaps most powerful rearticulation in Toril Moi's *Sexual/Textual Politics*:

> Any attempt to formulate a general theory of femininity will be metaphysical. This is precisely Irigaray's dilemma: having shown that so far femininity has been produced exclusively in relation to the logic of the Same, she falls for the temptation to produce her own positive theory of femininity. But . . . to define 'woman' is necessarily to essentialize her. (1985, 139)

Is it true that any definition of 'woman' must be predicated on essence? And does Irigaray, in fact, define 'woman'? Though I will later argue that the problem of an idealism based on the body, on an essential femininity, is fundamentally a misreading of Irigaray, suffice it to say here that Moi's assumption that "to define 'woman' is necessarily to essentialize her" is by no means self-evident.

While Irigaray has been criticized by both psychoanalysts and materialists alike, the most impassioned critiques have come primarily from the materialists. Monique Plaza's " 'Phallomorphic Power' and the Psychology of 'Woman,' " first published in the French radical feminist publication *Questions féministes* and later reprinted in the British marxist journal *Ideology and Consciousness*, offers the most sustained and unremittingly critical indictment of Irigaray's apparent essentialism. According to Plaza, Luce Irigaray's great mistake (second only to her general failure to interrogate adequately psychoanalytic discourse) is a tendency to confuse social and anatomical categories; Irigaray's theorization of female pleasure and her "search for the feminine 'interior' " lead her to abjure the category of the social and to practice a dangerous form of "pan-sexualism which is only a coarse, disguised naturalism" (1978, 8-9). Plaza, along with Monique Wittig and Christine Delphy, argues from the materialist standpoint that "nature" is always a product of social relations and that sex is always a construction of oppression and never its cause. It is the move to desocialize "women," Plaza insists, which leads Irigaray into the fallacy of essentialism:

> The absence of a theory of oppression, the belief in the unavoidable and irreducible sexual Difference, the psychologistic reduction, the inflation of the notion of "women" which one finds in Luce Irigaray's investigation, can only result in this essentialist quest. In the gap left by the statement of woman's non-existence, Luce Irigaray will set up a "new" conception of woman. (28)

Plaza goes on to accuse Irigaray of positivism, empiricism, and negativism (31). Toril Moi, another materialist critic, adds two more weighty epithets: ahistorcism and apoliticism (1985, 147-48). If this were a critical barbecue, Irigaray would surely be skewered.

Luce Irigaray, however, is not without her defenders. Jane Gallop, in "Quand nos lèvres s'écrivent: Irigaray's Body Politic," interprets Irigaray's persistent focus on the female labia as a *construction* rather than a *reflection* of the body; Irigaray's essentialism is thus read within a larger anti-essentialist project of re-creating, re-metaphorizing the body (1983, 77-83). Margaret Whitford takes a similarly sympathetic (which is not to say uncritical) approach to the question of essentialism in Irigaray's work. In "Luce Irigaray and the Female Imaginary: Speaking as a Woman," Whitford concludes that while Irigaray does sometimes blur the distinctions between the social and the biological, "this is obviously a stategy adopted within a particular historical and cultural situation" (1986, 7).[4] This particular response to the problem of essentialism in Irigaray strikes me as the most promising line of argument to follow, for rather than foreclosing the discussion on essentialism before it has truly begun, this approach asks the more difficult question: if Irigaray appeals to a mode of feminine specificity, and if she attempts to speak the female body, what might such strategic forays into the territory of essentialism allow her to accomplish? What might Irigaray's work amount to *if she refused* such admittedly risky ventures into "this sex which is not one"?

"BY OUR LIPS WE ARE WOMEN"

Let me begin to answer these questions by re-examining the place and function of the "two lips" in Irigaray's theorization of female pleasure. This concept is perhaps most responsible for generating the charges of essentialism. Three words neatly summarize for Irigaray the significance of the two lips: "Both at once." Both at once signifies that a woman is simultaneously singular and double; she is "already two—but not divisible into one(s)," or, put another way, she is "*neither one nor two*" (1985c, 24, 26). It is the two lips which situate women's autoeroticism, their pleasure, in a different economy from the phallic, in an economy of ceaseless exchange and constant flux:

> Woman's autoeroticism is very different from man's. In order to touch himself, man needs an instrument: his hand, a woman's body, language. . . . And this self-caressing requires at least a minimum of activity. As for woman, she touches herself in and of herself without any need for mediation, and before there is any way to distinguish activity from passivity. Woman "touches herself" all the time, and moreover no one can forbid her to do so, for her genitals are formed of two lips in continuous contact. Thus, within herself, she is already two—but not divisible into one(s)—that caress each other. (1985c, 24)

It would be hard to deny, on the basis of this particular passage, that Irigaray proposes to give us an account of female pleasure based on the body's genitalia; and it would be hard to deny that her account of the phallus is any less morphological.[5] Why the essentialist language here? Why the relentless emphasis on the two lips?

Let me turn first to the Irigarian critique of the phallus to demonstrate what appears to be a strategic misreading of male genitalia. According to Irigaray, Western culture privileges a mechanics of solids over a mechanics of fluids because man's sexual imaginary is isomorphic; as such, the male imaginary emphasizes the following features: "production, property (propriété), order, form, unity, visibility, erection" (1985a, 77). The features

associated with a female imaginary, as we might expect, more closely approx-
imate the properties of liquids: "continuous, compressible, dilatable, viscous,
conductible, diffusable" (1985c, 111). The problem here is simply that many
of the properties Irigaray associates with the two lips might also describe the
penis. As K.K. Ruthven points out:

> A good deal depends here on the accuracy of Irigaray's charac-
> terization of the penis as "one" in comparison with the "not
> one" of the vulva. Certainly, her theory seems to require the
> penis to be always inflexibly erect and quite without metamor-
> phic variation, and also to be circumcised, as the presence of a
> foreskin endows it with most of the properties she attributes to
> the labia. (1984, 100-101)

Irigaray's reading of phallomorphism as a kind of isomophism, however, is
not so much a misreading as an *exposure* of one of the dominant metaphors in
poststructuralist psychoanalysis. It is not Irigaray who erects the phallus as a
single transcendental signifier but Lacan: Irigaray's production of an apparently essentializing notion of female sexuality functions strategically as a reversal and a displacement of Lacan's phallomorphism.

Irigaray's critique of Lacan centers primarily on his refusal to listen to
women speak of their own pleasure; she finds most untenable Lacan's insistence that, on the subject of pleasure, women have nothing to say. In his
Seminar XX on women, Lacan listens not to women but to art, not to Saint
Theresa but to Bernini's statue of Saint Theresa: "you only have to go and
look at Bernini's statue in Rome to understand immediately that she's coming, there is no doubt about it" ("God and the Jouissance of The Woman," in
Mitchell and Rose 1982, 147). Irigaray's interrogatory response in "Così Fan
Tutti" deftly unmasks the phallocentrism at play here: "In Rome? So far
away? To look? At a statue? Of a saint? Sculpted by a man? What pleasure are
we talking about? Whose pleasure?" (1985c, 90-91) Her logic is irrefutable:
why would a woman need to go all the way to Rome to discover the "truth" of
her pleasure? Why, after all, is "the right to experience pleasure . . . awarded
to a statue" (1985c, 90)?

Irigaray's "When Our Lips Speak Together" provides an explanatory gloss
on Lacan's efforts to arrive at the truth of woman's pleasure through an appeal
to a statue: "Truth is necessary for those who are so distanced from their body
that they have forgotten it. But their truth immobilizes us, turns us into statues . . ." (1985c, 214). If women are turned into statues through the process
of specularization—through the agency of the look—how can this specular
economy be undone? How, in other words, can women begin to speak their
own pleasure? Throughout both *Speculum of the Other Woman* and *This Sex
Which Is Not One*, Irigaray supplants the logic of the gaze with the logic of
touch: it is the "contact of *at least two* (lips) which keeps woman in touch

with herself but without any possibility of distinguishing what is touching from what is touched" (1985c, 26). This shift of focus from sight to touch affords Irigaray another opportunity to challenge Lacan, this time on the subject of his obsession with veiling: "Veiling and unveiling: isn't that what interests them? What keeps them busy? Always repeating the same operation, every time. On every woman" (1985c, 210). A woman's exchange of herself with herself, without the agency of the literal penis or the Symbolic phallus, is exactly what puts into question the prevailing phallocratic and specular economy.

It is tempting to compare Monique Wittig's concept of "lesbian" and Irigaray's notion of the "two lips," since both work to rethink the place and status of the phallus in Western culture. For Wittig, "lesbian" operates as a new transcendental signifier to replace the phallus; it is outside the system of exchange and keeps the system open. Irigaray's "two lips," while also outside of a phallic economy, do not function in the same way, since the lips articulate a female imaginary and not a cultural symbolic.[6] Still, it is not always easy to distinguish the imaginary from the symbolic in Irigaray, especially since the female imaginary is repeatedly theorized in relation to the symbolic agencies of language and speech. Margaret Whitford comes closest to pinpointing Irigaray's departure from Lacan; in the Irigarian account of female sexuality, "what is needed is for the female imaginary to accede to its own specific symbolisation" (1986, 4).

This symbolisation of the female imaginary is precisely what Irigaray seeks to elaborate through her conceptualization of the two lips. The sustained focus in her work on this particular trope operates in at least two ways. First, it has the desired effect of historically foregrounding "the more or less exclusive—and highly anxious—attention paid to erection in Western sexuality" and it demonstrates "to what extent the imaginary that governs it is foreign to the feminine" (1985c, 24). Second, it poses a possible way out of one of the most troubling binds created for feminist psychoanalysts: the problem of how to acknowledge the formative role of the Symbolic, the arm of phallocracy, while still subscribing to the notion of feminine specificity. To turn once again to that lyrical lover letter, "When Our Lips Speak Together," Irigaray's testing of the essentialist waters becomes total submersion: "no event makes us women," she explains, rather "by our lips we are women" (1985c, 211, 209-10). Unlike Wittig, who severs the classification "woman" from any anatomical determinants, there can be little doubt that, for Irigaray, a woman is classified as such on the basis of anatomy:

> Your/my body doesn't acquire its sex through an operation.
> Through the action of some power, function, or organ. Without any intervention or special manipulation, you are a woman already. (1985c, 211)

The point, for Irigaray, of defining women from an essentialist standpoint is not to imprison women within their bodies but to rescue them from enculturating definitions by men. An essentialist definition of "woman" implies that there will always remain some part of "woman" which resists masculine imprinting and socialization:

> How can I say it? That we are women from the start. That we don't have to be turned into women by them, labeled by them, made holy and profane by them. That has always already happened, without their efforts. . . . It's not that we have a territory of our own; but their fatherland, family, home, discourse, imprison us in enclosed spaces where we cannot keep on moving, living, as ourselves. Their properties are our exile. (1985c, 212)

To claim that "we are women from the start" has this advantage—a political advantage perhaps pre-eminently—that a woman will never be a woman solely in masculine terms, never be wholly and permanently annihilated in a masculine order.

"ROLLED UP IN METAPHORS"

Perhaps what most disturbs Irigaray's critics is the way in which the figure of the two lips becomes the basis for theorizing a speaking (as) woman, a *parler femme*. Many American feminists are disturbed by the French feminist tendency to link language and the body in any way, literally or metaphorically. It bothers Elaine Showalter, for example, that "while feminist criticism rejects the attribution of literal biological inferiority, some theorists seem to have accepted the metaphorical implications of female biological difference in writing." Showalter believes that "simply to invoke anatomy risks a return to the crude essentialism, the phallic and ovarian theories of art, that oppressed women in the past" (1982, 17). Mary Jacobus concurs, arguing that "if anatomy is not destiny, still less can it be language" (1982, 37), and Nancy K. Miller similarly insists in her criticism of the French feminists that a "woman-text" must be sought in "the body of her writing and not the writing of her body" (1980, 271). It is interesting to note, as Jane Gallop does, that all the critics included in *Writing and Sexual Difference* (a volume which includes Showalter's "Feminist Criticism in the Wilderness" and Jacobus's "The Question of Language: Men of Maxims and The Mill on the Floss") have difficulty accepting the metaphoricity of the body; they demand that metaphors of the body be read literally, and they then reject these metaphors as essentialistic (1982, 802).[7]

The debate over Irigaray's essentialism inevitably comes down to this question of whether the body stands in a literal or a figurative relation to language and discourse: are the two lips a metaphor or not? What I propose to argue here is that, for Irigaray, the relation between language and the body is neither literal nor metaphoric but *metonymic*. Though Irigaray disparages what she calls the " 'masculine' games of tropes and tropisms" (1985b, 140), she is not without her own favorite tropes, chief among them the figure of metonymy. But before examining the way in which Irigaray deconstructs the predominance of metaphoricity in Western culture and creates a space for metonymy, a brief consideration of what Irigaray actually says about speaking (as) woman is in order.

Irigaray's project is to explore the "distinction of the sexes in terms of the way they inhabit or are inhabited by language" (1985c, 100); her work represents "an attempt to define the characteristics of what a differently sexualized language would be" (1985a, 84). This line of inquiry leads her to ask how women can "already speak (as) women." Her answer? "By going back through the dominant discourse. By interrogating men's 'mastery.' By speaking to women. And among women" (1985c, 119). The chapter entitled "Questions" in *This Sex Which Is Not One* provides us with a series of clarifications on what a speaking (as) woman might be and how it can be put into practice:

> Speaking (as) woman . . . implies a different mode of articulation between masculine and feminine desire and language. (1985c, 136)

> Speaking (as) woman is not speaking of woman. It is not a matter of producing a discourse of which woman would be the object, or the subject. (1985c, 135)

> There may be a speaking-among-women that is still a speaking (as) man but that may also be the place where a speaking (as) woman may dare to express itself. (1985c, 135)

> Speaking (as) woman would, among other things, permit women to speak *to* men. (1985c, 136)

> It is certain that with women-among-themselves . . . something of a speaking (as) woman is heard. This accounts for the desire or the necessity of sexual nonintegration: the dominant language is so powerful that women do not dare to speak (as) woman outside the context of nonintegration. (1985c, 135)

Parler femme appears to be defined not so much by what one says, or even by how one says it, but from whence and to whom one speaks. Locus and audience distinguish a speaking (as) woman from a speaking (as) man: "by *speaking (as) woman*, one may attempt to provide a place for the 'other' as feminine" (1985c, 135). Is it only *from* this "place" that women can speak to women, or is it precisely by speaking to women that the speaker can achieve a *parler femme*? Irigaray's response would be "both at once" since for a woman to speak she must establish a locus from which to be heard, and to articulate such a space, she must speak.

Closely connected to the notion of *parler femme* is Irigaray's conception of two syntaxes (one masculine, one feminine) which cannot accurately be described by the number "two" since "they are not susceptible to comparison" (1985b, 139). These syntaxes are "irreducible in their strangeness and eccentricity one to the other. Coming out of different times, places, logics, 'representations,' and economies" (1985b, 139). The two syntaxes cannot be compared since the relation between them is not based on similarity but contiguity, in other words, not on metaphor but on metonymy. Like the "two lips," they "touch upon" but never wholly absorb each other. Contiguity, it turns out, operates as the dominant feature of a *parler femme*, the distinguishing characteristic of a feminine syntax:

> what a feminine syntax might be is not simple nor easy to state, because in that "syntax" there would no longer be either subject or object, "oneness" would no longer be privileged, there would no longer be proper meanings, proper names, "proper" attributes . . . Instead, that "syntax" would involve nearness, proximity, but in such an extreme form that it would preclude any distinction of identities, any establishment of ownership, thus any form of appropriation. (1985c, 134)

Impacted within this list of what a feminine syntax is not—subject, object, oneness, appropriation, and so on—a positive description emerges: nearness and proximity. We return to the figure of the two lips as a model for a new kind of exchange:

> Ownership and property are doubtless quite foreign to the feminine. At least sexually. But not *nearness*. Nearness so pronounced that it makes all discrimination of identity, and thus all forms of property, impossible. Woman derives pleasure from what is *so near that she cannot have it, nor have herself.* She herself enters into a ceaseless exchange of herself with the other without any possibility of identifying either. This puts into question all prevailing economies. . . . (1985c, 31)

To speak (as) woman is ceaselessly to embrace words and persistently to cast them off. To touch upon but never to solidify, to put into play but never to arrive at a final telos or meaning, isn't this another way to speak about "différance"? Carolyn Burke seems to think so when she proposes that Irigaray offers us a "vaginal" fable of signification to supplement, but not replace, Derrida's "hymeneal" fable (1987, 293 and 303). I don't believe, however, that Irigaray would ever use such a term or endorse such a concept as "vaginal fable" since it limits female pleasure to a single erogenous zone by over-privileging the vagina and denying that a woman's sexuality is plural: in fact, "a woman's erogeneous zones are not the clitoris or the vagina, but the clitoris and the vagina, and the lips, and the vulva, and the mouth of the uterus, and the uterus itself, and the breasts . . ." (1985c, 63-4). The sites of woman's pleasure are so diffuse that Irigaray wonders whether the qualifier "genital" is still even required (1985c, 64).

If the trope of nearness does not function in the way Burke suggests, as yet another non-synonymic term for "différance,"[8] it does appear to facilitate a deconstruction of the metaphor/metonymy binarism operative in Western philosophical discourse. Roman Jakobson defines these two polar figures of speech in "Two Aspects of Language and Two Types of Aphasic Disturbances," a study of speech disorders in which he demonstrates that all varieties of aphasia can be identified as an impairment either of the faculty for "selection and substitution" (metaphor) or of the faculty for "combination and contexture" (metonymy). Metaphor operates along the axis of similarity whereas metonymy operates along the axis of contiguity (Jakobson and Halle 1956, 76).[9] In theories of language, metaphor has long dominated over metonymy.[10] We see this dominance played out in Lacanian psychoanalysis where the phallus stands in a privileged metaphoric relation to the body (it "stands for" sexual difference), and where the "paternal metaphor" emerges as the privileged signifier. Why is metaphor validated over metonymy? Exactly what role does the paternal metaphor play in Lacan's theorization of sexual difference and its construction? Jacqueline Rose identifies three symbolic functions:

> First, as a reference to the act of substitution (substitution is the very law of metaphoric operation), whereby the prohibition of the father takes up the place originally figured by the absence of the mother. Secondly, as a reference to the status of paternity itself which can only ever logically be inferred. And thirdly, as part of an insistence that the father stands for a place and function which is not reducible to the presence or absence of the real father as such. (Mitchell and Rose 1982, 38-39)

Rose goes on to defend Lacan against the charge of phallocentrism, arguing that we must recognize that for Lacan "the status of the phallus is a fraud" (because castration is a fraud) and so we must not literalize the phallus and reduce it to the level of the penis (40 and 45).

While this line of argument is compelling enough, and certainly faithful to Lacan's own conception of the phallus, still the contiguity between the penis and the phallus, the proximity and nearness of these two terms, gives one pause. Mary Ann Doane puts the problem this way:

> [D]oes the phallus really have nothing to do with the penis, no commerce with it at all? The ease of the description by means

> of which the boy situates himself in the mode of "having" one
> would seem to indicate that this is not the case. . . . There is
> a sense in which all attempts to deny the relation between the
> phallus and the penis are feints, veils, illusions. The phallus,
> as signifier, may no longer be the penis, but any effort to con-
> ceptualize its function is inseparable from an imaging of the
> body. (1981, 27-28)[11]

The problem, put another way, is simply that the relation between the penis
and the phallus is as much one of association or metonymy as similarity or
metaphor. The same might be said of Irigaray's treatment of the "two lips,"
the only difference being that Irigaray allocates the metonymic function to
the two lips and relegates metaphor to the realm of Lacan's phallomorphism.

Irigaray has this to say about a woman's historical relation to metaphoricity: a woman is "stifled beneath all those eulogistic or denigratory metaphors" (1985b, 142-43); she is "hemmed in, cathected by tropes" (1985b,
143) and "rolled up in metaphors" (1985b, 144). One wonders to what extent it is truly possible to think of the "two lips" as something other than a
metaphor. I would argue that, despite Irigaray's protestations to the contrary,
the figure of the "two lips" never stops functioning metaphorically. Her insistence that the two lips escape metaphoricity provides us with a particularly
clear example of what Paul de Man identifies as the inevitability of
"reentering a system of tropes at the very moment we claim to escape from it"
(1984, 72). But, what is important about Irigaray's conception of this particular figure is that the "two lips" operate as a metaphor *for* metonymy; through
this collapse of boundaries, Irigaray gestures toward the deconstruction of the
classic metaphor/metonymy binarism. In fact, her work persistently attempts
to effect a historical displacement of metaphor's dominance over metonymy;
she "impugns the privilege granted to metaphor (a quasi solid) over metonymy (which is much more closely allied to fluids)" (1985c, 110). If Freud was
not able to resist the seduction of an analogy,[12] Irigaray insists that no analogy, no metaphoric operation, completes her:

> Are we alike? If you like. It's a little abstract. I don't quite un-
> derstand 'alike.' Do you? Alike in whose eyes? in what terms?
> by what standards? with references to what third? I'm touching
> you, that's quite enough to let me know that you are my body.
> (1985c, 208)

Lacan writes that the play of both displacement and condensation (metaphor
and metonymy) mark a subject's relation to the signifier; they operate, in
fact, as the laws which govern the unconscious. A question oft-repeated in
Irigaray is "whether the feminine *has* an unconscious or whether it *is* the unconscious" (1985c, 73). Is it possible that the feminine neither has an uncon-

scious of its own nor represents man's unconscious but rather articulates itself as a specific operation within the unconscious: the play of metonymy?

A POLITICS OF ESSENCE

Irigaray's favorite topics—the two lips, *parler femme*, a feminine syntax, an economy of fluids—all seem to suggest that she is more interested in questions of subjectivity, desire, and the unconscious than in questions of power, history, and politics. In one sense, this is true; as a "psychophilosopher," Irigaray places greater emphasis on the "physical" than on the "social." However, her work is not entirely without what one might call a certain political perspicacity. Monique Plaza, Beverly Brown, Parveen Adams, and Ann Rosalind Jones all question whether a psychoanalytic investigation of the feminine can adequately account for women's social oppression. As Jones puts it,

> feminists may still doubt the efficacy of privileging changes in subjectivity over changes in economic and political systems; is this not dangling a semiotic carrot in front of a mare still harnessed into phallocentric social practices? (Jones 1985, 107)[13]

Plaza goes further and indicts Irigaray for providing not a theory of oppression but an oppressive theory (1978, 24-25). While I think it is true that Irigaray does not provide us with a blueprint for social action, I also find her work politically aware and even practically useful. Any discussion of Irigaray's "politics of essence" must begin with her own understanding of politics and, specifically, with her comments on what a feminist politics might be.

Irigaray's explicit remarks on political practice, the women's movement in France (the MLF), and women's social oppression are largely concentrated in the selection from her interviews, seminar remarks, and conversations published under the title "Questions" in *This Sex Which is Not One*. It seems that readers and students of Irigaray most want her to talk about the political significance of her work, its impact on social practice, and its relation to current political activism in France, perhaps because *Speculum* appears, on the surface, to jettison so completely the category of the political in favor of the philosophical and psychoanalytic. Irigaray seems eager to respond to her critics. If Plaza and others see her work as reactionary because it is apolitical, Irigaray is likely to respond that they are working with too limited or rigid a notion of politics, that they are perhaps thinking only in terms of a masculine politics:

> Strictly speaking, political practice, at least currently, is masculine through and through. In order for women to be able to

make themselves heard, a 'radical' evolution in our way of
conceptualizing and managing the political realm is required.
(1985c, 127)

For Irigaray, politics—a "feminine" politics—is inseparable from the project
of putting the feminine into history, into discourse, and into culture. Because
of the contingent, future condition of this latter project, Irigaray acknowledges that in fact "we cannot speak . . . of a feminine politics, but only of
certain conditions under which it may be possible" (1985c, 128).

The nascent condition of a feminine politics, however, does not preclude
discussion of a feminist politics. "Liberation" (loosely understood by Irigaray
as the introduction of the feminine into practice) is not an "individual" task:

> A long history has put all women in the same sexual, social,
> and cultural condition. Whatever inequalities may exist
> among women, they all undergo, even without clearly realiz-
> ing it, the same oppression, the same exploitation of their
> body, the same denial of their desire. That is why it is impor-
> tant for women to be able to join together, and to join to-
> gether "among themselves". . . . The first issue facing libera-
> tion movements is that of making each woman "conscious" of
> the fact that what she has felt in her personal experience is a
> condition shared by all women, thus *allowing that experience to
> be politicized.* (1985c, 164)

A different notion of politics does seem to emerge here—a politics based not
so much on group militancy or open confrontation as on shared "experience." But this notion of politics sounds suspiciously like the popular approved method of politicization in the early years of the Women's Movement
in both France and America: consciousness-raising. And as such, it is subject
to many of the same criticisms—especially the charge by numerous "marginal" feminists that what white, heterosexual, middle-class, and educated
women feel in their personal experience does not necessarily represent "a
condition shared by all women." Irigaray might rightly be accused here of a
certain tendency to universalize and to homogenize, to subsume all women
under the category of "Woman." Still, her work is not always insensitive to
the axes of difference which divide "women-among-themselves." Consider:

> I think the most important thing to do is to expose the exploi-
> tation common to all women and to find the struggles that are
> appropriate for each woman, right where she is, depending
> upon her nationality, her job, her social class, her sexual expe-
> rience, that is, upon the form of oppression that is for her the
> most immediately unbearable. (1985c, 166-67)

Here we see the typical Irigarian double gesture: Irigaray proposes a feminist
politics that will work on two fronts at once—on one side, a "global" politics

that seeks to address the problem of women's universal oppression, and on the other side, a "local" politics that will address the specificity and complexity of each woman's particular situation. In order to accomplish "both at once," Irigaray believes that "it is essential for women among themselves to invent new modes of organization, new forms of struggle, new challenges" (1985c, 166). The phrase "women-among-themselves" suggests a call for separatism, and indeed Irigaray does, cautiously, endorse separatism as a valid political strategy for feminists:

> For women to undertake tactical strikes, to keep themselves apart from men long enough to learn to defend their desire, especially through speech, to discover the love of other women which, sheltered from men's imperious choices, put them in the position of rival commodities, to forge for themselves a social status that compels recognition, to earn thier living in order to escape from the condition of prostitute . . . these are certainly indispensable stages in their escape from their proletarization on the exchange market. But if their aim were simply to reduce the order of things, even supposing this to be possible, history would repeat itself in the long run, would revert to sameness: to phallocratism. (1985c, 33)

Irigaray believes that separatism can be a legitimate means to escape from a phallic economy but not an adequate goal; she sees it as a tactical option rather than a final telos. Above all, she does not want to foreclose the possibility that the politics of women-among-themselves might itself be a way to put the feminine into practice.

Through her comments on what a feminist politics might be, Irigaray broadens the notion of politics to include psychic resistance. She does not rule out direct political activism; she simply insists that resistance must operate on many levels:

> Women must of course continue to struggle for equal wages and social rights against discrimination in employment and education, and so forth. But that is not enough: women merely "equal" to men would be "like them," therefore not women. (1985c, 165-66)

Irigaray seems to imply here both that women already have an identity on which to base a politics and that they are striving to secure an identity through the practice of politics. In either case, the concept of "identity" has long been a problem for feminist poststructuralists seeking to base a politics on something other than "essence." Is it possible to generate a theory of feminine specificity that is not essentialist? How do we reconcile the poststructuralist project to displace identity with the feminist project to reclaim it? For

Irigaray the solution is again double: women are engaged in the process of both constructing and deconstructing their identities, their essences, simultaneously.[14]

The process of laying claim to "essence" at first appears to be a politically reactionary maneuver; but one needs to place Irigaray's essentialism in the larger historical context of Western philosophy in order to comprehend how she might be using it strategically. In Aristotelian philosophy, "woman" has a very specific relation to essence, distinct from "man's" relation to essence. Only man properly *has* an essence; subjecthood is attained as he strives, in Irigaray's words, "to realize his essence as perfectly as he can, to give full expression to his *telos*" (1985b, 164).[15] Because only subjects have access to essence, "woman" remains in unrealized potentiality; she never achieves "the wholeness of her form"—or if she has a form, it is merely "privation" (1985b, 165). Woman is the ground of essence, its precondition in man, without herself having any access to it; she is the ground of subjecthood, but not herself a subject:

> Is she unnecessary in and of herself, but essential as the non-subjective sub-jectum? As that which can never achieve the status of subject, at least for/by herself. Is she the indispensable condition whereby the living entity retains and maintains and perfects himself in his self-likeness? (1985b, 165)

In a phallocratic order, woman can never be more than "the passage that serves to transform the inessential whims of a still sensible and material nature into universal will" (1985b, 225).

Irigaray's reading of Aristotle's understanding of essence reminds me of Lacan's distinction between *being* and *having* the phallus: a woman does not *possess* the phallus, she *is* the Phallus.[16] Similarly, we can say that, in Aristotelian logic, a woman does not *have* an essence, she *is* Essence. Therefore to give "woman" an essence is to undo Western phallomorphism and to offer women entry into subjecthood. Moreover, because in this Western ontology existence is predicated on essence, it has been possible for someone like Lacan to conclude, *remaining fully within traditional metaphysics*, that without essence, "woman does not exist." Does this not cast a rather different light on Irigaray's theorization of a woman's essence? A woman who lays claim to an essence of her own undoes the conventional binarisms of essence/accident, form/matter, and actuality/potentiality. In this specific historical context, to essentialize "woman" can be a politically strategic gesture of displacement.

To say that "woman" does not have an essence but *is* Essence, and at the same time to say that she has no access herself to Essence as Form, seems blatantly contradictory. Moreover, has not Western philosophy always posited an essence for woman—an essence based on biology and, as everyone knows, defined by the properties of weakness, passivity, receptivity, and emotion, to name just a few? The problem, I would argue, is not with Irigaray; it is precisely Irigaray's deployment of essentialism which clarifies for us the contradiction at the heart of Aristotelian metaphysics. In his philosophy, we see that the figure of "woman" has become the site of this contradiction: on the one hand, woman is asserted to have an essence which defines her as woman and yet, on the other hand, woman is relegated to the status of matter and can have no access to essence (the most she can do is to facilitate man's actualizing of his inner potential). I would go so far as to say that the dominant line of patriarchal thought since Aristotle is built on this central contradiction: woman has an essence and it is matter; or, put slightly differently, it is the essence of woman to have no essence. To the extent that Irigaray reopens the question of essence and woman's access to it, essentialism represents not a trap she falls into but rather a key strategy she puts into play, not a dangerous oversight but rather a lever of displacement.

What, then, constitutes woman's essence? Irigaray never actually tells us; at most she only approximates—"touches upon"—possible descriptions, such as the metonymic figure of the two lips. In fact, she insists that "woman" can never be incorporated in any theory, defined by any metaphysics. "What I want," Irigaray writes, "is not to create a theory of woman, but to secure a place for the feminine within sexual difference" (1985c, 159). She explains that "for the elaboration of a theory of woman, men, I think, suffice. In a woman('s) language, the concept as such would have no place" (1985c, 123). Irigaray works towards securing a woman's access to an essence of her own, without actually prescribing what that essence might be, or without precluding the possibility that a subject might possess multiple essences which may even contradict or compete with one another. Thus Irigaray sees the question "Are you a woman?" to be precisely the wrong question. Let me conclude with her playful challenge to all those who would press her to define the essence of "woman": " 'I' am not 'I,' I am not, I am not one. As for woman, try and find out . . ." (1985c, 120).

NOTES

1. Heath (1978), Jardine (1987), Schor (1987), and Spivak (1987) have all endorsed a renewed consideration of essentialism.

2. The phrase is Carolyn Burke's (1981, 289).

3. Two earlier introductory pieces to French feminist theory also appear in Signs: see Marks (1978) and Burke (1978).

4. For another sympathetic reading of Irigaray, and an application of her deconstructive feminism, see Féral (1981).

5. Irigaray makes a distinction between "morphological" and "anatomical" in "Women's Exile" (1977, 64), but I agree with Monique Plaza (1978, 31) and Toril Moi (1985, 143) that the distinction is too imprecise to be helpful.

6. The Imaginary and the Symbolic are here used in the Lacanian sense. The Imaginary refers to the primary narcissism (the illusionary oneness with the maternal body) which characterizes

the child's psychical development in the pre-oedipal stage. The symmetry of the mother-child dyad is broken by the introduction of the Law of the Father during the Oedipal stage, facilitating the child's accession to subjectivity through the order of language, speech, and sociality. In Lacan, the Symbolic is always valued over the Imaginary (see Lacan 1977).

7. Carolyn Burke makes a similar argument in defense of Irigaray: to reduce "the subtlety of Irigaray's thought to a simple argument 'from the body,' in order to then point out that such arguments are, indeed, essentialist" amounts to a circular argument based on a rather questionable initial reading (1981, 302).

8. Vincent Leitch writes that, by the early 1980's, Derrida had formulated more than three dozen such substitutions (see Leitch 1983, 43).

9. For a recent rereading and application of Jakobson's terms, see Johnson (1984, 205-19).

10. Studies of metaphor have also dominated over studies of metonymy in the comparatively recent history of linguistic and semiotic research. Jakobson explains: "Similarity in meaning connects the symbols of a metalanguage with the symbols of the language referred to. Similarity connects a metaphorical term with the term for which it is substituted. Consequently, when constructing a metalanguage to interpret tropes, the researcher possesses more homogeneous means to handle metaphor, whereas metonymy, based on a different principle, easily defies interpretation. Therefore nothing comparable to the rich literature on metaphor can be cited for the theory of metonymy" (1956, 81).

11. Jane Gallop's *Reading Lacan* (1985) also addresses the penis/phallus distinction, focussing specifically on the linguistic sources of the confusion. See especially chapter 6, "Reading the Phallus," pp. 133-156. See also Gallop's "Phallus/Penis: Same Difference" in *Men by Women, Women and Literature* (1981).

12. The reference is to Freud's "Constructions in Analysis" (1937): "I have not been able to resist the seduction of an analogy." Jane Gallop has cleverly suggested that Irigaray's general resistance to analogical reasoning is based on a prior repudiation of Freud's anal-logical model of sexual difference. Irigaray's refusal of analogy can thus be read within the wider frame of a deep scepticism concerning the anal fixation of Freud's own theories (see Gallop 1982a, 68-69).

13. See also Plaza (1978) and Adams and Brown (1979).

14. Naomi Schor has made a similar point which I find compelling: "in both Cixous and Irigaray the anti-essentialist aspect of their work is that which is most derivative, that is most Derridean. When Cixous and Irigaray cease to mime the master's voice and speak in their own voices, they speak a dialect of essentialese, the language of what they construe as the feminine, and wishing it weren't so won't make it go away. Rather than simply wanting to excise this unsightly excrescence, I think it would be ultimately more interesting and surely more difficult to attempt to understand just how and why a Cixous and an Irigaray deconstruct and construct femininity at the same time" (see Schor 1986, 98-99).

15. Most of Irigaray's remarks on Aristotle can be found in the chapter entitled "How to Conceive (of) a Girl" in *1985b*, 160-67. For Aristotle's own comments on essence, see especially *Categories, Physics, Metaphysics,* and *On the Generation of Animals,* all of which can be found in McKeon 1941.

16. For Lacan's distinction between being and having the phallus, see "The Meaning of the Phallus" in Mitchell and Rose 1982, esp. 82-84. Both girl and boy are the phallus in the pre-oedipal stage; that is, both are the phallus *for* the mother. But during the crucial ascension to sexual difference through the recognition and representation of lack (the castration complex) the possession of a penis allows the boy to *have* the phallus while the girl continues to *be* it. For Lacan, it is this distinction between being and having the phallus which facilitates the taking on of a sexed subject position, the production of masculine or feminine subjects.

REFERENCES

Abel, Elizabeth, ed. 1982. *Writing and sexual difference.* Chicago: The University of Chicago Press.

Adams, Parveen and Brown, Beverly. 1979. The feminine body and feminist politics. *m/f* 3: 35-50.

Burke, Carolyn. 1978. Report from Paris: Women's writing and the women's movement. *Signs* 3 (4): 843-55.

———. 1981. Irigaray through the looking glass. *Feminist Studies* 7 (2): 288-306.

De Man, Paul. 1984. *The rhetoric of romanticism*. New York: Columbia University Press.

Delphy, Christine. 1984. *Close to home: A materialist analysis of women's oppression*. Trans. Diana Leonard. Amherst: The University of Massachusetts Press.

Doane, Mary Ann. 1981. Woman's stake: Filming the female body. *October* 17: 23-36.

Fauré, Christine. 1981. The twilight of the goddesses, or the intellectual crisis of french feminism. *Signs* 7 (1): 81-6.

Féral, Josette. 1981. Towards a theory of displacement. *Substance* 32: 52-64.

Gallop, Jane. 1981. Phallus/penis: Same difference. In *Men by women*. Vol. 2 of *Women and literature*, ed. Janet Todd. New York and London: Holmes & Meier, 243-51.

———. 1982a. *The daughter's seduction: Feminism and psychoanalysis*. Ithaca, New York: Cornell University Press.

———. 1982b. *Writing and sexual difference*: The difference within. *Critical Inquiry* (Summer).

———. 1983. Quand nos Lèvres s'écrivent: Irigaray's body politic. *Romanic Review* 74 (1): 77-83.

———. 1985. *Reading Lacan*. Ithaca and London: Cornell University Press.

Heath, Stephen. 1978. Difference. *Screen* 19 (3): 50-112.

Irigaray, Luce. 1977. Women's exile. *Ideology and Consciousness* 1 (May): 62-76.

———. 1985a. Is the subject of science sexed? *Cultural Critique* 1 (Fall): 73-88.

———. 1985b. *Speculum of the other woman*. Trans. Gillian C. Gill. Ithaca, New York: Cornell University Press. Trans. of *Speculum de l'autre femme*. Paris: Minuit, 1974.

———. 1985c. *This sex which is not one*. Trans. Catherine Porter with Carolyn Burke. Ithaca, New York: Cornell University Press. Trans. of *Ce Sexe qui n'en est pas un*. Paris: Minuit, 1977.

Jacobus, Mary. 1982. The question of language: men of maxims and *The mill on the floss*. In *Writing and sexual difference*; ed. Elizabeth Abel. Chicago: The University of Chicago Press, 37-52.

Jakobson, Roman and Halle, Morris. 1956. *Fundamentals of language*. 'S-Gravenhage: Mouton.

Jardine, Alice and Smith, Paul, eds. 1987. *Men in feminism*. New York and London: Methuen.

Jardine, Alice. 1987. Men in feminism: Odor di uomo or compagnons de route? In Men in feminism, eds. Alice Jardine and Paul Smith. New York: Methuen, 54-61.

Johnson, Barbara. 1984. Metaphor, metonymy and voice in Their eyes were watching god. In Black literature and literary theory, ed. Henry Louis Gates, Jr. New York: Methuen, 205-219.

Jones, Ann Rosalind. 1985. Inscribing femininity: French theories of the feminine. In Making a difference: Feminist literary criticism, eds. Gayle Greene and Coppélia Kahn. London and New York: Methuen, 80-112.

Lacan, Jaques. 1977. Écrits. Trans. Alan Sheridan. New York: W. W. Norton & Company.

Leitch, Vincent. 1983. Deconstructive criticism: An advanced introduction. New York: Columbia University Press.

Marks, Elaine. 1978. Women and literature in France. Signs 3 (4):832-42.

McKeon, Richard, ed. 1941. The basic works of Aristotle. New York: Random House.

Miller, Nancy K. 1980. Women's autobiography in France: For a dialectics of identification. Women and language in literature and society, eds. Sally McConnell-Ginet, Ruth Borker, and Nelly Furman. New York: Praeger.

Mitchell, Juliet and Rose, Jacqueline. 1982. Feminine sexuality: Jacques Lacan and the école freudienne. New York: W. W. Norton and Company.

Moi, Toril. 1985. Sexual/textual politics. New York: Methuen.

Plaza, Monique. 1978. "Phallomorphic power" and the psychology of "woman." Ideology and Consciousness 4 (Autumn):57-76. Originally published in Questions féministes 1 (1978).

Ruthven, K. K. 1984. Feminist literary studies: An introduction. Cambridge: Cambridge University Press.

Schor, Naomi. 1986. Introducing feminism. Paragraph 8. Oxford University Press: 94-101.

———. 1987. Dreaming dissymmetry: Barthes, Foucault, and sexual difference. In Men in feminism. Jardine and Smith, 98-110.

Showalter, Elaine. 1982. Feminist criticism in the wilderness. In Writing and sexual difference, ed. Elizabeth Abel. Chicago: The University of Chicago Press, 9-36.

Spivak, Gayatri Chakravorty. 1987. In other worlds: Essays in cultural politics. New York and London: Methuen.

Whitford, Margaret. 1986. Luce Irigaray and the female imaginary: Speaking as a woman. Radical Philosophy 43 (Summer):3-8.

Wittig, Monique. 1980. The straight mind. Feminist Issues (Summer): 103-111.

———. 1981. One is not born a woman. Feminist Issues (Fall): 47-54.

Lacanian Psychoanalysis and French Feminism: Toward an Adequate Political Psychology

DOROTHY LELAND

This paper examines some French feminist uses of Lacanian psychoanalysis. I focus on two Lacanian influenced accounts of psychological oppression, the first by Luce Irigaray and the second by Julia Kristeva, and I argue that these accounts fail to meet criteria for an adequate political psychology.

The use of psychoanalysis as a feminist theoretical tool is a precarious enterprise. In classical psychoanalytic theory, female psychosexual development, only marginally and infrequently discussed, is measured against a masculine norm and found deficient. During the early 1970's, the concept of penis envy, developed by Freud in his account of the female version of the castration complex, came to represent for many North American feminists the misogynist bias of psychoanalytic theory. Moreover, many feminists considered this misogyny a sufficient ground for rejecting psychoanalysis as a feminist theoretical tool.

During the middle to late 1970's, feminists such as Juliet Mitchell (1974), Gayle Rubin (1975), Dorothy Dinnerstein (1976), and Nancy Chodorow (1978) moved beyond this initial rejection of psychoanalysis to explore its feminist potential. These efforts were premised less on a denial of the misogynist character of psychoanalytic theory than on a reinterpretation of it. Gayle Rubin, for example, argued that the feminist critique of psychoanalysis is justified to the extent that Freudian theory is a rationalization of women's subordination. But, Rubin proposed, this is not the only legitimate way to understand Freud's theory. It can also be read as "a description of how phallic culture domesticates women, and the effects in women of their domestication" (Rubin 1975, 197-98). Thus, Rubin concluded, to the extent that Freudian theory is a description of processes that contribute to women's oppression, the feminist critique of psychoanalysis is mistaken.

I thank Sandra Bartky, Nancy Fraser, Terry Winant, and Iris Young for encouraging me to write this paper.

Hypatia vol. 3, no. 3 (Winter 1989) © by Dorothy Leland

Whereas the work of Dinnerstein and Chodorow draws on the tradition of object-relations theory, Rubin followed Mitchell in drawing on the psychoanalytic theory of Jacques Lacan. Indeed, it was the work of Mitchell and Rubin that served to introduce Lacanian psychoanalysis to North American feminists. However, most of the effort to effect a *rapprochement* between feminism and Lacanian psychoanalysis has been undertaken by feminists in France. The adoption in the early 1970's of the name *psychanalyse et politique* by an influential wing of the French Women's Liberation Movement is just one indicator of the importance assumed by psychoanalysis in French feminist politics. This importance is also reflected in Julia Kristeva's division of French feminism into two distinct generations or phases: a first, "socialist" phase, dominated by the politics of equality and a second, "psychoanalytic" phase, dominated by a politics of difference (Kristeva 1981, 37-38).

In this paper, I examine some French feminist uses of Lacanian psychoanalysis in order to evaluate its adequacy as a political psychology. On my interpretation, one primary concern of French psychoanalytic feminisms is with so-called "psychological" or "internalized" oppression, oppression that results when schemas of thought and valuation are internalized and function as intruments of domination. In the case of women's oppression, the relevant schemas of thought and valuation include, but are not necessarily limited to, the sexual ideologies of male-dominated societies.

One central claim of French psychoanalytic feminisms is that the psychological oppression of women is primarily, if not exclusively, a function of the process of oedipalization. This process begins when a child comprehends its society's sexual rules and gender prescriptions (e.g., kinship relations, the incest taboo) and ends when these rules and prescriptions are internalized or acceded to. For French psychoanalytic feminists, then, the Oedipus complex is the mechanism whereby a neonate comes to recognize itself as an I-she or an I-he and hence becomes subject to whatever sexual rules and gender prescriptions this entails in her or his society.

My standards for assessing the adequacy of Lacanian psychoanalysis as a feminist political psychology reflect a familiar socialist feminist position (Jaggar 1983, 150). I invoke two criteria.[1] First, an adequate political psychology must recognize the grounding of internalized oppression in culturally and historically specific institutions and practices. Second, an adequate political psychology must be non-deterministic; it must allow that psychological oppression can, at least under some conditions and to some extent, be transcended.

In what follows, I use these criteria to evaluate Lacanian theory through an analysis of works by Luce Irigaray and Julia Kristeva. My intent is not to provide a comprehensive account of the writings of these French feminists. Rather, I invoke selected themes that illustrate important problems associated with the appropriation of Lacanian psychoanalysis as a feminist theoretical tool. I begin with a discussion of Luce Irigaray's account of internalized oppression in "Women on the Market." I examine her uncritical appropriation of empirically suspect Lévi-Straussian and Lacanian claims, and I argue that her account of psychological oppression lacks the cultural and historical specificity required by criterion one. Then, I turn to the work of Julia Kristeva. I examine her use of *avant-garde* literature as a model for feminist political practice, and I argue that her view of internalized oppression involves a form of determinism that violates criterion two and deadends in political pessimism.

I

> The emergence of symbolic thought must have required that women, like words, should be exchanged. . . . This was the only means of overcoming the contradiction by which the same woman was seen under two incompatible aspects: on the one hand, as the object of personal desire, thus exciting sexual and proprietorial instincts; and, on the other hand, as the subject of the desire of others, and seen as such, i.e., as the means of bending others through alliance with them.
>
> (Lévi-Strauss 1969, 496)

> Where on earth would one situate the determinations of the unconscious if not in those nominal cadres in which marriage ties and kinship are always grounded?
>
> (Lacan 1968, 128)

Lacanian psychoanalysis, unlike object-relations theory, ascribes a central role to the Oedipus complex in the acquisition of sexual identity.[2] Consequently, in Lacanian-based accounts of internalized oppression, the emphasis is less on concrete relations between a mother and her infant than on the familial power of the father   in Lacanian parlance, the father's "name" and "no." Moreover, in Lacanian theory, the Oedipus complex is posited as a universal of psychosexual development. Lacanian theory thus implicitly rejects the claim that the Oedipus complex is about or limited to the nuclear family. It also implicitly rejects the view that the Oedipus complex is a psychic structure grounded in culturally and historically specific forms of praxis.

For Lacan and his followers, the universality of the Oedipus complex is a function of its status as a condition of sociality or culture as such. Lacan draws support for this view from Claude Lévi-Strauss's *The Elementary Structures of Kinship* (1969), where kinship is viewed as a social/symbolic organization that marks the passage from nature to culture. More specifically, Lévi-Strauss argues that what transforms biological relationships into cultural kinship systems is the institution of exogamy—the systematic exchange of women by

men. This view is aptly summarized by Juliet Mitchell, whose own appropriation of Freud draws heavily on the intersection of Lacanian and Lévi-
Straussian theory:

> The universal and priomordial law [of society] is that which
> regulates marriage relationships and its pivotal expression is
> the prohibition of incest. This prohibition forces one family to
> give up one of its members to another family; the rules of mar-
> riage within 'primitive' societies function as a means of ex-
> change and as an unconsciously acknowledged system of com-
> munication. The act of exchange holds a society together: the
> rules of kinship . . . *are* the society. (Mitchell 1974, 370)

According to Mitchell, even though "visible" kinship structures play only a
residual role in advanced as compared to so-called primitive societies, they
are nonetheless "definitional" of society or culture as such. The same is true
of the "subjective" expression of exogamy, the incest taboo. Thus, Mitchell
proposes that the "myth Freud rewrote as the Oedipus complex epitomizes
man's entry into culture itself. It reflects the original exogamous incest taboo,
the role of the father, the exchange of women and the consequent differences
between the sexes" (Mitchell 1974, 377).

Among the texts of French psychoanalytic feminisms, Luce Irigaray's
"Women on the Market" (1985) is the most explicit attempt to provide an
account of women's oppression drawing on the intersection of Lévi-
Straussian and Lacanian theory. Irigaray's essay turns on two theoretical piv-
ots. First, she reinterprets Lévi-Strauss's account of the passage from nature to
culture *via* the institution of exogamy as the reign of *hom(m)osexualité* or
man's [*homme*] desire for the same [*homo*]. Second, she draws on an (unorthodox) interpretation of Marx's analysis of commodities as "the elementary
form of capitalist wealth" to examine the alienation of women's desire under
this reign.[3] For Irigaray, the alienation that results when women's desire is reduced to men's desire (the desire for the same) is constitutive of women's psychological oppression. Moreover, she argues, in patriarchal societies,
women's alienated sexuality has the status of a commodity.

Although Irigaray's use of Marx and of the concept of a commodity might
suggest that her account is intended to cover the situation of women in capitalist societies only, this is not the case. Rather, her analysis is intended to be
universal in scope; it purports to reveal what remains the same about women's
oppression throughout historical variations of social regimes and productive
relations. According to Irigaray, the "organization of partriarchal societies,
and the operation of the symbolic system on which this organization is based
. . . contains in a nuclear form the developments that Marx defines as characteristic of capitalist regimes" (1985, 172-3). Irigaray does not explicitly explain why she thinks this is so. But her text hints at possible answers. For

Irigaray, exogamy is itself an economic arrangement, one which subtends "the economy" in the narrower sense:

> The exchange of women as goods accompanies and stimulates exchanges of other 'wealth' among groups of men. The economy—in both the narrow and broad sense—that is in place in our societies thus requires that women lend themselves to alienation in consumption, and to exchanges in which they do not participate, and that men be exempt from being used and circulated like commodities. (1985, 172)

Elsewhere, in "The Power of Discourse" Irigaray proposes that the earliest oppression, identified by Engels as the oppression of women by men *via* the institution of monogamy, remains in effect today, and that the problem for feminists "lies in determining how it is articulated with other oppressions" (Irigaray 1985, 83).

Although Irigaray does not credit Lévi-Strauss for suggesting the analogy between women and commodities, a passage from *The Elementary Structures of Kinship* is its likely source:

> There is no need to call upon the matrimonial vocabulary of Great Russia, where the groom was called the 'merchant' and the bride the 'merchandise' for the likening of women to commodities, not only scarce but essential to the life of the group (Lévi-Strauss 1969, 36).

Like Lévi-Strauss, Irigaray proposes that culture or society as we know it is based on the exchange of women among men according to the rule known as the incest taboo: "whatever familial form this prohibition may take in a given state of society . . . [the incest taboo] assures the foundation of the economic, social, and cultural order that has been ours for centuries" (1985, 170).

However, Irigaray rejects Lévi-Strauss's explanation of why women, not men, are the objects of exchange. According to Lévi-Strauss, this is due to the "deep polygamous tendency, which exists among all men, [and which] makes the number of available women *seem* insufficient" (1969, 38). Irigaray deems this inadequate because it presupposes but does not acknowledge a more fundamental asymmetry between the sexes: it assumes that women are the objects of men's desire, but not *vice versa*, and that only men have a tendency toward polygamy. Irigaray writes:

> Why are men not objects of exchange among women? It is because women's bodies—through their use, consumption, and circulation—provide for the condition making social life and culture possible, although they remain an unknown 'infras-

tructure' of the elaboration of the social life and culture. . . .
In still other words: all the systems of exchange that organize
patriarchal societies and all the modalities of productive work
that are recognized, valued, and rewarded in these societies
are men's business. The production of women, signs, and commodities is always referred back to men . . . , and they always
pass from one man to another. The work force is thus always
assumed to be masculine, and 'products' are objects to be used,
objects of transaction among men alone. (1985, 171)[4]

Irigaray thus proposes that the exchange of women among men, an exchange that Lévi-Strauss and Lacan view as essential for the passage from nature to culture, should be understood more fundamentally as the institution
of the reign of hom(m)osexualité. By this, she means a social order whose laws
are the "exclusive valorization of men's needs/desires, of exchange among
men" (Irigaray 1985, 171). More specifically, Irigaray defines
hom(m)osexualité as a social order in which the value of symbolic and imaginary production is superimposed on and even substituted for the value of nature and corporeal (re)production. Women's bodies, as commodities exchanged by men, are also subjected to this superimposition and substitution
of value. As a result, Irigaray concludes, "in this new matrix of History, in
which man begets man as man in his own likeness, wives, daughters, and sis-
ters have value only in that they serve as the possibility of, and potential ben-
efit in, relations among men" (1985, 172).

Like Juliet Mitchell, Irigaray finds that women's sexual identity is determined by their utilization as exchange objects. Women's bodies, sexualized as
female by means of the Oedipus structure, are held to be part of the nature or
"matter" acted upon by the (masculine) subject, and women's identity,
grasped as the product of this labor, is assumed to be an objectification of
men's needs and desires. In this social order, Irigaray finds that so-called feminine sexuality (i.e., "normal" feminine sexuality as described by psychoanalytic theory) resembles a commodity in four main respects. First, just as a
commodity is produced by subjecting nature to "man", so feminine sexuality
is produced by subjecting women to the "forms and laws" of masculine activity. Second, just as exchange functions override the natural utility of things
when they become commodities, so the natural properties of women's bodies
are suppressed and subordinated when they are made into objects of circulation among men. Third, just as a commodity is incapable of imaging or
mirroring itself, so women's self-image becomes an image of and for men.
Fourth and finally, just as commodities must be measured in terms of an extrinsic standard, monetary value, in order to be exchanged, so women must
be submitted to the extrinsic standard of male sexual desire in order that
they, too, can be exchanged among men.

Viewed as an intertextual weaving of Marxian, Lévi-Straussian, and Lacanian theory designed to undercut their presumptions of gender neutrality, "Women on the Market" is a *tour de force*.[5] But if we examine Irigaray's own account of women's psychological oppression as the alienation through commodification (oedipalization) of women's desire, a number of critical questions arise. Some of these concern the empirical adequacy of her claims. For example, Irigaray's contention that in patriarchal societies the work force is *always* masculine (and so expressive of *hom(m)osexualité*) is false. The situation of Western women during and after the industrial revolution, when women became a relatively permanent part of the conventionally-defined paid labor force, provides just one counterexample. Irigaray could, of course, counter this objection with the claim that the entry of women into the labor force does not negate the latter's masculine character. Or she could claim that in industrialized societies, men control women's labor even outside the reproductive sphere. But Irigaray makes none of these claims. The issue of empirical warrants does not enter into her analysis at all.

This lack of attention to the empirical bases of theoretical claims is characteristic of Irigaray's approach. For example, although she criticizes Freud, Lacan and Lévi-Strauss for not acknowledging that their respective psychological and anthropological descriptions are descriptions of the situation of women under conditions of oppression, she also uncritically adopts claims that are central to these accounts. Irigaray assumes that all cultures have been patriarchal or male-dominated, that the incest taboo is a cultural universal, and that all kinship structures are based on the exchange of women. Yet there is considerable controversy surrounding each of these claims.[6]

Similarly, Irigaray fails to question the presumed universality of key Lévi-Straussian, Freudian and Lacanian concepts. For example, "Women on the Market" relies heavily on a genderized nature/culture dichotomy invoked both by Lévi-Strauss and by Freud and Lacan, where the feminine is linked with nature and the masculine with culture. Into this framework, Irigaray deftly inserts Marx's conception of productive labor, according to which labor is seen as the means whereby "man duplicates himself, not only in consciousness, intellectually, but also actively, in reality, [so that] he sees himself in a world he has created" (Marx and Engels 1975, 277). By redescribing productive labor as the means whereby "man begets *man* as *man* in his own likeness," and by calling this "the reign of *hom(m)osexualité*," Irigaray foregrounds Marx's tendency to conceive of the human being as male, his modeling of productive labor on traditional masculine activities, and his focus on the sphere of object production in general and commodity production in particular as the matrix and main stage of history. What she does not consider is the possibility that the genderized nature/culture distinction retained in her account is not a cultural universal but rather specific to modern, Western society—a view supported by several anthropological studies.[7] As a result, Irigaray leaves herself open to the charge that her universal generalizations about patriarchal cultures are products of the spurious practice of projecting historically specific (and ideologically suspect) concepts onto other societies and other historical periods.

Irigaray's claim that in patriarchal societies, women's alienated sexuality has the status of a commodity illustrates this problem. While it may be true that women's sexual alienation presupposes sexual objectification, it does not follow that men universally value women as sex objects as objects in general are valued under capitalism—as commodities. Irigaray offers no empirical evidence for her claim. Nor does she consider whether the sexual objectification of women assumes different forms in other historical periods and cultures. Instead, she develops her claim by analogy, relying on concepts shared by Marx, Lévi-Strauss, and Lacan (including the genderized nature/culture distinction), without considering the cultural and historical limits of these concepts. Thus, while Irigaray's analysis of sexual objectification as commodification may illuminate aspects of our own sexual alienation, its claim to universality is suspect.

An adequate political psychology must recognize, as Irigaray's does not, that women's psychological oppression is rooted in historically specific social relations and structures. This criterion does not rule out the possibility that some aspects of psychological oppression have remained relatively constant thoughout the history of, say, Western societies. But it does demand that these long-term continuities be situated with respect to the specific social relations and social structures that actually sustain them at various times. Irigaray's appeal to "the exchange of women by men" does not meet this requirement. It does not describe any specific social structure but serves as an abstract formula for a system of structural possibilities consisting in three types of family relations—consanguinity, affinity and descent. Moveover, the exchange of women by men is at best only a partial expression of the social structures and relations that link together members of a given culture, particularly in modern industrialized and class stratified societies.[8] Given that the social relations of male domination vary in different societies and in different historical periods as well as across class and ethnic lines, explanations of women's psychological oppression that focus on only one type of social relation, in Irigaray's case marriage relations, risk being either over simplified or reductionistic.

Irigaray's discussion of the alienation of women's desire highlights an important aspect of women's psychological oppression: the symbolic and ideological dimension of men's control of women's sexuality, which includes the "terms" and processes under which women come to identify themselves as sexual beings and as women. But she views this alienation abstractly as a feature of sociality *per se*, as something that ineluctably attends the passage from "nature" to "culture." Irigaray does not consider the different ways, even in modern Western societies, in which men control the expression and direction of women's desire or the variety of practices and institutions that engender and reinforce women's sexual alienation.

Irigaray's appeal to *hom(m)osexualité* as a causal (if not *the* causal) factor in women's sexual alienation illustrates one important problem created by the abstract character of her analysis. As the principle of sociality governing patriarchal societies, *hom(m)osexualité* is everywhere, "subtending," as Irigaray puts it, the vast and variegated texts of social, political, and economic life. But, and for the same reason, *hom(m)osexualité* is nowhere. It is independent of any historically and culturally specific institutions and practices, a free-floating ideological and psychological structure. As such, *hom(m)osexualité* lacks explanatory force; it cannot *explain* how specific institutions and practices contribute to the causes and maintenance of women's sexual alienation. Rather, of such institutions and practices, *hom(m)osexualité* can at best say: man's desire for the same resides, as it does everywhere, here.

For Irigaray, although historically and culturally specific practices and institutions express or embody *hom(m)osexualité*, they do not engender it. Consequently, to attribute women's sexual alienation to *ho(m)osexualité*, as Irigaray does, effectively severs this alienation, its causes and maintenance, from concrete social relations of power and dominance, the seat of all oppression. Irigaray's appeal to *hom(m)osexualité* to explain women's sexual alienation, interpreted as the commodification of women's desire, is thus inadequate. For it falsely assumes that sexual alienation is independent of the institutions and practices in which men's control of women's sexuality is enforced and enacted.

These defects in Irigaray's account of the alienation of women's desire illustrate two pitfalls associated with the appropriation of Lacanian psychoanalysis as a feminist theoretical tool. The first is the questionable empirical adequacy of Lacanian claims about universal structures of psychic life, particularly the Oedipus complex understood as the "subjective" expression of exogamy. The second is the excessively abstract character of Lacan's account of these universals.

One striking feature of "Women on the Market" is the absence of references, even for the purpose of illustration, to concrete social relations. This is also a striking, and troublesome, feature of Lacan's account of the Oedipus complex. Following Lévi-Strauss, Lacan holds that "the primordial law [of sociality] is . . . that which in regulating marriage ties superimposes the kingdom of culture on that of nature abandoned to the law of copulation" (Lacan 1977, 63). This law is the incest taboo, and its subjective, psychological pivot is the Oedipus complex, which governs for each individual his or her passage from "nature" to "culture." As viewed by Lacan, the Oedipus complex prescribes the limits and possibilities of the socialization/humanization process regardless of the actual nature of relations between children and their caretakers, and more generally, regardless of historically and culturally specific social relations. From this perspective, the Oedipus complex is not only or even primarily a familial drama, the psychic counterpart of some concrete organization of social relations like the nuclear family. Rather, it is an inexorable structural mechanism that operates independently of the human content it organizes. The abstract character of Irigaray's analysis in "Women on the Market" is in large measure a consequence of her identification of the alienation of women's desire with Lacan's structural version of the Oedipus complex, reinterpreted as the installation within psychic life of the reign of hom(m)osexualité. [9]

In this section, I have argued that Irigaray's account of the alienation of women's desire through commodification and oedipalization rests on questionable empirical grounds and fails adequately to link internalized oppression to culturally and historically specific institutions and practices. Thus, it fails to meet criterion one. In the next section, I turn to my second criterion, which requires that an adequate political psychology must be nondeterministic. I will examine the adequacy of Lacanian psychoanalysis with respect to this criterion through an analysis of selected themes from the work of Julia Kristeva.

II

"As soon as she speaks the discourse of the community, a woman becomes phallus."

(Kristeva 1974, 6)

One important feminist objection to psychoanalysis has been its biologistic leanings—for instance, the biological determinism reflected in Freud's remark that "anatomy is destiny." Simone de Beauvoir's counter slogan, "one is not born but rather becomes a woman," captures the spirit of feminist quarrels with the view that human sex and gender identities, behaviors and desires are determined by the anatomical/biological differences necessary for reproduction. Against this view, a growing body of feminist research is providing support for a politically important counter-thesis: gender and sexuality are social constructs that are in principle susceptible to intervention and change.

Part of the appeal to feminists of Lacanian psychoanalysis is its rejection of the strand of Freud associated with the view that "anatomy is destiny." This rejection is clearly evident in Lacan's treatment of the castration and Oedipus complexes. Here, fears and desires that have been interpreted as pertaining to actual body parts are held instead to pertain to these body parts only as symbolic entities or signifiers. For example, in Lacan's account of the castration complex, it is not the penis as an anatomical structure but rather the "phallus" as a symbolic bearer of culturally conferred meanings that plays a causal role. Penis envy thus becomes the desire to have what the phallus signifies, namely the social prestige and power that those who lack phallic signifiers (penises) are denied.

Thus, Lacanian psychoanalysis does not base sexual identity (the recognition of oneself as an I-he or I-she) on biology or on any other innate structures. Rather, it holds that sexual identity is acquired through processes of identification and language learning that constitute the psychological becoming of the social person. Lacan divides this process into two main stages—the Imaginary and the Symbolic. The Imaginary corresponds to the pre-Oedipal period governed by a diadic relation between mother and child. During this stage, the child forms its first self-conception by identifying with a unified corporeal image which more or less corresponds to its mother's body.[10] This identification is gradually replaced by an identification with the object of the mother's desire: the child wants to be "all" for the mother, to please and to fuse with her. The Symbolic, on the other hand, corresponds to the Oedipal and post-Oedipal periods during which the child comes to individuate itself from others and to recognize itself as an I-he or I-she. This identificatory change requires the child to renounce its desire to fuse with its mother. Psychic castration, then, is the awareness of this separation. According to Lacan, the Oedipal crisis occurs during the process of language acquisition when the child learns its society's sexual rules. It ends when these rules are internalized or acceded to. In taking over the identity functions prescribed by society, the child represses its desire for the mother and enters what Lacan calls the Symbolic Order which, as andro-or phallocentric, is governed by the father's law (the incest taboo).

Lacan thus rejects biological determinism and offers in its place an account of the social construction of sex and gender. Normally, the political significance of the view that sexuality and gender are socially constructed is linked to the assumption that social constructs, unlike innate biological structures, are susceptible to intervention and change. Lacan, however, is more pessimistic:

> Woman is introduced into the symbolic pact of marriage as an object of exchange along basically androcentric and patriarchal lines. Thus, the woman is engaged in an order of exchange in which she is an object; indeed, this is what causes the fundamentally conflictual character of her position—I would say *without exit*. The symbolic order literally submerges and transcends her. (1954-5, 304) [My emphasis]

Here, Lacan's pessimism about the possibility of change is linked to his view of the relation between women and the Symbolic Order. Elsewhere, his pessimism implicates both men and women:

> Symbols . . . envelop the life of man in a network so total that they join together, before he comes into the world, those who

> are going to engender him 'by flesh and blood'; so total that
> they bring to his birth . . . the shape of his destiny; so total
> that they give the words that will make him faithful or
> renegrade; the law of the acts that will follow him right to the
> very place where he *is* not yet and even beyond his death.
> (Lacan 1977, 65)

Given Lacan's view of the phallic structuring of sex and gender as a function of the reigning social symbolics, the possibility of transcending or modifying the rule of phallic law is dim. Julia Kristeva puts the matter this way: we are caught in a "profound structural mechanism concerning the casting of sexual difference in the West . . . and [we] can't do much about it" (1986, 155).

Kristeva's pessimism concerning the possibility of transcending or modifying the phallocentric Symbolic Order is reflected in her account of the possibilities open to us for revolutionary change. This account is developed by way of an analysis of what she calls *le sujet en proces* and its disruptive effects as exhibited in the writings of the late-nineteenth century *avant-garde* (Kristeva 1984). Although this may seem like a circuitous way to address the problem of revolutionary change, Kristeva thinks otherwise. She claims that the "revolution in language" effected in the texts of the literary *avant-garde* is homologous to revolutionary disruption in the social and political sphere: "The [*avant-garde*] text is a practice that can be compared to political revolution: the one brings about in the subject what the other introduces into society" (1984, 17).

In her analysis of the late nineteenth century *avant-garde*, Kristeva focuses on the presence in these texts of "poetic language" and its effect of "unsettling" the identity of meaning and of the speaking subject:

> . . . one should begin by positing that there is within poetic
> language . . . a *heterogeneousness* to meaning and signification.
> This *heterogeneousness*, detected genetically in the echolalias
> of infants as rhythms and intonations anterior to the first pho-
> nemes, morphemes, lexemes, and sentences . . . operates
> through, despite, and in excess of [signification], producing in
> poetic language 'musical' as well as non-sense effects that de-
> stroy not only accepted beliefs and significations but, in radi-
> cal experiments, syntax itself, that guarantee of thetic con-
> sciousness. (1980a, 133)

For Kristeva, then, poetic language is marked by the presence of rhythmic, tonal, or syntactical features that bear either a negative or surplus relation to meaning and signification, that is, to the *symbolic* modality of language use. This symbolic modality, which corresponds to the Lacanian Symbolic Order, is language as it is mobilized in the circuit of social communication, a circuit within which the phonemic, lexemic, morphemic, and syntactical structures of language are harnessed to the existing "social contract." Thus, the symbolic modality encompasses those features of language that enable it to function as an instrument of communication, for instance, syntactical structures and grammatical categories, intersubjectively fixed and reiterable units of meaning, established social contexts of use and shared conventions. According to Kristeva, at work in poetic language and giving rise to its "unsettling" effects is another modality of language radically distinct from the symbolic dimension. This modality, which she calls the *semiotic*, springs from the archaisms of the instinctual body. It is the manifestation in language of instinctual drives.

Kristeva's account of this semiotic modality is elaborated in terms of Freudian and Lacanian theory. Her "speaking subject" is the split subject of psychoanalytic theory, a subject divided between psychosomatic processes and social constraints. Accordingly, Kristeva proposes that the signifying practices of the split subject can be analyzed in terms of two dispositions or modalities—the semiotic, linked to instinctual drives, and the symbolic, linked to the installation of the subject into a social network and the assumption of social identity. The semiotic refers to tensions or forces discernible in language that represent a kind of residue from the pre-Oedipal phase of development. As Terry Eagleton explains,

> The child in the pre-Oedipal phase does not yet have access to language . . . , but we can imagine its body as criss-crossed by a flow of 'pulsions' or drives which are at this point relatively unorganized. This rhythmic pattern can be seen as a form of language, though it is not yet meaningful. For language as such to happen, this heterogeneous flow must be, as it were, chopped up, articulated into stable terms, so that in entering the symbolic order this 'semiotic' process is repressed. This repression, however, is not total: for the semiotic can still be discerned as a kind of pulsional pressure within language itself, in tone, rhythm, the bodily and material qualities of language, but also in contradiction, meaninglessness, disruption, silence and absence. (Eagleton 1983, 188)

Kristeva describes this libidinal-signifying organization as instinctual, maternal, and feminine. It is held to be *instinctual* because the organization is dictated by primary processes such as displacement and condensation, absorption and repulsion, rejection and stasis, all of which function as innate preconditions for language acquisition. It is held to be *maternal* because of the child's direct dependence on the mother. Finally, it is held to be *feminine* because this semiotic realm of rhythmic, corporeal rapport with the mother has been gendered as such by our culture.

Kristeva holds that the semiotic and symbolic modalities of signification are necessarily intertwined in language use. She also asserts that differences in the dialectical interplay between the two signifying modalities give rise to importantly different kinds of signifying practices. At one extreme is scientific discourse which tends to reduce as much as possible the semiotic component. At the other extreme is poetic language in which the semiotic gains the upper hand. More precisely, Kristeva contends that in poetic language the semiotic and the symbolic exist in a kind of internal tension such that poetic language in effect "posits itself . . . as an undecidable process between sense and non-sense, between *language* and *rhythm*" (Kristeva 1980, 135). Insofar as it is a socially communicable form of discourse, poetic language partakes of the semantic/syntactical organization of language. But it also displays a "sonorous distinctiveness" which exists in either a surplus or negative relation to the symbolic dimension of language use. According to Kristeva, in the literary texts of the *avant-garde*, this sonorous distinctiveness disrupts the flow of signification, setting up a play of unconscious drives that undercuts the stability of received social meaning. For readers of these texts, the result of such disruptions is a momentary release of libidinal pleasure (*jouissance*).

What is the relation between Kristeva's analysis of the "revolution in language" effected in *avant-garde* texts and her views on feminist politics? For Kristeva, the *avant-garde* text is to language what feminism is (or should be) to society—a disruptive element. Just as poetic disruption depends on a "permanent contradiction" between the semiotic and symbolic, so feminist disruption depends on an equally permanent contradiction between masculine/paternal and feminine/maternal identifications. Kristeva views these "permanent contradictions" as rooted in the Oedipal structuring of desire, a "profound structural mechanism" which we women "can't do much about."

The political pessimism suggested by this remark is echoed in Kristeva's analysis of the options available to women given the Oedipal structure. As presented by Kristeva, these options are bounded by two undesirable extremes, father-identification and mother-identification, which effectively create for women a double-bind. The father identified woman is exemplified by the figure of Electra, who has her mother, Clytemnestra, killed in order to avenge her father. In so doing, Electra takes the point of view of her father *vis-à-vis* her mother. As interpreted by Kristeva, the mother's crime against the father has been to expose her *jouissance* to the world by taking a lover, a *jouissance* forbidden by patriarchal law. Electra's act is an expression of her fear and hatred of the *jouissance* not only of her mother's body but also of her own. She must abhor in herself what she abhors in her mother and as a result she perpetuates the patriarchal social/symbolic order.

If this picture of the father-identified woman is unpalatable, Kristeva nonetheless accepts the view of Freud and Lacan that repression of both instinctual pleasure and continuous relation to the mother is the price one must pay to enter history and social affairs. This is why the alternative of mother-identification is equally undesirable: it condemns us to "forever remain in a sulk in the face of history, politics, and social affairs" (1986, 156). According to Kristeva, then, mother-identification results in a failure to enter the symbolic order, a path that ends in psychosis. On the other hand, father-identification entails taking over patriarchal conceptualizations and valuations. In the extreme case, this results in a rejection of attributes gendered as feminine insofar as these attributes are considered to be incompatible with entry into the (masculine) realm of culture and history. [11]

For Kristeva, both identificatory options are captured in the gender categorizations operative in patriarchal culture: mother-identification by feminine categories such as nature, body and the unconscious, and father-identification by contrasting masculine categories such as culture, mind, and ego. While Kristeva believes that these gender categories are always at work in the formation of one's identity as an I-she or I-he, she also asserts that the extremes of mother and father identification can be avoided. Moreover, she recommends such an avoidance as a desirable feminist practice.

> Let us refuse both extremes. Let us know that an ostensibly masculine, paternal identification . . . is necessary in order to have a voice in the chapter of politics and history. . . . [But] let us right away be wary of the premium on narcissism that such an integration can carry; let us reject the development of a 'homologous' woman [i.e. an Electra], who is finally capable and virile; and let us rather act on the socio-politico-historical stage as her negative: that is, act first with all those who refuse and 'swim against the tide'—all who rebel against the existing relations of production and reproduction. But let us not take the role of Revolutionary either, whether male or female: let us on the contrary refuse all roles to summon [a] truth outside time, a truth that is neither true nor false, that cannot be fitted into the order of speech and social symbolism. (1986, 156)

This "truth" is Kristeva's semiotic order—the instinctual pleasure one must repress in order to gain entry into the symbolic/social domain. Thus, the politics that Kristeva recommends requires an "impossible dialectic," a "permanent alternation" between the semiotic ("maternal" *jouissance*) and the symbolic ("paternal" power or law).

This politics is supposed to be an analogue of poetic language. But there are problems concerning the manifestation, aim, and efficacy of the practice Kristeva recommends. Terry Eagleton argues that Kristeva's vision of politically revolutionary activity as a semiotic force that disrupts stable meanings and institutions leads to a kind of anarchism that fosters private libidinal pleasure. He also criticizes Kristeva for failing to see the need to move beyond internal fragmentation to new forms of social solidarity (Eagleton 1983, 190-91). Likewise, Toril Moi finds that Kristeva's focus on negativity and disruption rather than on building new solidarities leads to an undesirable anarchist and subjectivist political position (Moi 1985, 170-71). I have a good deal of sympathy for these criticisms, for, as I will argue, the aspects of Kristeva's views they call into question are symptomatic of an untenable political pessimism. This pessimism is a consequence of the view that the patriarchal Symbolic Order is not susceptible to feminist intervention and change. For Kristeva, as for Lacan, the Symbolic Order is an "implacable structure" and the only escape is psychosis.

For both Lacan and Kristeva, the Symbolic Order is the realm of culture and language definitive of human being. Hence, entry into the Symbolic Order is identified with the process of humanization, the assumption of social identity and social roles. What is essential to this process is the submission of presocial desire to the laws of organization and exchange within a sexually differentiated group. Insofar as one successfully negotiates the passage from natural to social being, the identity functions prescribed by the Symbolic Order are inescapable.

Lacan seems to hold that there is only one Symbolic Order, that in which identity functions are prescribed by the Law of the Father. Kristeva, in contrast, contends that the Symbolic Order described by Freud and Lacan is specific to Western (Mosaic) monotheistic culture.[12] Thus, although Kristeva holds that symbolic mediation is required in the passage from nature to culture, she does not subscribe to the view that all cultures are based on the same symbolic system. Because it marks a sensitivity to the problem of ethnocentrism with respect to the identification of cultural universals, this qualification is important. However, it does not alter Kristeva's position on the more general issue concerning the symbolic determination of psychic life. Insofar as a Westerner successfully negotiates the passage from natural to social being, she maintains, the identity options prescribed by the patriarchal symbolic system specific to Western monotheism are inescapable.

Kristeva's account of these identity options presupposes the Freudian dictum that what is today an act of internal restraint was once an external one. Although this dictum presumably holds for any external restraint, Freud focused on aggression, the so-called "primal" father's restraint of the sons, which presupposed his possession of all the primal horde's women. Thus, for Freud, the historical origin of the Oedipal structuring of psychic life is a situation of oppression in which women are dominated by men. With the internalization of the father's external restraint (the incest taboo), this situation of oppression is transformed into one of repression. In the history of individual persons, the Oedipal structuring of psychic life is a repetition of this epochal event, which Freud identifies with the origins of civilization proper. External restraint is replaced by its symbolic expression: the father comes to represent the cultural reality principle, the symbolic, while the mother represents the sensual substratum, the semiotic, that must be repressed if a child is to enter culture at all.

Since Freud views the psychological mechanism of Oedipal repression as the symbolic/psychological expression of women's "primal" oppression, he grounds the Oedipus complex in an hypothetical historical situation of oppression. However, once the (primal) father's external restraint is internalized, the resulting psychic structure and symbolism is severed from the social sphere. For Freud, this autonomy of the psychological from the social is a consequence of the hypothesis that a "primaeval and prehistoric demand has . . . become part of the organized and inherited endowment of mankind" (Freud 1953-74, 13:188). What was originally social (the primal father's threat of castration, the sons' responses, etc.) became "natural," an internal disposition or instinctual structure. From this perspective, the Oedipus complex is not exclusively or even primarily the psychological counterpart of some particular socio-familial structure but rather an autonomous function of psychic life.

The autonomy thus ascribed to the Oedipus complex is at the root of Kristeva's political pessimism. Once set in motion, the Oedipal mechanism, like the Deist's universe, functions of its own accord. It runs on and on in both the individual and her culture, impervious to changing social and economic relations and to ongoing feminist interventions.

Given her adoption of Lacan's "de-biologized" Freud, the implacable character of the Oedipal structuring of desire does not entail, for Kristeva, a crude biological determinism. Anatomy is not destiny. Instead, it is the psychic symbolism and structure definitive of the Oedipus complex that plays this determining role.

Kristeva's view on this matter reflects a hyperbolic but nonetheless faithful interpretation of a basic Lacanian claim: "Images and symbols *for* the woman cannot be isolated from images and symbols *of* the woman . . . [for] it is the representation of sexuality which conditions how [sexuality] comes into play" (Lacan 1982, 90). On some interpretations, this claim is unobjectionable. In fact, some version of it is central to the project of feminist political psychology, a psychology whose task it is to explain the processes whereby patriarchal representations and gender-differentiated categories take root within our psychic lives, affecting our desires, feelings, thoughts, and valuations. This task presupposes, first, that at least some patriarchal representations of women also serve as representations *for* women. In addition, it presupposes, that in so serving, they function as instruments of male domination. But the project of feminist political psychology rests on yet another, equally crucial premise. Feminist psychology is *political* psychology precisely because its accounts of internalized oppression are given in the service of a liberatory project. It thus assumes that psychological oppression, at least under some conditions and to some extent, can be transcended. But Kristeva's Lacanian account of psychological oppression does not allow for the political hope expressed by this third assumption. This is not because she rejects on empirical grounds the possibility of transcending the patriarchal Symbolic Order. It is rather a consequence of her acceptance of the Lacanian view that social personhood (at least for Western women) requires subjection or submission to Oedipal identity functions and laws.

Lacan and Kristeva allow for only two alternatives: subjection to the Law of the Father or psychosis. I-hood, having a coherent self-identity over time, is impossible without submission through oedipalization to the patriarchal Symbolic Order, which structures and sustains subjectivity. Submission to the Symbolic Order thus is not just a diachronic, developmental event but a permanent condition of social being. The political pessimism engendered by this view can be expressed as the claim that the Oedipal structuring of subjectivity is "total"—i.e., once in place, we cannot escape the identificatory options circumscribed by patriarchal representations and gender categories. This claim, however, is unwarranted. For even if we accept the (arguable) view that we enter society *via* the Oedipus complex and submission to the Law of the Father, it does not follow that we cannot *subsequently* reject, at least in part, our paternal heritage. [13]

Part of what feminism is about is breaking free of damaging representations and gender categories, and I see no reason not to believe that this project is in principle possible or that, indeed, it has not already met with some success. As long as there are slippages or "contradictions" between patriarchal representations of women and other features of a woman's symbolically-mediated lived experience, as long as such representations do not dictate the entire structure and content of such experience, they are susceptible to feminist interventions. [14]

Lacan's contention that there is no such slippage is made on *a priori* grounds. Yet I believe that the history of feminist interventions provides an empirical challenge to the view that we cannot transcend the identity options and laws definitive of the patriarchal Symbolic Order. The practice of consciousness raising provides just one example. One of the primary aims of this type of feminist intervention is to help women discover facets of internalized oppression by "showing up" the sexual ideology that affects our desires, feelings, thoughts, and valuations. This process both presupposes and utilizes the slippage between this sexual ideology and the symbolically-medited reality of women's lives. To "show up" sexual ideology involves exposing it for what it is, to make it the subject of our thoughts, feelings, and valuations rather than their determining content. Of course, "showing up" sexual ideology in this way does not necessarily involve freeing oneself from it. But to grant this project some success, one need not deny that patriarchal representations and gender categories are deeply rooted in our psychic lives, so much so that they can appear implacable. Rather it is to deny that they exhaust the entire symbolic dimension mediating experience. In addition, it is to affirm that gradually we can loosen the hold of patriarchal representations, see through them and beyond them, and perhaps one day even overcome their domination of our psychic lives.

Many of the writings of French feminists influenced by Lacan, including writings by Kristeva and Irigaray, can be seen as contributions to the feminist practice of consciousness raising. The site of their analyses is the unconscious cultural symbolism, particularly sex and gender symbolism, which subtends individual psychic life. The aim is to make the unconscious conscious and in doing so to assist women in overcoming internalized oppression.[15] Yet the political hope presupposed by such a project often exists in uneasy tension with the political pessimism that Lacanian theory engenders.

Julia Kristeva's politics provides an extreme example of this pessimism. It combines the pessimism of the Lacanian view that the Oedipal structuring of female subjectivity is "total" with Freud's pessimism concerning "civilization's" demands for instinctual renunciation. As a result, the feminist politics Kristeva commends emerges as just one expression of an eternal war between (feminine) *jouissance* and (masculine) power/law, where the only possible revolutions are temporary transgressions, limited "returns of the repressed." For Kristeva, what makes feminism genuinely revolutionary is not its opposition to and transformation of historically specific relations of *oppression*. Rather, feminism's revolutionary moment consists in its opposition to the *repressive* or *sacrificial* character of sociability or culture *per se*.[16] Accordingly, Kristeva holds that if feminism has a role to play in revolutionary politics,

> it is only by assuming a negative function: reject
> everything finite, definite, structured, loaded with meaning in
> the existing state of society. Such an attitude places women on
> the side of the explosion of social codes: with revolutionary
> moments. (1980b, 166)

If everything finite, definite, structured, loaded with meaning in the existing state of society contributes to women's oppression, then Kristeva's prescription for feminist politics might make some sense. But there is no good reason for thinking this to be so. Of course, in our own society, women are socially and economically subordinated to men. However, this does not mean that all aspects of society are harmful to women and hence legitimate targets of feminist opposition. Moreover, feminism needs to move beyond the rejection of existing social codes to the construction of new, more equitable social, economic, and political relations.[17] Kristeva's view of revolutionary feminist politics is thus inadequate for two reasons: it rejects too much and it hopes or aims for too little.

III

In this paper, I have claimed that an adequate feminist political psychology must meet at least two requirements. First, it must treat internalized oppression as grounded in culturally and historically specific institutions and practices. Second, it must understand such oppression non-deterministically and allow for the possibility that it could, under some circumstances, be overcome. I have argued that the theories of Luce Irigaray and Julia Kristeva do not meet these requirements. I would like to conclude on a more positive note with some brief reflections as to the sort of theory that might better provide for an adequate political psychology.

Let me begin by observing that the two requirements I have invoked are not unrelated. To see internalized oppression as based in historically specific institutions and practices is to see it non-deterministically. It is to suppose that to dismantle those institutions and practices is to begin to dismantle psychological oppression. It is to assume, in addition, that under alternative, egalitarian and non-sexist arrangements, patriarchal symbolic representations could lose their hold on our psyches.

A feminist political psychology that began from these assumptions would have an interest in investigating certain matters that Lacanian theory ignores. For example, it would want to examine the history and character of infant care, the concrete and variable contexts where language learning and early identity formation occurs. The point would be to uncover the actual empirical links between different practices and different symbolic constructions of social identity. Moreover, an adequate political psychology would situate the child care practices it studies in their larger social-structural context. It would try to understand the connections, including the tensions, among familial and extra-familial factors in society that contribute to the formation of sex and gender identity. Further, an adequate political psychology would attend to the experiences and activities of the "post-Oedipal person." Here, the task would be to understand what social and economic relations tend to reinforce or resist early sex and gender socialization. Finally, an adequate political psychology would approach all of its inquiries with a view to eventually determining what sorts of alternative arrangements are both possible and desirable. In so doing, it would be committed to demystifying the patriarchal-ideological illusion that women's internalized oppression is inescapable.

NOTES

1. The criteria I invoke here are not the only relevant ones. In addition, an adequate political psychology must be non-idealistic, that is, it must recognize that social relations of domination

cannot be adequately defined in terms of ideational or symbolic structures. I do not discuss this criterion here.

2. Lacanian theory does not draw on the familiar distinction between sex and gender identity according to which sexual identity is a function of differentiating *biological* features and gender identity is a function of *socially defined* meanings and roles. For Lacan and his followers, sexual identity is itself a socially mediated phenomenon rather than a purely biological datum. This view is reflected in Irigaray's claim that bodies are "sexualized as female [*sexué feminin*] in and through discourse" (Irigaray 1985,90). Similarly, Kristeva asserts that the categories 'man' and 'woman' should be viewed in terms of how biological and physiological differences are "translated by and translate a difference in the relationship of subjects . . . to power, language, and meaning" (Kristeva 1981,39).

3. For purposes of the present discussion, it is not necessary to take up the question of the accuracy of Irigaray's reading of Marx. Let me simply suggest that it strikes me as suspect.

4. It should be noted that *both* Irigaray and Lévi-Strauss give circular answers to the question of why women rather than men are the objects of exchange.

5. In "Women on the Market," Irigaray uses the rhetorical strategy she calls "mimicry"—a deliberate imitation of male-generated discourse that aims to flaunt or parody its androcentric biases. However, her essay as a whole is not a parody. The analogy it develops between oedipalization and commodification is taken seriously by Irigaray, who also invokes it elsewhere.

6. For an extended argument against the claim that all cultures have been male-dominated, see Leacock (1982). Duley and Edwards (1986, 26-47) review current anthropological literature on this issue. Millett (1971) and Firestone (1971) contain classic feminist criticisms of Freud on the universality of the Oedipus complex. Leach (1970) provides an accessible critical analysis (based on ethnographic data) of Lévi-Strauss's account of the elementary structures of kinship.

7. Ortner (1974) invokes Lévi-Strauss, among others, in developing the claim that in all societies, culture has been associated with masculinity and nature with femininity. For anthropological criticisms of this claim, see Ortner and Whitehead (1981).

8. In modern industrialized societies, even marriage relations cannot be adequately characterized as an exchange of women (daughters and wives) by men (fathers and husbands). Although some marriage ceremonies include a symbolic gesture in which a father "gives away" his daughter to some other man's son, marriage is apt to be seen by its participants as an emotional, religious, or legal contract between free individuals. This perception is not without ideological components that mask the extent to which marriage as an institution is oppressive to women. Nonetheless, the claim that marriage is based on the exchange of women by men hardly suffices to capture the complexity of this institution, including the ideological dimensions that may contribute to a woman's psychological oppression.

9. Ragland-Sullivan (1986, 267-280) criticizes Irigaray, among others, for reading Lacan substantively rather than structurally by equating Lacan's Symbolic Order with patriarchy and the Oedipal structure with the alienation of women's desire under patriarchy. On my interpretation, in contrast, Irigaray does not *misread* Lacan; rather, she foregrounds matters she believes he slighted or overlooked, for example, the universality of male domination and the role played by the Oedipal structure in women's oppression. Thus unlike Ragland-Sullivan, Irigaray rejects the claim that the "Lacanian phallic signifier [is] neutral in its own right" (273) rather than an artifact or emblem of male domination.

10. I am assuming that Lacan's notion of "the mirror stage" is best understood metaphorically and that it is early maternal identification, rather than a mirror image, that is at the base of the pre-Oedipal "moi."

11. I have not discussed two assumptions central to understanding Kristeva's claim that both mother and father identification are undesirable. The first, relatively uncontroversial assumption, is that psychosis is undesirable. The second, more controversial assumption, is that the rejection by women of so-called "feminine" in favor of "masculine" attributes is undesirable. Kristeva's "Women's Time" (1981) contains a useful discussion of this second assumption.

12. Kristeva's *Des Chinoises* (1974) is an extended argument for this claim.

13. Although the sex and gender structuring of our psychic lives begins in early childhood, it does not end there. The social institutions and practices that tend to reinforce or resist childhood sex and gender-structuring should be of special interest to feminists concerned with psychological oppression.

14. The phrase "a woman's lived experience" does not denote a substratum of experience unmediated by representations. My point is that our experience or perception of reality does not always conform to *patriarchal* representations of it.

15. See Whitford (1988) for an interpretation of Luce Irigaray along these lines.

16. Kristeva does not deny that it is important for women to fight against specific social and economic oppressions. But she does not consider this fight genuinely revolutionary unless it is also a fight against the psychologically repressive character of the Symbolic Order. She views revolutionary feminist politics as part of a broader cultural revolt, exemplified by the *avant-garde* in literature, painting, and music, against the inhibitions and prohibitions of the social-symbolic order.

17. Kristeva does have a vision of a better world which is less repressive, less body- and pleasure-denying, less "totalizing" and "equalizing" than our own. However, this vision can never find effective *social* and *institutional* realization if revolutionary political practice is limited to perpetual demystification of the status quo. In part, it is because the realization of her political vision seems to be confined to the "corporeal and desiring space" of individuals that Eagleton (1983), Moi (1985), and others have labelled Kristeva's politics of negation or rejection "individualistic anarchism".

REFERENCES

Chodorow, Nancy. 1978. *The reproduction of mothering.* Berkeley: University of California Press.

Dinnerstein, Dorothy. 1976. *The mermaid and the minotaur: sexual arrangements and the human malaise.* New York: Harper and Row.

Duley, Margot and Mary Edwards, ed. 1986. *The cross-cultural study of women: a comprehensive guide.* New York: The Feminist Press.

Eagleton, Terry. 1983. *Literary theory.* Minneapolis: University of Minnesota Press.

Firestone, Shulamith. 1971. *The dialectics of sex: the case for feminist revolution.* New York: Bantam.

Freud, Sigmund. 1953-74. The claims of psycho-analysis to scientific interests. 1913. In *The standard edition of the complete psychological works of Sigmund Freud*, vol 13. Trans. and ed. James Strachey, *et al.* London: The Hogarth Press and the Institute of Psycho-analysis.

Irigaray, Luce. 1985. *Ce sexe qui n'en est pas un.* 1977. *This sex which is not one.* Trans. Catherine Porter. New York: Cornell University Press.

Jaggar, Alison. 1983. *Feminist politics and human nature.* New Jersey: Rowman and Allanheld.

Kristeva, Julia. 1974. Sujet dans le langage et pratique politique. In *Psychanalyse et politique.* Paris: Verdiglione.

———. 1977. *Des chinoises.* 1974. *About chinese women.* Trans. Anita Barrows. London: Aron Boyars.

———. 1980a. D'une identite l'autre. 1975. From one identity to another. Trans. Tom Gora and Alice Jardine. In *Desire in language: a semiotic approach to literature and art.* Ed. Leon Roudiez. New York: Columbia University Press, 124-148.

——. 1980b. Oscillation between power and denial. 1974. In *New French feminisms*. Ed. Elaine Marks and Isabelle de Courtivron. New York: Schocken.

——. 1981. Le temps des femmes. 1979. Women's time. Trans. Margaret Waller. *Signs* 7, 13-35.

——. 1984. *La revolution du langage poétique*. 1974. *Revolution in poetic language*. Trans. Margaret Waller. New York: Columbia University Press.

——. 1986. *Des chinoises*. 1974. Excerpted as About Chinese Women. Trans. Sean Hand. In *The Kristeva Reader*. Ed. Toril Moi. New York: Columbia University Press, 138-159.

Lacan, Jacques. 1954-55. Seminaire II. Paris: Editions du Seuil.

——. 1956. "De l'usage de la parole et des structures de langage dans la conduite et dans le champ de la psychanalyse." In *La psychanalyse*, vol. 1, 202-55.

——. 1977. *Ecrits*. 1966. Ecrits: a selection. Trans. and ed. Alan Sheridan. New York: Norton.

Leach, Edmund. 1970. *Claude Lévi-Strauss*. New York: The Viking Press.

Leacock, Eleanor B. 1982. *Myths of male domination*. New York: Monthly Review Press.

Lévi-Strauss, Claude. 1969. *Les structures élémentaires de la parenté*. Trans. 1949. *The elementary structures of kinship*. Boston: Beacon Press.

Marx, Karl and Frederick Engels. 1975. *Collected works*. Vol. 3. New York: International Publishers.

Millett, Kate. 1971. *Sexual politics*. New York: Avon.

Mitchell, Juliet. 1974. *Psychoanalysis and feminism*. New York: Vintage

Moi, Toril. 1985. *Sexual/textual politics*. London: Methuen.

Ortner, Sherry. 1974. Is female to male as nature is to culture? In *Women, culture, and society*. Ed. M.Z. Rosaldo and L. Lamphere. Palo Alto: Stanford University Press.

Ortner, Sherry and Harriet Whitehead, eds. 1981. *Sexual meanings: the cultural construction of gender and sexuality*. New York: Cambridge University Press.

Ragland-Sullivan, Ellie. 1986. *Jacques Lacan and the philosophy of psychoanalysis*. Chicago: University of Illinois Press.

Rubin, Gayle. 1975. The traffic in women: Notes on the political economy of sex. In *Toward an anthropology of women*. Ed. Rayna R. Reiter. New York: Monthly Review Press, 157-210.

Whitford, Margaret. 1988. Luce Irigaray's critique of rationality. In *Feminist perspectives in philosophy*. Ed. Morwenna Griffiths and Margaret Whitford. Bloomington: Indiana University Press, 109-130.

The Subversion of Women's Agency in Psychoanalytic Feminism: Chodorow, Flax, Kristeva

DIANA T. MEYERS

Despite the well deserved reputation for misogyny psychoanalysis has gained, psychoanalytic feminists have sought to capitalize on and to augment its liberatory possibilities. In this essay, I explicate and assess the efforts of three prominent psychoanalytic theorists—Nancy Chodorow, Jane Flax, and Julia Kristeva—to develop a feminist account of women's agency. In section 1, I argue that gender dichotomies subvert both Chodorow's valorization of traditional feminine capacities and Flax's more circumspect synthesis of traditional masculine capacities with traditional feminine capacities. In section 2, I turn to Julia Kristeva's more complex view. Not only does Kristeva reject the association of agency with masculinity and thus reconstrue femininity, but also she scrambles gender associations that lie at the root of the Freudian theory of development. I argue, however, that gender makes a pernicious reappearance in Kristeva's conceptualization of social criticism and political action. Thus, Kristeva, too, is defeated by gender polarities. Finally, in section 3, I assess more generally the prospects for a psychoanalytic theory of women's agency. While psychoanalytic feminism has offered important insights regarding women's potential as agents as well as proposals for realizing this potential, I urge that this school of thought has thus far remained too much in the grip of the gender bifurcation Freud codified to supply an account of the individual agent and human interaction that is altogether satisfactory from a feminist point of view.

Only the most intransigent empiricists and skeptics fail to see the power of Freud's mythic, eroticized tale of the unformed infant coming into the world and embarking upon the travail of personality consolidation, with its attendant torments and triumphs. Acknowledging not only that psychoanalysis taps a deep layer of people's self-concepts but also that it helps to perpetuate those very self-understandings, psychoanalytic feminists have not dismissed psychoanalysis as a soon-to-be-extinct patriarchal dinosaur. They have, instead, sought to capitalize on and to augment its liberatory tradition.

Yet, all variants of psychoanalytic feminism face a common fundamental problem. Psychoanalysis is premised on the claim that the self is fundamentally divided. What becomes evident as psychoanalytic feminists strive to adapt psychoanalysis to feminist purposes is that psychoanalysis is itself fundamentally fractured along gender lines. The problem is not merely that Freud mars his theory of psychic structure and psychodynamics by associating his view with repugnant gender norms, for it seems possible that his insights in these areas could be purged of these meretricious associations. The deeper and more difficult problem is that Freud divides every capacity involved in human agency according to gender. Feeling and submission are feminine; thought and control are masculine. Moreover, Freud hardly saw traditional feminine capacities as capacities. Whereas masculinity, which is linked with civilization through the censorious superego's respect for principles, exacts independence and activity, femininity, which is linked with regression through the insistent primary processes of the unconscious, requires dependence and passivity. Thus, Freud's entire schema of interpretation is premised on a system of assumptions about gender that no feminist could endorse.

Still, the consuming and skewed gender polarity that Freud placed at the center of his theory has not deterred psychoanalytic feminists. They have sought to correct Freud's oversights regarding women's role in human development as well as his overtly misogynous view of women. Moreover, they have sought to harness the power and scope of psychoanalysis to emancipatory purposes. That is, they have begun to ask how the developmental process and social relations might be transformed so as to free masculinity and femininity from their links to domination and subordination.

Much of the attraction of psychoanalytic accounts of gender stems from their grasp of the embeddedness of gender imperatives in personality structure (Young 1983, 135; Jaggar 1983, 126). Women's recent entrance into the labor market shows that reshuffling institutional roles does not metamorphize gender. Assuming economic responsibilities seldom reduces women's concern for their children, and men whose wives are working continue to resist sharing equally in childcare and housekeeping. Plainly, the gender syndrome that is in place cannot easily be demolished, and psychoanalytic feminism gives a vivid and compelling account of the tenacity of gender identity. But a feminist theory could hardly stop there. Not only must it defend the feminine capacities Freud so glibly belittled, but also it must criticize traditional gender norms in order to indicate what shape women's personalities might assume in an egalitarian world.

Unfortunately, these tasks are in tension with one another. To explain both how gender identity comes to be deeply entrenched in individual psychology and also how gender can be transformed seems to require a simultaneously backward- and forward-looking account. Indeed, providing a psychoanalytic explanation of how gender identity comes to be lodged at the core of psychic structure seems to require reiterating a variant of the Freudian story, tainted though it is with retrograde gender associations, whereas a psychoanalytic explanation of how gender can be finessed and how novel modes of agency can be established seems to require dispensing with that very set of concepts and line of argument. Likewise, although the claim that, relative to traditional masculinity, traditional femininity has been misrepresented and underrated is plainly compatible with the claim that neither gender modality is ideal, it is not clear that psychoanalytic feminism is capable of doing justice to both of these points.

The question, then, is whether feminist theory that seeks to rid foundational psychoanalytic concepts of misogyny and to elevate feminine capacities to the status they deserve can retain the capacity to account for the strength of gender identities without sacrificing the capacity to use the framework for progressive purposes. In short, can psychoanalytic feminism explain the inbred handicaps limiting women's life prospects while generating a vision of human agency that would eliminate those handicaps?

I shall address this problem by examining the accounts of agency presented in three versions of psychoanalytic feminism—the theories of Nancy Chodorow, Jane Flax, and Julia Kristeva. In Section 1, I consider the unidimensional yet opposed strategies of Nancy Chodorow and Jane Flax. Whereas Chodorow undertakes to construct an account of agency relying exclusively on materials salvaged from traditional feminine norms, Jane Flax tries to achieve the same end by building elements of traditional masculinity into her account. I argue that both projects are subverted by the persistence of gender dichotomies and the failure to supersede them. Then, in Section 2, I turn to the more complex strategy of Julia Kristeva. Kristeva not only rejects the association of agency with masculinity and thus reconstrues femininity, she also scrambles gender associations that lie at the root of the Freudian theory of development. I argue, however, that gender makes a pernicious reappearance in Kristeva's conceptualization of social criticism and political action. Thus Kristeva, too, is defeated by gender polarities. Finally, in Section 3, I assess more generally the prospects for a psychoanalytic theory of women's agency. While psychoanalytic feminism has offered important insights regarding women's potential as agents as well as proposals for realizing this potential, I urge that this school of thought has thus far remained too much in the grip of the gender bifurcation Freud codified to supply an account of the individual agent and human interaction that is altogether satisfactory from a feminist point of view.

1. THE DILEMMA OF GENDER IN RECENT OBJECT RELATIONS THEORY

In formulating her conception of subjectivity and agency, Nancy Chodorow seems to start from the relational capacities of women, which she positively values. Then, responding to the perceived need to furnish women with a capacity to resist others' unwarranted demands and influence, she incorporates a compensatory independence component—the self-nurturing capacity. The result she describes as a "relational rather than a reactive autonomy" (Chodorow 1980, 10).

Alone, the relational capacity inclines one to merge with others—to identify so completely with their interests and values that one loses any determinate sense of independent selfhood and gladly nullifies one's own interests and values.[1] The servile wife and mother who invariably puts her family's desires ahead of her own and who is never critical of her family's demands becomes the victim of her relational capacity. As a corrective to such excessive identification with others, Chodorow proposes self-nurturance—the presence within oneself of a sense of being cared for and affirmed that gives one a sense of confident distinctness. For Chodorow, it is a sense of confident distinctness that enables one to regard oneself as a subject among subjects—to have agency and authenticity without denying relatedness (1980, 10-11; 1986, 203-4).

Caretakers support the emergence of confident distinctness by protecting the infant from intrusions and from need, by supplying a tolerably consistent, though complex, set of images for the child to internalize, and by attending to and acknowledging the child's feelings instead of projecting their own feelings onto the child (Chodorow 1980, 9-10). A parent who is experienced as overdenying or, conversely, as overwhelming will derail this development process and leave the child so fiercely independent as to be sociopathic or so clingingly dependent as to be abjectly conformist (Chodorow 1978, 60; 1980, 11). In contrast, a parent who is experienced as warmly solicitous will be internalized as a "good internal mother" (Chodorow 1980, 10). The "thereness" of a good caretaker, says Chodorow, becomes an "internal sense of another who is caring and affirming"—a sense of "self-in-good-relationship" (1980, 10). People who have such a relational, self-nurturing capacity are not only able to be alone but also to acknowledge their inextricable connections to others (Chodorow 1980, 10-11).

Now, it seems to me that there is a troubling ambiguity in Chodorow's exposition of self-nurturance. Sometimes self-nurturance appears to be nothing more than a permanent internal representation of the good mother's warm solicitude. As Chodorow puts it, "A 'capacity to be alone' . . . develops because of a sense of the ongoing presence of another" (1980, 10). I take this to mean that one can be alone because one does not feel alone, and one does not feel alone because one is always accompanied by the imprint of another caring, but not overbearing, person. Yet, since self-nurturance is supposed to function as an antidote to self-destructive interpersonal connectedness—it is supposed to provide women with a firm sense of personal identity and self-esteem that will enable them to proffer or withhold care freely (Chodorow

1974, 60)—there must be more to self-nurturance. It must involve a capacity to care for and to affirm oneself, that is, to pay attention to those of one's interests and values that compete with others' and also to express those interests and values, sometimes despite others' contrary preferences or beliefs. Yet, stressing the affective dimension of the good mother's image while ignoring the cognitive and interpersonal skills required for good mothering, Chodorow gives us no account of any critical or oppositional capacities.

For Chodorow, self-nurturing capacities provide a foundation of self-definition on the basis of which one can safely enter into close relationships:

> Once this confident separateness is established, one's relational self can become more central to one's life. Differentiation is not distinctness and separateness, but a particular way of being connected to others. This connection to others, based on early incorporations, in turn enables us to feel that empathy and confidence that are basic to the recognition of the other as a self. (1980, 11)

In this passage, Chodorow denies that self-nurturing capacities demarcate boundaries between oneself and others or that they tell one when to break connections with others. Apparently, to have self-nurturing capacities is not to be able to discern one's own core needs, desires, and values and to defend and act on them when they are jeopardized. It is to have an alter ego that affirms one's distinctness while one mainly devotes oneself to securing bonds to other people.

It seems to me, then, that Chodorow has not sufficiently distinguished between what might be characterized as a self-soothing capacity and what she labels a self-nurturing capacity. Having a self-soothing capacity would reassure one of one's own existence and worth in the face of opposition and defeat. No doubt, this sort of resilience is a consolation. But women gain nothing from being pacified in their inability to withstand unwarranted familial pressures and in their inability to reconcile their feminine sense of responsibility for their family life with their personal aspirations. In conjunction with self-soothing capacities, relational capacities make women liable to conflate being manipulated with mutuality.

In professing her support for a self-nurturing self, yet describing only a self-soothing self, Chodorow echoes a traditional feminine tendency to reduce care and nurturance to conflict minimization and uncritical support (Blum et al. 1973-74). Indeed, it is not surprising that a devalued good mother should be internalized as nothing more than a self-soothing capacity, for a devalued good mother, as Chodorow herself observes, cannot mother as well as a valued one could (1974, 60). Despite Chodorow's explicit project of according due respect to women's traditional contribution and to the psychological structure that makes it possible, the devaluation of women resurfaces in this disguised form. Integrated relational, self-nurturing capacities would provide the basis for egalitarian reciprocity. However, Chodorow's account capitulates to traditional feminine norms, and, in dispensing with self-nurturing capacities, leaves women defenseless.[2]

For Chodorow, gender becomes problematic when she maneuvers to avoid condemning femininity, as it is traditionally understood, while explaining both why femininity is harmful and how women need to change. Feminist discussion of autonomy is typically ambivalent, and this ambivalence is evident in Chodorow's work. After writing as if autonomy were clearly a good that women need but lack—indeed, after having endorsed a relational form of autonomy—Chodorow declares that autonomy should not be seen as a major goal of psychic development (1980, 10 and 11). I take this reluctance to decisively ally herself with the value of autonomy to be symptomatic of Chodorow's justifiable concern to avoid trading women's virtues for a set of oppressive masculine norms. Nevertheless, her determination to stay clear of such discredited values combines with her background association of self-assertion and control with masculinity to rule out any conception of the self that includes oppositional capacities.

Convinced that a self devoid of oppositional capacities condemns women to frustration and submission, Jane Flax unequivocally affirms that women need autonomy. Not the embattled, ostensibly heroic isolation that has long passed for autonomy, but rather something that might well go under the appellation she suggests—interactive autonomy. Flax, therefore, sets out to secure for women the oppositional capacities that are necessary to autonomy.

Taking issue with Chodorow's excessive valorization of relational capacities, Flax explicitly undertakes to frame an account of a self that integrates self-assertion with deep emotional bonds. According to Flax, the " 'unitary,' mentalist, deeroticized, masterful, and oppositional selves" that are commonly associated with masculinity are not the only alternatives, and women sorely need a feminist account of subjectivity (1987a, 93). Basing her contribution to this project on her clinical experience, Flax contends that the repressed is gendered—that women and men repress different sorts of desires—and that women can only overcome the distortions and damage of this repression through an unrepressed, interactive form of autonomy.

According to Flax, women repress aspects of the self concerning autonomy, aggression, ambition, mastery, and sexuality (1987a, 92, 101, and 104). In women, the social self—a self whose relational mode may be limited to letting others use one to fulfill their ends—is often dominant, but false (Flax 1987a, 98-99). The sexual self and especially the autonomous self are typically repressed (Flax 1987a, 98). Not only does this repression of sexuality and autonomy consume energy that women could otherwise put to productive use, but women are also victimized by counterproductive outlets, such as self-hatred and attraction to self-destructive relationships, that this repressed material finds (Flax 1987a, 94, 98; 1980, 35).

Yet, Flax is not disposed to recommend a masculine form of autonomy. Noting that in our society the mother represents nurturance and the father autonomy, Flax stresses that supplanting mother-daughter identification with father-daughter identification exacts a high price. The latter identification means giving up maternal nurturance, becoming contemptuous of women as a group, and losing one's sense of feminine identity.[3] Moreover, this conflictual dynamic often sabotages the prospective rewards of identifying with the father, including career success (Flax 1980, 37; 1981, 63). Yet, if women in our society have a repressed autonomous self, it could only be the internalized image of engagement in work and politics, of freedom from entanglement in the family, and of wielder of power and authority that the father represents in Western, male-dominated culture (Flax 1980, 33). Plainly, this form of autonomy is not compatible with any authentic expression of women's social self or sexual self. Social responsiveness could only be reduced to perceptiveness deployed in order to control others, and sexuality would become a means to possess another person, not a means of achieving intimacy and mutuality.

Nevertheless, Flax holds that, for women, wholeness is integration of the social self and the sexual self under the aegis of the autonomous self, and autonomy is choice relieved of the burden of gendered repression (1987a, 105; also see Flax 1986, 335). Now, this burden of gendered repression must be compound. Which capacities are repressed depends on gender—women repress the autonomous self; men do not. Moreover, since the capacities that are repressed are gendered, women's repressed autonomy takes a distinctly masculine form. Thus, women's agency, in the sense that Flax endorses, requires not only the "return" of the repressed autonomous self but also its transformation into a self that can accommodate women's social and sexual selves.

Flax sketches a conception of the autonomous self—an unrepressed, interactive self—that women could have. She concurs with Chodorow in denying that autonomy involves antisocial indifference to others and in affirming that an autonomous individual could enjoy being alone. However, in contradistinction to Chodorow, Flax stresses autonomous activity rather than an autonomous state of mind. An autonomous self would "enjoy mastery, aggression, competition, and define its desires independently of, even against, the wishes of others"; it would recognize its interdependence, but also its own uniqueness; it could acknowledge the uses of logic and objectivity without being overawed by them; it could enjoy sexuality on its own terms; it could cope with lapses in adherence to its own "rational" plans (Flax 1987a, 105). In mentioning mastery, aggression, and competition as modes of activity women should learn to enjoy, Flax may leave her readers with the impression that she advocates a merely additive approach to agency—that is, women should learn to exercise masculine style autonomy whenever it is appropriate and advantageous to do so. However, in view of her critique of girls identifying with their fathers and thereby acquiring masculine capacities, I think she is best understood as reaching for a vision of autonomy that respects and incorporates all of women's capacities in a unified personality.

Of course, Flax is hardly sanguine about the prospects of achieving this sort of autonomy in light of the pervasive and powerful forces of patriarchal repression in contemporary culture (1987a, 105). Still, she thinks progress can be made through friendships between women: "Only through relationships with other women can women heal the hurts suffered through their psychological development. The rift between identifying with the mother and being oneself can only be closed within a *relationship in which one is nurtured for being one's autonomous self*" (1981, 60; emphasis added). The value of friendship among women who are actively resisting passivity and subordination cannot be gainsaid. Still, how such relations are supposed to reconcile the repressed masculine autonomous self with the feminine social self remains unclear.

If the repressed capacity for autonomy is understood on the traditional masculine model—as a collocation of inclinations to proclaim preferences, to exert authority, to take control, to compete for benefits, and so forth—autonomy can only conflict with connectedness. It is hard to see, then, how bringing the autonomous self to consciousness could bring about an "increase in energy, sense of competence, and positive feelings" (Flax 1981, 61). Quite the contrary, one would expect a distressing awareness of dividedness and a sense of frustration and helplessness.

Moreover, one would expect the friendships in which women are supporting one another's autonomous forays to establish a precarious balance between conflicting needs and desires, if not to collapse under their weight, unless mutual revelation and interpretation were supplemented with a program to adapt these autonomous inclinations to the needs of close, reciprocal interpersonal ties.[4] In her discussion of conflicts within the women's movement between activists who saw consciousness raising as a mere preliminary to political action and women who primarily sought emotional sustenance through consciousness raising groups, Flax makes it clear that she is aware of this problem (1981, 65-66). Though she laments this reenactment of unconscious conflicts within feminism, she offers no solution to this impasse. Nothing less than a transformed conception of autonomy—one that jettisons its gendered character—could support Flax's ideal of personal integration and friendship among women. But as long as psychoanalysis identifies autonomy with the image of the father, the requisite notion of autonomous mutuality will remain beyond the reach of psychoanalytic feminism.

Chodorow and Flax each undertake to wrest a feminist account of women's agency from psychoanalysis without violating the framework of gender divisions that Freud set forth. Chodorow, who explicates agency exclusively in terms of traditionally feminine relational concepts, fails to extricate her account from the well-known liabilities of other-directedness. She succeeds in appreciating the feminine characteristics Freud denigrated, but she errs in idealizing them. Flax's account, which incorporates both traditionally feminine and traditionally masculine concepts, locks the antithetical feminine and masculine components in irresolvable conflict. Coming perilously close to prescribing masculinity as the remedy for the liabilities of femininity, yet resisting this solution, Flax fails to generate a cogent account of agency. Julia Kristeva's thought can be seen as an attempt to overcome the collision between rigidly gendered concepts that paralyzes the views of Chodorow and Flax.

2. JULIA KRISTEVA'S QUESTIONABLE SUBJECT-IN-PROCESS

Julia Kristeva sees the bonds implicit in gender-differentiated psychoanalytic concepts as even more pervasive and profound than do Chodorow and Flax.[5] Not only does she hold that early childhood culminating in the Oedipus complex brands each child as feminine or masculine, but in addition she maintains that language, and thus every utterance, is shot through with gender meaning. Specifically, Kristeva associates the realm of the symbolic—the language of referential semantics and logical syntax that scientific writing typifies—with the Phallus or the Name of the Father, and she associates the realm of the semiotic—communicative, yet undecidable rhythm, intonation, figures of speech, and the like that poetic writing brings to the fore—with the maternal (1980, 132-35). In so doing, she transposes the Freudian pictographic nightmare of castration into the abstract formalizations of linguistics (1986, 150, 198). Yet, the familiar gender connotations remain intact—femininity coupled with fusion, subjection, unconscious drive, and indefiniteness; masculinity coupled with separation, power, inhibition, and lucidity. No one is more aware of this patriarchal drag than Kristeva herself, and she responds to it by synthesizing her psychoanalytic linguistic theory with a program for feminist politics.

Kristeva is forthright about her bleak assessment of the bond between patriarchy, language, and agency. On her view, to establish coherent subjectivity or, in other words, to become a self, the infant must repress the maternal semiotic realm and enter the phallic symbolic order. The symbolic order is a linguistic system that artificially divides the undifferentiated world into distinct categories and that furnishes syntactical structures for relating these categories. Not only does the symbolic order enable people to understand the world around them, but, more fundamentally, it enables them to identify and locate themselves as discrete individuals. People are dependent, then, on a patriarchal linguistic order for their very existence as agents who are intelligible to themselves and others.

For Kristeva, the division of the sexes, along with the asymmetrical valuation of them, lies at the foundation of monotheistic, patrilineal, capitalist culture. As long as one remains within this symbolic order, one cannot deny this division without succumbing to "fetishism" (Kristeva 1986, 145). To claim that women and men are fundamentally the same or that women are not inferior to men is to attach feeling, desire, or value to what does not warrant it—in Kristeva's psychoanalytic parlance, it is to believe in the maternal phallus and therefore to be deluded in the belief that the symbolic order is not masculine.

Now, Kristeva maintains that sophisticated communication is impossible outside the symbolic order. Though poetry taps the semiotic, what distinguishes it from unintelligible psychotic babbling is its appropriation of codified signs from the symbolic order (Kristeva 1980, 132-34). Likewise, if women decide to identify with the maternal unconscious and seek to represent it, their representations must enter into and be coopted by the paternal symbolic order. In a now notorious aside, Kristeva comments, "A woman finds herself caught here, and can't do much about it" (1986, 155).

Nevertheless, Kristeva adds two mitigating qualifications to this otherwise dismal view. First, she contends that all communications partake of both the semiotic and the symbolic, the mix of these two signifying dispositions determining the type of discourse produced. Characteristically, scientific discourse minimizes and attempts to hide the ambiguous semiotic within it, but this maternal unconscious dimension cannot finally be altogether extirpated (Kristeva 1980, 135).

Second, she raises doubts about the inherent masculinity of symbolic language. It is clear that Kristeva regards the conflictual split between the amorphous unconscious and its unruly drives, on the one hand, and unified consciousness and the superego's imposition of regulation, on the other, as necessary to culture and that she also holds that this split cannot come about unless the developing infant confronts a figure representing power (1986, 209; 1987a, 372, 383). Yet, it is not clear that she is equally convinced that the unconscious and consciousness are inextricable from their respective gender identities.

In Tales of Love, one of Kristeva's central projects is to undercut the gender identity of Freud's "father of individual prehistory" and to raise doubts about the link between femininity and nondifferentiation. In Freud's account of human development, the infant's first task is to emerge from a state of fusion with the mother and thereby to acquire a distinct sense of self. Freud holds that individuation comes about as a result of primary identification—the infant's apprehension of and attraction to an individual other than its mother. For Freud, the object of primary identification is the father of individual prehistory, whose role is to secure an escape from oneness with the mother.

But Kristeva questions the masculinity of this paternal figure. Not only is this "father" loving (not severe), this figure is "both parents" and "endowed with the sexual attributes of both," a "father-mother conglomerate" or, alternatively, the "maternal desire for the Phallus": " . . . is it he or is it she?" (1987a, 26, 33, 40, 41, 43, 46). Whichever it may be, this "father" is decidedly not the Phallus (1987a, 30). Furthermore, the idea of the infant's harmonious, frustration-free idyll of primal bonding with an omnipotent mother is a myth that badly needs iconoclastic reconsideration (Kristeva 1986, 205). From the perspective of the infant, gender duality is confounded in the earliest stages of psychic development; gender must, then, remain confounded to the extent that the traces of the period preceding the Oedipus complex and language acquisition stay lodged in the unconscious.

Remarkable as well, Kristeva occasionally dissociates power from the Phallus. "Whatever the organ," she states, "confrontation with power remains" (1987a, 81). Apparently, something other than the Phallus could in principle represent power. In a radically different system of production and reproduction, there could be nonphallic power manifest in nonphallic symbolic language (Kristeva 1986, 145).

Still, according to Kristeva, power and symbolic language are masculine in Western culture. This contention has led one of Kristeva's most insightful commentators to suggest that she "has meticulously mapped an impossible situation" (Nye 1987, 681). Indeed, it is undeniable that the tenor of Kristeva's writings is that of a virtually unwinnable contest with smothering gendrification. Still, Kristeva regards this contest as one that is necessary to wage.

Along with the rebel, the psychoanalyst, and the writer, Kristeva lists women as dissidents (1986, 295-96). For Kristeva, the dissident is a "questionable subject-in-process"—an agent who acknowledges that fixed identity is illusory and yet sustains a tenable subjectivity by alternating between destabilization and "provisional unity" (1980, 135-37; 1987a, 380; 1987b, 9). Since mothers epitomize the questionable subject-in-process, Kristeva discerns a redemptive aspect of women's experience of maternity, and she positively values this experience.[6] Describing the confusion of identities she associates with pregnancy as an "institutionalized form of psychosis" and the responsibilities and emotions that accompany maternity as a "bridge between singularity and ethics," Kristeva regards mothers paradoxically as "the guarantee and a threat to [society's] stability" (1986, 297; also see 1980, 146). The threat to social stability stems from the fusion experiences some mothers report in tandem with the experience of gradual separation from the developing child, for these processes decenter the self (Kristeva 1986, 167-68, 173, 179). In such cases, the indissoluble attachment the mother feels for her child throws the bounds of her identity into doubt, and this destabilization makes her receptive to long-submerged memories of her own childhood connections to her mother (Kristeva 1986, 172). According to Kristeva, the destabilization brought on by maternity constitutes an implicit critique of the repression society enforces and is, therefore, disruptive of social norms.

Like Chodorow and Flax, Kristeva holds that political and economic arrangements dictate patterns of repression.[7] Thus, needless social repression is not merely a source of personal distress to be assuaged in the privacy of the analyst's chamber; it must be confronted politically. Moreover, since Kristeva, concurring again with Chodorow and Flax, holds that the repressed is gendered, she regards women's tapping of the unconscious not only as a source of self-understanding but also as a source of feminist direction. But whereas Chodorow and Flax rely on cultural gender norms to flesh out the idea of gendered repression—women repress autonomy, men repress connectedness—Kristeva insists on probing the unconscious anew.

Calling upon dissidents generally to "give voice to each individual form of the unconscious, to every desire and need," Kristeva calls further for the "demassification of the problem of *difference*"—for attending to the "multiplicity of female expressions and preoccupations" with the aim of discovering the "intersection of these differences" (1986, 295, 209, 193). She urges that "one needs to listen, more carefully than ever, to what mothers are saying today" (1986, 179). But Kristeva has more in mind than merely cataloging mothers' joys and complaints. She advocates "an *interiorization of the founding separation of the socio-symbolic contract*" in order to confront the "potentialities of *victim/executioner* which characterize each identity, each subject, each sex" (1986, 210). The aim is to make personal and sexual identity "disintegrate in its very nucleus," in other words, to recognize "the *relativity of* [each individual's] *symbolic as well as biological existence*, according to the variation of his/her specific symbolic capacities" (1986, 209, 210). Kristeva admonishes " . . . let the seeming take itself seriously, let sex be as unessential because as important as a mask or a written sign—dazzling outside, nothing inside" (1987a, 380).

There are several important points here. First, Kristeva refuses to understand gender primarily in terms of standard cultural images of sexual difference. She sees capacities for both victimization and domination in all people. Moreover, for conventional gender norms, she proposes to substitute whatever points of commonality inquiring into difference between individual women and men reveals. Second, sexual differences are not to be found primarily at the level of everyday experience. They are buried in the unconscious. Third, these differences have a complex status. On the one hand, they are fabrications, and, as fabrications, they are susceptible to debunking. On the other hand, since they permeate our conceptual apparatus and therefore our self-concepts, they cannot simply be dispensed with. Thus, Kristeva condemns the conception of the self to which the symbolic order gives rise as "that anthropomorphic identity which *currently* blocks the horizon of the discursive and scientific adventure of our species," and yet she retains the gendered linguistic distinction between the semiotic and the symbolic (1986, 211, emphasis added).

Still, Kristeva's call for the demassification of the problem of difference—for individual women to undertake to discover themselves in their
"singularity"—in conjunction with her refusal to abandon theoretical language shows that she cannot think that the masculine nature of symbolic language dooms women to stereotypical self-images (1980, 146). She must think
it possible for individual women to find their own voices and to express their
own experience in and through the symbolic order.[8] To call symbolic language phallic, then, is not to assert that only phallocentric thoughts can be
articulated in this language. Rather, it is to contend that women cannot
avoid reckoning with issues of gender difference and differential valuation,
for the grid of gender difference and differential valuation will always be imposed on their self-understandings. In one respect, then, Kristeva's claim that
symbolic language is phallic is misleadingly hyperbolic, but, in another respect, it serves to alert women to what Kristeva deems a virtually ineradicable
conceptual undercurrent and to the need to trust in destabilization in order to
bend language to the expression of women's own apprehension of the repressed dimension of their lives.

In addition, I think that Kristeva's point can be read politically as a re-
minder of the pervasiveness of gender-based power relations and of the contribution that destabilization can make to eroding their hold. Indeed, she
contends that as a result of their experience of destabilization mothers can
pose a profound challenge to the political and economic status quo (1986,
156, 206). At this juncture, however, it is important to consider the dimension of maternity that Kristeva counts on to secure social stability.

Of course, Kristeva denies that the unconscious can simply be released
from repression; its sexual determinants, especially the cruel and violent
ones, must be dissolved, often through analysis (1980, 145). In the case of
the mother, however, her very love for her child and her concern for its welfare constitute a built-in barrier against the wild propensities of the unconscious and therefore a bulwark against extreme radicalism. The mother's pre-
servative orientation secures her commitment to society. Thus, Kristeva suggests that mothers and women who want to be mothers are ideally situated to
found a new ethics—a "heretical ethics," a "herethics" (1986, 185).[9] This
herethics would not avoid "the embarrassing and inevitable problematics of
the law [of social expectations and conventions]" but would give the contes-
tability of these practices "flesh, language, and *jouissance*" (Kristeva 1986,
185). Since the destabilizations of motherhood provide a point of departure
for questioning social norms, but since the responsibilities of maternity coun-
teract the hostile potentialities of its destabilizations, mothers can be relied
upon to be provocative, but not crazed, dissidents.

In practice, Kristeva recommends a stance of permanent ambivalence—achieving "ostensibly masculine" paternal identification in order to
be politically effective, but refusing to assimilate while maintaining one's al-

legiance to what remains unspoken, unsatisfied, repressed, incomprehensible.[10] Wholeness is an illusion; destabilization is good. Strategic switching between political activism or professional attainment and dipping into the springs of the unconscious is not only a practical necessity but also a desirable way to live. Moreover, it is only by alternating between the exigencies of politics and the replenishing reservoir of the unconscious that women can avoid the trap of losing themselves in somebody else's values and institutions or of retreating into bitter reverse sexism and separatism.

Here, Kristeva simply circumnavigates the tension between traditional masculinity and traditional femininity. Admittedly, there is a tension, but the hope of reconciling these two aspects of life is misguided and forlorn. In other respects, however, Kristeva takes measures to dissolve the tension between traditional masculinity and traditional femininity. As we have seen, she resists attributing genders to the figures that are constitutive of the pre-Oedipal unconscious, and she stresses the need to reexamine gender in light of the reality of each unconscious. Inasmuch as she sees unconscious desire as the prime impetus behind oppositional activity, this muting of the iconic gender status of the unconscious helps to neutralize the traditional link between masculinity and oppositional capacities.[11]

Yet, the price of this success is Kristeva's resuscitation of the cultural stereotype of women as self-sacrificial mothers. Kristeva's account of oppositional capacities generates distinctive problems. For Kristeva, the unconscious ruptures fixed identity and endows the agent with an inexhaustible store of oppositional potential. However, this view of social criticism sets the oppositional process adrift. Since her account does not rely on established cultural values or a rational procedure to validate opposition, but instead draws on the untamed forces of the unconscious, Kristeva's theory needs a way of differentiating between legitimate demands and mad clamor. To demarcate legitimate demands, Kristeva introduces the mother's resistance to any form of extremism that might jeopardize her child's future. Thanks to their inherent conservatism, mothers can be trusted to confine their initiatives to reasonable proportions.

While calling for the demassification of sexual difference, Kristeva here remassifies difference by invoking a shopworn but unrealistic image of motherhood. As we have seen, Kristeva assumes that plumbing women's unconscious will yield a point (or points) of intersection that can be taken as definitive of femininity. Now, we find that this assumption betrays her commitment to the singularity of each unconscious and dissolves what appeared to be an open-ended, unpredictable investigation into a stipulative theory of the feminine. The "real *fundamental difference* between the two sexes" (Kristeva 1986, 193) proves to be none other than sentimentalized motherhood. It would seem, then, that singularity is reduced to pathology—a distinctive feminine unconscious is just one that has been driven from the track of normal development that leads to sublimation through maternity. If Kristeva's view does not imply that only mothers or maternally inclined women are qualified to press their political demands, thereby establishing a hierarchy among women in which mothers outrank the rest, it implies that all women are intrinsically mothers or maternally inclined, regardless of their professed desires. The former claim reinstates Freud's vision of mature femininity in the guise of reverse elitism; the latter imposes an essentialist account of femininity that Freud would not quarrel with. Yet, Kristeva herself expressly repudiates both reverse sexism and essentialism (1986, 161, 202-4).

Now, it might be urged that Kristeva is not committed to the claim that being a mother or wanting to be one is necessary in order to access the unconscious while limiting the demands one makes on the basis of that experience. If this is so, Kristeva might be read as proposing motherhood, not as a condition that must be met, but as a paradigm for the type of constrained commerce with the unconscious that she is recommending. Admittedly, Kristeva holds that there are other ways to explore the unconscious and to defuse its explosive power—psychoanalytic therapy, for example. Nevertheless, it seems to me that Kristeva's psychoanalytic approach dictates a more literal reading of her position.

Not only does Kristeva explicitly advocate inquiring into the unconscious desires of mothers and giving motherly women a voice in ethical thought, but also the peculiar problem of distinguishing warranted social criticism from psychotic diatribe that her view poses cannot be solved by a maternal paradigm, as opposed to mothers. Kristeva undertakes to explain how one can criticize patriarchal norms without altogether losing one's moorings. Mainstream psychoanalysis assigns the superego the task of certifying acceptable conduct and condemning unacceptable conduct. But, since the superego is the repository of socially transmitted values and standards, it reinforces socially sanctioned repression. Thus, Kristeva needs a functional equivalent for Freud's superego that will not merely echo patriarchal values, and she nominates the nonviolent, caring dispositon of mothers. But, just as it is people who actually have a well-developed superego who can be trusted to exercise control over their behavior, so it is people who have actually developed the dispositions of motherhood who can safely contest social conventions. Neither a superego paradigm nor a maternal paradigm will prevent people from running amuck.

Gender does not undercut Kristeva's view in the way one would expect. Her partitioning of language into the phallic symbolic and the feminine semiotic is not fatal. Indeed, it may be necessary, for it is the vehicle of Kristeva's acknowledgment that her cultural context enshrines gender bifurcation and steadily pulls in the direction of gendered accounts. Still, this division is problematic, for it sometimes obfuscates what is most innovative and valuable in Kristeva's work from a feminist point of view, namely, her challenges to standard psychoanalytic images of gender. Not only does Kristeva convincingly attack the association of femininity with an infantile state of harmonious symbiotic suspension and the association of masculinity with individuation and agency; she also proposes to jettison conventional views of gender in order to discover what forms of repression society in fact imposes and what forms of liberation women should be seeking. However, Kristeva ultimately fails to sustain her critique.

It turns out that gender invades Kristeva's theory at a new level. To be sure, she avoids the oversimplifications of Chodorow's and Flax's gender-driven diagnoses of the problem of women's agency. For Kristeva, women's agency is subverted neither by an incompletely actualized feminine relationality nor by a repressed masculine autonomy. Kristeva is agnostic regarding the content of the repression that subverts women's agency, but she does contend that unnecessary, differential social repression is at work. Thus, Kristeva's remedy is to analyze that repression on a case by case basis with the dual aim of discovering the patterns it assumes and devising socially tenable ways to satisfy these repressed desires. But, since Kristeva does not pretend to know in advance what women have been obliged to repress, she recognizes that the thrust of some of their repressed desires might well prove horrifying.

Plainly, however, Kristeva cannot appeal to the patriarchal authority of the superego and the codification of its principles in the symbolic order to curb the unconscious desires of women, for these desires stand in need of liberation from oppressive patriarchal norms. Thus, she seeks out a disposition that might serve as the feminine counterpart of the superego and comes up with maternal solicitude. What is most damaging to Kristeva's theory from a feminist point of view, then, is her revival of the sentimental ideal of maternal devotion to tame the sinister forces of destruction that she ascribes to women's unconscious. Unfortunately, within a psychoanalytic framework, to do away with familiar, tolerably civilized images of gender at the level of the unconscious is to introduce these selfsame images at the level of values and conscience.

3. FREUD'S LEGACY AND PSYCHOANALYTIC FEMINISM

Each of the three psychoanalytic feminist theories I have considered successfully parries Freud's contempt for women by instating the attributes associated with femininity as capacities involved in agency and by conferring a measure of value on these capacities. Nevertheless, in different yet related ways, the polarization of psychoanalytic concepts according to gender thwarts the work of Kristeva, Chodorow, and Flax. Kristeva and Chodorow both defy longstanding contempt for femininity by grounding their accounts of agency in traditional feminine norms, and, though they differ about which forces disrupt the unity of the self, each defends a dispersed view of the self. It turns out, however, that to endorse a dispersed view of the self in a psychoanalytic context is to reinforce the intolerable constraints of male domination—submissiveness, in Chodorow, and mandatory motherhood, in Kristeva. Similarly, Kristeva and Flax concur in deploring gendered repression, and they discern a liberatory potential in the reclamation of this repressed material. But, if the irreconcilability of gender-typed capacities does not then subvert the account, as it does in Flax's view, the vacuum left by rejected masculine capacities will be filled by feminine stereotypes, as in Kristeva's view. If the evidence of these theories is reliable, then, the prognosis for a psychoanalytic feminist account of agency that is not mired in the unacceptable gender norms inherited from Freud is not favorable. Still, it remains to be asked whether psychoanalysis might sustain a feminist account of agency.

The power of the psychoanalytic account of the tenacity of gender is partly a consequence of the two-tiered configuration of the psychoanalytic theory of the subject. Gender is conceived not merely as a pair of collocations of traits—landscapes that are readily susceptible to redesigned pruning and planting—but, more fundamentally, in terms of personality structure itself—the geological foundation undergirding the landscape. Femininity is not a superficial matter of preoccupation with family, lack of self-confidence, and so forth; it is a structural problem of weak or, less contentiously, permeable ego boundaries. Accordingly, the gendered outcomes psychoanalysis envisages seem less tractable than those that other psychological accounts propose, for the former maintains that feminine and masculine behaviors and traits are manifestations of a refractory infrastructure.

I shall not rehearse the well-known general psychoanalytic account of how personality traits and abiding desires—including, but not limited to, gendered traits and desires—become embedded in the deep structure of the psyche through mechanisms that harness emotionally charged encounters at our earliest and most impressionable stage of life. Since I believe that psychoanalysis supplements this general etiological theory with two strategies peculiar to its account of the formation and the tenacity of gender identity, I shall focus on them. On the one hand, I shall urge, gender is integral to the concepts psychoanalysis fields to explain psychological development, and, on the other hand, this theory posits that satisfactory development aims at gendered outcomes. By coupling gendered explanatory concepts with a gendered telos, psychoanalysis secures a compelling account of the bond between individual identity and gender identity. But, in so doing, psychoanalysis hampers its prospects of generating an account of agency that is satisfactory from a feminist point of view.

In regard to gendered explanatory concepts, consider some well-known features of Freud's account of the emergence of gendered personalities. Girls, he tells us, discover that they do not have penises, and, perceiving their own deficiency, contract penis envy (Freud 1966, 589). The decisive force in a woman's life, penis envy shapes her character—she will become vain, capricious, and jealous—along with her aims in life—she will want to have a baby, preferably a boy, to compensate for her missing organ (1966, 589, 592, 593, 596). On the question of feminine character, penis envy is a term of art that figuratively summarizes the undesirable qualities traditionally assembled under the feminine stereotype. Freud captures the purportedly feminine foibles by ascribing the mean yet pitiable vice of envy to women, and he captures women's alleged inferiority to men in the suggestion that what is envied is male anatomy. As for the aim of motherhood, it is arrived at through a process of reconciliation and substitution. Whereas the boy's castration complex, which develops when he discovers that women do not have penises, represents his fear of loss and issues in his determination to prevent this loss, the girl's castration complex, which develops when she discovers her lack, represents the onset of disillusionment and irreversible disappointment (1966, 588-89, 593). The girl relinquishes any personal aspirations she may have had and submits to her maternal fate. Thus, Freud's notion of the castration complex, in its masculine and feminine variants, symbolizes activity and passivity, respectively.

The psychological forces Freud sees driving the process of feminine and masculine development are themselves gendered.[12] It is not surprising, then, that this account should impress readers with the inextricability of gender from personality. I would urge, moreover, that feminist reformulations of Freud's account, though they show respect for feminine capacities, nonetheless rely on the same rhetorical strategy.

Chodorow's theory, for example, adverts to the unbroken emotional bonds between mothers and daughters, that is, the ongoing relational experiences of girls, to explain the empathic and nurturant capacities of adult women. To account for the independence and emotional detachment of men, she points out the boy's need to break free of the maternal emotional orbit in order to form a masculine identity. The emotional warmth and interpersonal connectedness that Chodorow considers to be predominant in girls' childhood experience are themselves components of our prevailing cultural view of femininity. Likewise, the separation from others and the willingness to sacrifice emotional ties that Chodorow considers to be decisive in boys' development recapitulate familiar components of our prevailing cultural view of masculinity. Like its progenitor, psychoanalytic feminism invokes gendered forces to account for gendered personalities, and therein lies much of its compellingness as an account of the persistence of gender.

As long as psychoanalysis relies on gendered psychological forces to explain the emergence of gendered individuals, however, it cannot deliver a feminist account of agency. As others have remarked, this quandary raises doubts about the feasibility of Chodorow's coparenting recommendation (Rossi 1981, 497-99). If Chodorow's theory of feminine and masculine personality development is correct, women will suffer acutely when they are evicted from the nursery, and men will prove too detached and insensitive to respond to the emotional needs of young children. Moreover, on this theory, there is no reason to predict that coparented children will be better off in virtue of having acquired the strengths, without the weaknesses, of each parent. Since, as we have seen, it is doubtful that these sharply dichotomized strengths can be combined, Chodorow's account gives us equally good reason to anticipate that coparented children will end up confused. To make sense, the coparenting proposal requires that the personality extremes Chodorow's theory attributes to women and men be mitigated and therefore that the psychic forces shaping development be redescribed.

To my knowledge, no psychoanalytic feminist has attempted to tell the story of the psychodynamics of successful coparenting in detail. My suspicion is that this narrative would be virtually unrecognizable as a piece of psychoanalytic theory. In order to convey the tenacity of personality outcomes, the narrative would have to retain psychoanalysis's evocative, imagistic characterizations of psychic forces. However, in order to palliate gender polarities, the narrative would have to be cast in nongendered, or, perhaps, benignly gendered, language. This language would represent a radical departure from familiar psychoanalytic narratives. Indeed, such a reconstrual of psychic forces would severely weaken psychoanalytic feminism's capacity to account for the formation of polarized gendered personalities. If this reformulation did not render these outcomes unintelligible, it would surely stigmatize gender extremes as perversions of normal development.

Here it is worth noting that psychoanalytic feminism's defense of the domestic contribution that women have traditionally made along with the capacities that equip women for this role compounds the difficulty of supplying a convincing account of development under coparenting and the form of agency this practice might bring about. Though psychoanalytic feminists bring various types of argument to bear on their defense of femininity, a pivotal component of this line of thought is an extension of the rhetorical method I have been sketching. Acknowledging the impact of labels, psychoanalytic feminists have invented terminology that transmutes the misogynist connotations of Freud's vocabulary. Thus, dependence becomes nurturance and connectedness in Chodorow's work, while emotional irrationality becomes the heterogeneity that gives the semiotic its creative and dissident propulsion in Kristeva's work.

However, conveying the worth of women's capacities through language that implicitly celebrates them preempts renouncing these capacities in order to seek out an alternative vision of agency. The commitment to these capacities befitting the positive connotations of psychoanalytic feminism's revisionist language argues for building on feminine capacities, instead of forging a new conception. It is not surprising, then, that the accounts of women's agency that Kristeva and Chodorow advance prove reducible to revalued reprises of traditional femininity.[13]

Still, it might seem that psychoanalytic feminism need not resort to the disfiguring measure of casting its account of the genesis of gender in radically different language. Since, according to psychoanalytic theory, many features of personality are rooted in childhood identifications, repressions, and the like that are heavily invested with psychic energy, and since psychoanalytic clinical theory furnishes a procedure through which detrimental personality structures can be overcome, it might seem that gender is no less malleable in principle than other dispositions and desires with similar antecedents.[14] If so, the psychoanalytic view of gender should pose no insuperable obstacle to a psychoanalytic feminist account of agency. Though psychoanalytic clinical theory holds out the hope of an account of agency rescued from the distortions of gender, I shall urge that psychoanalysis's gendered telos has prevented psychoanalytic clinical theory from realizing this apparent emancipatory potential.

Certainly, the process of psychoanalytic treatment—self-revelation through dream reports, free association, and the transference relationship; self-discovery as one's resistances are probed; self-transformation as a result of assimilating revelations about one's unconscious life in light of the analyst's interpretations—is not conspicuously gendered. Thus, the account of how the analysand repeatedly confronts and gradually works through repressed materials—how, as Richard Wollheim aptly puts it, one comes to affectively understand the contents of one's unconscious (1984, 232-34)—and thereby gains greater flexibility and control might yield a view of agency that is not torn between antithetically gendered capacities.

Undeniably, Freud's figurative characterizations of the therapeutic process belie this apparent neutrality. For Freud, transference phenomena involve a "struggle between the doctor and patient [the authority and the dependent], between intellect and instinctual life [culture and nature], between understanding and seeking to act [control and impulse]" (1971, 106). Likewise, he advises that the patient must be persuaded that his or her illness is an "enemy worthy of his [sic] mettle."[15] The masculine imagery of battle is pervasive in Freud's essays on clinical practice. Countering this view, feminists have sought to place a feminine stamp on this part of psychoanalytic theory. Flax disputes Freud's scientific self-image and urges that the analyst's task is akin to mothering (1986, 343). Chodorow insists on the relational, that is, feminine, structure of the analytic process (1986, 207). Likewise, just as Kristeva describes maternity in terms of the mother's intensely tender feelings for her child, the concomitant blurring of the boundaries between them, and the access to the unconscious this experience affords, so she describes psychoanalysis in terms of loving individuals whose interaction facilitates rebirth through destabilization. In recent psychoanalytic feminism, then, the gender of the therapeutic dynamic has been reversed, but it has by no means been eliminated.

Still, one may ask whether this metatheoretical survival of gender bifurcation infects the account of agency implicit in psychoanalytic clinical theory. Since Kristeva expounds her view of clinical practice more fully than Chodorow or Flax, I shall focus on her position. According to Kristeva, much of the originality of Freud's work resides in his appreciation of the role of love in human life. In love, Kristeva tells us, one open system is connected to another, and this interconnection brings about "destabilizing-stabilizing identification" (1987a, 15, 274; 1987b, 9). As Kristeva observes; "If it lives, your psyche is in love. If it is not in love, it is dead" (1987a, 15). Psychoanalysis regards love relationships as the model of optimal psychic functioning, for love is the condition for perpetual rejuvenation (Kristeva 1987a, 14).

According to Kristeva, a rich fantasy life is indispensable to the elaboration of the individual psyche and in turn to the individual's ability to idealize and identify with another, that is, to love. What brings people to analysis, then, is the "abolition of psychic space" that stems from lack of imagination—the inability to love (Kristeva 1987a, 9, 38, 373). In psychoanalysis, transference love collaborates with free association to rouse "desire-noise"—the residue of one's earliest, now repressed drives and identifications (Kristeva 1987a, 15). Desire-noise can be articulated through, but can also challenge, "memory-consciousness"—the conscious, too-often calcified systematization of one's experience (Kristeva 1987a, 15-16). Within the structure of psychoanalytic interaction, this encounter between conscious understandings and unconscious forces yields fresh metaphorical articulations and provides an ongoing occasion for provisional interpretation of these metaphors (Kristeva 1987a, 276; 1987b, 7). This process activates the individual's innovative powers, especially imagination, and initiates a "true process of self-organization" (Kristeva 1987a, 14, 15-16, 276, 381). The aim is not to grasp a truth, but to "provoke a rebirth"—to release the individual from emptiness, stagnation, and isolation (Kristeva 1987a, 381).

Kristeva characterizes the aims of psychoanalysis in terms that imply tremendous transformative power—rejuvenation, self-organization, and rebirth. Furthermore, as we saw earlier, Kristeva sometimes contemplates the possibility that living as a questionable subject-in-process might erode, if not dissolve, the effects of gendered development. It is disappointing, then, to learn that Kristeva lapses into standard Freudian dogma when she comments specifically on psychoanalytic treatment. She declares the Oedipus complex and its finalization of gender identity to be "unavoidable" (1987a, 46). She contends that "man's 'feminine' is not woman's 'feminine' " (1987a, 224). Whereas men come to terms with their feminine by creating art, women come to terms with theirs by having children (Kristeva 1987a, 228). Led by Kristeva's invocation of imagination, metaphor, and interpretation to expect fundamental change to be possible through psychoanalysis, one finds instead Kristeva's narrowly regimented view of gender and her prescription for a "playful and sublimational" reconciliation to one's sex-keyed fate (1987a, 46).

At this juncture, it is important to recall precisely what it is that psychoanalysis claims to accomplish. Psychoanalytic treatment affords an opportunity to repeat in imagination the pivotal incidents of the process of growing up and to self-consciously experience one's resulting pattern of affective responses. By opening these floodgates and systematically scrutinizing the material that comes out, psychoanalysis undertakes to undo the damaging and unnecessary repression that produces anxiety and exerts control over one's choices. Accordingly, the sort of change that psychoanalytic therapy brings about is limited to rearranging psychic materials and redistributing psychic energy. Moreover, psychoanalysis does not pretend to rid people of repression—repression is an inescapable feature of civilization—but only to rid people of damaging and unnecessary repression.

Kristeva seems to regard the repression associated with the Oedipus complex as necessary, at least, in Western culture, and other psychoanalytic feminists typically incorporate versions of the Oedipus complex into their developmental accounts. What is at stake in regard to this repression is the founding commitment of psychoanalysis to procreative heterosexuality as the normal and desirable developmental outcome—its gendered telos (Freud 1966, 599). Nevertheless, some psychoanalytic feminists who maintain that civilization can endure without imposing this psychosexual orientation on everyone conjecture that much Oedipal repression is dispensable (Mitchell 1975, 380, 403). That people need to consolidate a tolerably unified subjectivity is indisputable. That such subjectivity can only be attained through repression of one's attachment to a maternal figure and through the sublimation of exogamous heterosexuality is doubtful (Butler 1991, 162-176). Still, to my knowledge, no psychoanalytic feminist has attempted to describe an alternative process of the emergence of the subject as a schema for clinical interpretation.

When the gendered telos of psychoanalytic therapy is considered in the context of my earlier observations about the gendered nature of psychoanalytic explanatory concepts, it becomes clear that these two features of psychoanalytic theory are mutually reinforcing. The language in which psychoanalytic theory is couched reflects the gender divisions enforced by the Oedipus complex, and the Oedipus complex's inculcation of gender seems inevitable in a theory in which the forces driving psychic development are gender-coded. Perhaps, in a theory that traditionally divides all capacities pertinent to agency into feminine and masculine ones, all one can do is project a hypothetical plot line that would confound the patterns in which these capacities have usually been deployed and thereby adumbrate a possible alternative mode of agency. What is clear is that psychoanalytic feminism will be barred from directly describing a feminist vision of agency until it reformulates its account of psychic forces and liberalizes its assumptions about the ends of human development.

Now, if I am right that psychoanalytic feminism is so deeply embedded in Freudian gender bifurcation that it fails to provide a compelling account of women's agency, it could nonetheless be urged that psychoanalytic feminism is vindicated by its singular and outstanding achievement, namely, its account of the tenacity of gender identity and the role of gender in women's continuing subordination. Insofar as psychoanalysis claims to reflect social and psychological reality, it must record the persistence of obstacles to women's agency as well as the gains women make. The theories I have examined register the limits of contemporary psychoanalytic imagination with regard to gender and presage only what can be hoped for given the confines these limits set. With regard to the question of agency, psychoanalytic feminism has functioned as a barometer. As long as one does not mistake it for a bellwether, it is an invaluable instrument.

NOTES

I am grateful to Beth Ann Dobie, Eva Feder Kittay, Carole Steen, Linda Lois Till, and especially to the editors of this volume for their insightful comments on earlier drafts of this essay.

1. It is important to acknowledge that Chodorow's conception of women's capacities and limitations may well reflect white, middle-class gender norms. Later, we will see Kristeva relying on a different but also culturally biased view of motherhood.

2. Arguably, Carol Gilligan, in her account of post-conventional morality within the Care Perspective, provides a glimpse of a relational and self-nurturing person—that is, someone who is honest with herself about her own needs, desires, and so forth and who takes responsibility for caring for herself as well as for others (1986, 324-332).

3. Flax 1980, 37. In a discussion of Electra, Julia Kristeva makes a similar point. She stresses both the father-identified woman's coldness and rigid adherence to principle and also her hatred of the mother and the passionate feminine nature (1986, 151-52). Like Flax, Kristeva observes that this predicament highlights the way in which patriarchal culture boxes women in (1986, 152).

4. Elsewhere, I have argued that such a program would require training in new skills—skills that would enable women to distinguish what matters deeply to them from what can be sacrificed, skills that would enable women to communicate their own point of view and to insist on it when others seek to modify it or to dismiss it, and skills that would equip women to resolve conflicts between others and themselves without merely yielding to social pressure (Meyers 1987, 627; 1989, 76-91).

5. It should be acknowledged that Kristeva's account of early childhood is Lacanian and thus differs significantly from the accounts of Chodorow and Flax, who are object relations theorists. Nevertheless, insofar as they are all psychoanalysts, their views are threaded on a common stock of basic assumptions regarding the order of developmental stages and the major issues faced by the developing individual. Thus, there is good reason to examine them together.

6. There is good reason to question Kristeva's reenforcement of the conventional link between womanhood and motherhood as well as her reliance on the maternal as a model of creativity (Stanton 1986, 160-161, 171; Fraser this volume, pp. 185-190). However, in the interest of examining whether Kristeva's approach yields any insights that might be of use to feminists, I am setting these criticisms aside for the moment.

7. Since Chodorow's views regarding gendered repression have not been pertinent to my main line of argument, I have not discussed them. But this dimension of her thought can be seen in Chodorow 1981, 512.

8. For an interpretation of Kristeva that maintains that the symbolic order allows for no such individual self-expression, see Leland's essay in this volume.

9. It is interesting to note the similarities between Kristeva's account of motherhood and Sara Ruddick's account of the practice of mothering. Kristeva describes caring for a child as a "delightful apprenticeship in attentiveness, gentleness, forgetting oneself" and argues that an ethic is implicit in maternal experience (1986, 206). Ruddick's account goes far beyond these rudimentary remarks to exhibit a selection of values—such as holding, humility, resilient cheerfulness, and appreciability—that are implicit in mothering practice and to tie these values to social criticism (Ruddick 1986, 343-45, 350). Nevertheless, the overlap between them is striking.

10. Kristeva 1986, 156. I have quoted Kristeva's characterization of paternal identification as "ostensibly masculine" since I find her questioning of the masculinity of the paternal revealing. Elsewhere, she unsettles gender conventions in a similar way. Speaking of some feminists' identification with ideas of cyclical and monumental time, she observes that these attitudes are not "fundamentally incompatible with 'masculine' values" (Kristeva 1986, 192). Here, her scare quotes have the same effect as the qualification "ostensibly" in her other comment: what Western culture calls masculine is not necessarily so.

11. It is arguable that, insofar as Kristeva links the semiotic to the maternal, she is merely reversing the gender of oppositional capacities—though typically regarded as masculine, oppositional capacities are really feminine. In this connection, I would urge that Kristeva is engaged in a double project. In associating the maternal with the semiotic and the phallic with the symbolic, she sets up a theoretical structure that embodies pervasive cultural gender norms. Sometimes she argues that, if one is consistent within that structure, one will obtain surprising results regarding gender. For example, one will discover that the feminine unconscious is a powerful force in human agency and that the feminine is hardly equivalent to the passive. However, what I find most illuminating about Kristeva's work are her attempts to show that the gendered concepts that are constitutive of the theoretical structure are fundamentally misguided. Hence I have concentrated on this dimension of her work.

12. It should be noted that I am distinguishing psychological forces from psychic mechanisms—such as identification, sublimation, and repression—which are plainly not gendered. Whereas psychological forces represent configurations in which libido is channeled, psychic mechanisms represent managerial devices that organize and transform psychic materials. Furthermore, I do not mean to claim that in every case the psychological forces that psychoanalysis posits are gendered—for example, the pleasure principle is not. I am claiming only that those psychological forces that are invoked to explain the inculcation of gender are themselves gendered.

13. Of the three theorists I have discussed, Flax is least preoccupied with revaluing femininity. She wants to see the virtues associated with traditional feminine norms recognized, but she is sharply critical of some aspects of these norms. Thus, her view of agency does not merely repeat patterns familiar from traditional feminine norms. The difficulties in her view arise primarily from a problem which I shall discuss momentarily.

14. Nancy Chodorow takes this optimistic view of psychoanalysis's capacity to assist individuals in overcoming the effects of gender-laden socialization (1978, 216).

15. Freud 1971, 152. It is worth recalling in this context that many of Freud's most famous analysands were women.

BIBLIOGRAPHY

Blum, Larry, et al. 1973-74. "Altruism and women's oppression." *Philosophical Forum* 5: 222-47.
Butler, Judith. 1991. "The body politics of Julia Kristeva." This volume.

Chodorow, Nancy. 1974. "Family structure and feminine personality." In *Woman, culture, and society*, ed. Michelle Zimbalist Rosaldo and Louise Lamphere. Stanford: Stanford University Press.

———. 1978. *The reproduction of mothering*. Berkeley: University of California Press.

———. 1980. "Gender, relation, and difference in psychoanalytic perspective." In *The future of difference*, ed. Hester Eisenstein and Alice Jardine. Boston: G. K. Hall and Co.

———. 1981. "On *The reproduction of mothering*: A methodological debate." *Signs* 6: 500-514.

———. 1986. "Toward a relational individualism: The mediation of self through psychoanalysis." In *Reconstructing individualism: Autonomy, individuality, and the self in western thought*, ed. Thomas C. Heller, Morton Sosna, and David E. Wellbery. Stanford: Stanford University Press.

Flax, Jane. 1980. "Mother-daughter relationships: psychodynamics, politics, and philosophy." In *The future of difference*, ed. Hester Eisenstein and Alice Jardine. Boston: G. K. Hall and Co.

———. 1981. "The Conflict between nurturance and autonomy in mother-daughter relationships and within feminism." In *Women and mental health*, ed. Elizabeth Howell and Marjorie Bayes. New York: Basic Books.

———. 1986. "Psychoanalysis as deconstruction and myth: On gender, narcissism and modernity's discontents." In *Crisis of modernity*, ed. Gunter H. Lenz and Kurt L. Shell. Boulder: Westview Press.

———. 1987a. "Re-membering the selves: Is the repressed gendered?" *Michigan Quarterly Review* 26: 92-110.

———. 1987b. "Postmodernism and gender relations in feminist theory." *Signs* 12: 621-43.

Fraser, Nancy. 1991. "The uses and abuses of French discourse theories for feminist politics." This volume.

Freud, Sigmund. 1966. *The complete introductory lectures on psychoanalysis*. Trans. James Strachey. New York: W. W. Norton.

———. 1971. *The standard edition of the complete psychological works*. Vol. 12. London: The Hogarth Press.

Gilligan, Carol. 1982. *In a different voice*. Cambridge: Harvard University Press.

———. 1986. "In a different voice: Women's conceptions of self and of morality." In *Women and values*, ed. Marilyn Pearsall. Belmont, CA: Wadsworth Publishing Company.

Jaggar, Alison. 1983. *Feminist politics and human nature*. Totowa, NJ: Rowman and Allanheld.

Kristeva, Julia. 1980. *Desire in language: A semiotic approach to literature and art*. Trans. Thomas Gorz, Alice Jardine, Leon S. Roudiez. New York: Columbia University Press.

———. 1986. *The Kristeva reader*, ed. Toril Moi. New York: Columbia University Press.

———. 1987a. *Tales of love*. Trans. Leon S. Roudiez. New York: Columbia University Press.

———. 1987b. *In the beginning was love: Psychoanalysis and faith*. New York: Columbia University Press.

Leland, Dorothy. 1991. "Lacanian psychoanalysis and French feminism: Toward an adequate political psychology." This volume.

Meyers, Diana T. 1987. "Personal autonomy and the paradox of feminine socialization." *Journal of Philosophy* 84: 619-28.

———. 1989. *Self, society, and personal choice*. New York: Columbia University Press.

Mitchell, Juliet. 1975. *Psychoanalysis and feminism*. New York: Vintage.

Nye, Andrea. 1987. "Woman clothed with the sun: Julia Kristeva and the escape from/to language." *Signs* 12: 664-86.

Rossi, Alice S. 1981. "On *The reproduction of mothering*: A methodological debate." *Signs* 6: 492-500.

Ruddick, Sara. 1986. "Maternal thinking." In *Women and values*, ed. Marilyn Pearsall. Belmont, CA: Wadsworth Publishing Company.

Stanton, Domna C. 1986. "Difference on trial: A critique of the maternal metaphor in Cixous, Irigaray, and Kristeva." In *The Poetics of gender*, ed. Nancy K. Miller. New York: Columbia University Press.

Wollheim, Richard. 1984. *The thread of life*. Cambridge: Harvard University Press.

Young, Iris Marion. 1983. "Is male gender identity the cause of male domination?" In *Mothering: Essays in feminist theory*, ed. Joyce Trebilcot. Totowa, NJ: Rowman and Allanheld.

The Body Politics of Julia Kristeva

JUDITH BUTLER

Julia Kristeva attempts to expose the limits of Lacan's theory of language by revealing the semiotic dimension of language that it excludes. She argues that the semiotic potential of language is subversive, and describes the semiotic as a poetic-maternal linguistic practice that disrupts the symbolic, understood as culturally intelligible rule-governed speech. In the course of arguing that the semiotic contests the universality of the Symbolic, Kristeva makes several theoretical moves which end up consolidating the power of the Symbolic and paternal authority generally. She defends a maternal instinct as a pre-discursive biological necessity, thereby naturalizing a specific cultural configuration of maternity. In her use of psychoanalytic theory, she ends up claiming the cultural unintelligibility of lesbianism. Her distinction between the semiotic and the Symbolic operates to foreclose a cultural investigation into the genesis of precisely those feminine principles for which she claims a pre-discursive, naturalistic ontology. Although she claims that the maternal aspects of language are repressed in Symbolic speech and provide a critical possibility of displacing the hegemony of the paternal/symbolic, her very descriptions of the maternal appear to accept rather than contest the inevitable hegemony of the Symbolic. In conclusion, this essay offers a genealogical critique of the maternal discourse in Kristeva and suggests that recourse to the maternal does not constitute a subversive strategy as Kristeva appears to assume.

Kristeva's theory of the semiotic dimension of language at first appears to engage Lacanian premises only to expose their limits and to offer a specifically feminine locus of subversion of the paternal law within language. According to Lacan, the paternal law structures all linguistic signification, termed "the symbolic", and so becomes a universal organizing principle of culture itself. This law creates the possibility of meaningful language and, hence, meaningful experience, through the repression of primary libidinal drives, including the radical dependency of the child on the maternal body. Hence, the symbolic becomes possible by repudiating the primary relationship to the maternal body. The "subject" who emerges as a consequence of this repression itself becomes a bearer or proponent of this repressive law. The libidinal chaos characteristic of that early dependency is now fully constrained by a unitary agent whose language is structured by that law. This lan-

Hypatia vol. 3, no. 3 (Winter 1989) © by Judith Butler

guage, in turn, structures the world by suppressing multiple meanings (which always recall the libidinal multiplicity which characterized the primary relation to the maternal body) and instating univocal and discrete meanings in their place.

Kristeva challenges the Lacanian narrative which assumes that cultural meaning requires the repression of that primary relationship to the maternal body. She argues that the "semiotic" is a dimension of language occasioned by that primary maternal body which not only refutes Lacan's primary premise, but which serves as a perpetual source of subversion within the symbolic. For Kristeva, the semiotic expresses that original libidinal multiplicity within the very terms of culture, more precisely, within poetic language in which multiple meanings and semantic non-closure prevail. In effect, poetic language is the recovery of the maternal body within the terms of language, one that has the potential to disrupt, subvert, and displace the paternal law.

Despite her critique of Lacan, however, Kristeva's strategy of subversion proves doubtful. Her theory appears to depend upon the stability and reproduction of precisely the paternal law that she sought to displace. Although she effectively exposes the limits of Lacan's efforts to universalize the paternal law in language, she nevertheless concedes that the semiotic is invariably subordinate to the symbolic, that it assumes its specificity within the terms of a hierarchy which is immune to challenge. If the semiotic promotes the possibility of the subversion, displacement, or disruption of the paternal law, what meanings can those terms have if the symbolic always reasserts its hegemony?

The criticism of Kristeva which follows takes issue with several different steps in Kristeva's argument in favor of the semiotic as a source of effective subversion. First, it is unclear whether the primary relationship to the maternal body which both Kristeva and Lacan appear to accept is a viable construct and whether it is even a knowable experience according to either of their linguistic theories. The multiple drives that characterize the semiotic constitute a pre-discursive libidinal economy which occasionally makes itself known in language, but which maintains an ontological status prior to language itself. Manifest in language, in poetic language in particular, this prediscursive libidinal economy becomes a locus of cultural subversion. A second problem emerges when Kristeva maintains that this libidinal source of subversion cannot be maintained within the terms of culture, that its sustained presence leads to psychosis and to the breakdown of cultural life itself. Kristeva thus alternately posits and denies the semiotic as an emancipatory ideal. Though she tells us that it is a dimension of language regularly repressed, she also concedes that it is a kind of language which can never be consistently maintained.

In order to assess her seemingly self-defeating theory, we need to ask how this libidinal multiplicity becomes manifest in language, and what conditions its temporary lifespan there. Moreover, Kristeva describes the maternal body as bearing a set of meanings that are prior to culture itself. She thereby safe-guards the notion of culture as a paternal structure and delimits maternity as an essentially pre-cultural reality. Her naturalistic descriptions of the mater-nal body effectively reify motherhood and preclude an analysis of its cultural construction and variability. In asking whether a pre-discursive libidinal mul-tiplicity is possible, we will also consider whether what we claim to discover in the pre-discursive maternal body is itself a production of a given historical discourse, an effect of culture rather than its secret and primary cause.

Even if we accept Kristeva's theory of primary drives, it is unclear that the subversive effects of such drives can serve, via the semiotic, as anything more than a temporary and futile disruption of the hegemony of the paternal law. I will try to show how the failure of her political strategy follows in part from her largely uncritical appropriation of drive theory. Moreover, upon careful scrutiny of her descriptions of the semiotic function within language, it ap-pears that Kristeva reinstates the paternal law at the level of the semiotic it-self. In the end, Kristeva offers us a strategy of subversion that can never be-come a sustained political practice. In the final section of this paper, I will suggest a way to reconceptualize the relation between drives, language, and patriarchal prerogative which might serve a more effective strategy of subver-sion.

Kristeva's description of the semiotic proceeds through a number of prob-lematic steps. She assumes that drives have aims prior to their emergence into language, that language invariably represses or sublimates these drives, and that such drives are manifest only in those linguistic expressions which disobey, as it were, the univocal requirements of signification within the sym-bolic domain. She claims further that the emergence of multiplicitous drives into language is evident in the semiotic, that domain of linguistic meaning distinct from the symbolic, which is the maternal body manifest in poetic speech.

As early as *Revolution in Poetic Language* (1974), Kristeva argued for a nec-essary causal relation between the heterogeneity of drives and the plurivocal possibilities of poetic language. Differing from Lacan, she maintained that poetic language was not predicated upon a repression of primary drives. On the contrary, poetic language, she claimed, is the linguistic occasion on which drives break apart the usual, univocal terms of language and reveal an irrepressible heterogeneity of multiple sounds and meanings. Kristeva thereby contested Lacan's equation of the symbolic with all linguistic meaning by as-serting that poetic language has its own modality of meaning which does not conform to the requirements of univocal designation.

In this same work, she subscribed to a notion of free or uncathected energy which makes itself known in language through the poetic function. She claimed, for instance, that ". . . in the intermingling of drives in language . . . we shall see the economy of poetic language" and that in this economy, "the unitary subject can no longer find his place" (1984, 132). This poetic function is a rejective or divisive linguistic function which tends to fracture and multiply meanings; it enacts the heterogeneity of drives through the proliferation and destruction of univocal signification. Hence, the urge toward a highly differentiated or plurivocal set of meanings appears as the revenge of drives against the rule of the symbolic which, in turn, is predicated upon their repression. Kristeva defines the semiotic as the multiplicity of drives manifest in language. With their insistent energy and heterogeneity, these drives disrupt the signifying function of language. Thus, in this early work, she defines the semiotic as "the signifying function . . . connected to the modality [of] primary process."

In the essays that comprise *Desire in Language* (1977) Kristeva grounds her definition of the semiotic more fully in psychoanalytic terms. The primary drives that the symbolic represses and the semiotic obliquely indicates are now understood as *maternal drives*, not only those drives belonging to the mother, but those which characterize the dependency of the infant's body (of either sex) on the mother. In other words, "the maternal body" designates a relation of continuity rather than a discrete subject or object of desire; indeed, it designates that *jouissance* which precedes desire and the subject/object dichotomy that desire presupposes. While the symbolic is predicated upon the rejection of the mother, the refusal of the mother as an object of sexual love, the semiotic, through rhythm, assonance, intonations, sound play and repetition, re-presents or recovers the maternal body in poetic speech. Even the "first echolalias of infants" and the "glossalalias in psychotic discourse" are manifestations of the continuity of the mother-infant relation, a heterogeneous field of impulse prior to the separation/individuation of infant and mother, alike effected by the imposition of the incest taboo (1980, 135). The separation of the mother and infant effected by the taboo is expressed linguistically as the severing of sound from sense. In Kristeva's words, ". . . a phoneme, as distinctive element of meaning, belongs to language as symbolic. But this same phoneme is involved in rhythmic, intonational repetitions; it thereby tends toward autonomy from meaning so as to maintain itself in a semiotic disposition near the instinctual drive's body" (1980, 135).

The semiotic is described by Kristeva as destroying or eroding the symbolic; it is said to be "before" meaning, as when a child begins to vocalize, or "after" meaning as when a psychotic no longer uses words to signify. If the symbolic and the semiotic are understood as two modalities of language, and if the semiotic is understood to be generally repressed by the symbolic, then language for Kristeva is understood as a system in which the symbolic remains hegemonic except when the semiotic disrupts its signifying process through elision, repetition, mere sound, and the multiplication of meaning through indefinitely signifying images and metaphors. In its symbolic mode, language rests upon a severance of the relation of maternal dependency, whereby it becomes abstract (abstracted from the materiality of language) and univocal; this is most apparent in quantitative or purely formal reasoning. In its semiotic mode, language is engaged in a poetic recovery of the maternal body, that diffuse materiality that resists all discrete and univocal signification. Kristeva writes,

> In any poetic language, not only do the rhythmic constraints, for example, go so far as to violate certain grammatical rules of a national language . . . but in recent texts, these semiotic constraints (rhythm, vocalic timbres in Symbolist work, but also graphic disposition on the page) are accompanied by nonrecoverable syntactic elisions; it is impossible to reconstitute the particular elided syntactic category (object or verb), which makes the meaning of the utterance decidable . . . (1980, 134).

For Kristeva, this undecidability is precisely the instinctual moment in language, its disruptive function. Poetic language thus suggests a dissolution of the coherent, signifying subject into the primary continuity which is the maternal body:

> Language as symbolic function constitutes itself at the cost of repressing instinctual drive and continuous relation to the mother. On the contrary, the unsettled and questionable subject of poetic language (from whom the word is never uniquely sign) maintains itself at the cost of reactivating this repressed, instinctual, maternal element. (1980, 136)

Kristeva's references to the "subject" of poetic language are not wholly appropriate, for poetic language erodes and destroys the subject, where the subject is understood as a speaking being participating in the symbolic. Following Lacan, she maintains that the prohibition against the incestuous union with the mother is the founding law of the subject, a foundation which severs or breaks the continuous relation of maternal dependence. In creating the subject, the prohibitive law creates the domain of the symbolic or language as a system of univocally signifying signs. Hence, Kristeva concludes that "poetic language would be for its questionable subject-in-process the equivalent of incest" (1980, 136). The breaking of symbolic language against its own founding law or, equivalently, the emergence of rupture into language from within its own interior instinctuality is not merely the outburst of libidinal heterogeneity into language; it also signifies the somatic state of dependence on the maternal body prior to the individuation of the ego. Poetic language thus always indicates a return to the maternal terrain, where the maternal signifies both libidinal dependence and the heterogeneity of drives.

In "Motherhood According to Bellini", Kristeva suggests that, because the maternal body signifies the loss of coherent and discrete identity, poetic language verges on psychosis. And in the case of a woman's semiotic expressions in language, the return to the maternal signifies a pre-discursive homosexuality that Kristeva also clearly associates with psychosis. Although Kristeva concedes that poetic language is sustained culturally through its participation in the symbolic and, hence, in the norms of linguistic communicability, she fails to allow that homosexuality is capable of the same non-psychotic social expression. The key to Kristeva's view of the psychotic nature of homosexuality is to be understood, I suggest, in her acceptance of the structuralist assumption that heterosexuality is coextensive with the founding of the symbolic. Hence, the cathexis of homosexual desire can only be achieved, according to Kristeva, through displacements that are sanctioned within the symbolic, such as poetic language or the act of giving birth:

> By giving birth, the women enters into contact with her mother; she becomes, she is her own mother; they are the same continuity differentiating itself. She thus actualizes the homosexual facet of motherhood, through which a woman is simultaneously closer to her instinctual memory, more open to her psychosis, and consequently, more negatory of the social, symbolic bond. (1980, 239)

According to Kristeva, the act of giving birth does not successfully reestablish that continuous relation prior to individuation because the infant invariably suffers the prohibition on incest and is separated off as a discrete identity. In the case of the mother's separation from the girl-child, the result is melancholy for both, for the separation is never fully completed.

As opposed to grief or mourning, in which separation is recognized and the libido attached to the original object is successfully displaced onto a new substitute object, melancholy designates a failure to grieve in which the loss is simply internalized and, in that sense, *refused*. Instead of negating the attachment to the body, the maternal body is internalized as a negation, so that the girl's identity becomes itself a kind of loss, a characteristic privation or lack.

The alleged psychosis of homosexuality, then, consists in its thorough break with the paternal law and with the grounding of the female "ego", tenuous though it may be, in the melancholic response to separation from the maternal body. Hence, according to Kristeva, female homosexuality is the emergence of psychosis into culture:

> The homosexual-maternal facet is a whirl of words, a complete absence of meaning and seeing; it is feeling, displacement, rhythm, sound, flashes, and fantasied clinging to the maternal

> body as a screen against the plunge . . . for woman, a paradise
> lost but seemingly close at hand. . . . (1980, 239-40).

For women, however, this homosexuality is manifest in poetic language which becomes, in fact, the only form of the semiotic, besides childbirth, that can be sustained within the terms of the symbolic. For Kristeva, then, overt homosexuality cannot be a culturally sustainable activity, for it would constitute a breaking of the incest taboo in an unmediated way. And yet why is this the case?

Kristeva accepts the assumption that culture is equivalent to the symbolic, that the symbolic is fully subsumed under the "Law of the Father", and that the only modes of non-psychotic activity are those which participate in the symbolic to some extent. Her strategic task, then, is not to replace the symbolic with the semiotic nor to establish the semiotic as a rival cultural possibility, but rather to validate those experiences within the symbolic that permit a manifestation of the borders which divide the symbolic from the semiotic. Just as birth is understood to be a cathexis of instinctual drives for the purposes of a social teleology, so poetic production is conceived as the site in which the split between instinct and representation coexists in culturally communicable form:

> The speaker reaches this limit, this requisite of sociality, only by virtue of a particular, discursive practice called "art". A woman also attains it (and in our society, *especially*) through the strange form of split symbolization (threshold of language and instinctual drive, of the 'symbolic' and the 'semiotic') of which the act of giving birth consists. (1980; 240)[1]

Hence, for Kristeva, poetry and maternity represent privileged practices within paternally sanctioned culture which permit a nonpsychotic experience of the heterogeneity and dependency characteristic of the maternal terrain. These acts of *poesis* reveal an instinctual heterogeneity that exposes the repressed ground of the symbolic, challenges the mastery of the univocal signifier, and diffuses the autonomy of the subject who postures as their necessary ground. The heterogeneity of drives operates culturally as a subversive strategy of displacement, one which dislodges the hegemony of the paternal law by releasing the repressed multiplicity interior to language itself. Precisely because that instinctual heterogeneity must be re-presented in and through the paternal law, it cannot defy the incest taboo altogether, but must remain within the most fragile regions of the symbolic. Obedient, then, to syntactical requirements, the poetic-maternal practices of displacing the paternal law always remain tenuously tethered to that law. Hence, a full-scale refusal of the symbolic is impossible, and a discourse of 'emancipation', for Kristeva, is out of the question. At best, tactical subversions and displacements of the law challenge its self-grounding presumption. But, once again, Kristeva does not seriously challenge the structuralist assumption that the prohibitive paternal law is foundational to culture itself. Hence, the subversion of paternally sanctioned culture cannot come from another version of culture, but only from within the repressed interior of culture itself, from the heterogeneity of drives that constitutes culture's concealed foundation.

This relation between heterogeneous drives and the paternal law produces an exceedingly problematic view of psychosis. On the one hand, it designates female homosexuality as a culturally unintelligible practice, inherently psychotic; on the other hand, it mandates maternity as a compulsory defense against libidinal chaos. Although Kristeva does not make either claim explicitly, both implications follow from her views on the law, language, and drives.

Consider that for Kristeva, poetic language breaks the incest taboo and, as such, verges always on psychosis. As a return to the maternal body and a concomitant de-individuation of the ego, poetic language becomes especially threatening when uttered by women. The poetic then contests not only the incest taboo, but the taboo against homosexuality as well. Poetic language is thus, for women, both displaced maternal dependency and, because that dependency is libidinal, displaced homosexuality as well.

For Kristeva, the unmediated cathexis of female homosexual desire leads unequivocally to psychosis. Hence, one can satisfy this drive only through a series of displacements: the incorporation of maternal identity, i.e. by becoming a mother oneself, or through poetic language which manifests obliquely the heterogeneity of drives characteristic of maternal dependency. As the only socially sanctioned and, hence, non-psychotic displacements for homosexual desire, both maternity and poetry constitute melancholic experiences for women appropriately acculturated into heterosexuality. The heterosexual poet-mother suffers interminably from the displacement of the homosexual cathexis. And yet, the consummation of this desire would lead to the psychotic unraveling of identity, according to Kristeva. The presumption is that, for women, heterosexuality and coherent selfhood are indissolubly linked.

How are we to understand this constitution of lesbian experience as the site of an irretrievable self-loss? Kristeva clearly takes heterosexuality to be prerequisite to kinship and to culture. Consequently, she identifies lesbian experience as the psychotic alternative to the acceptance of paternally sanctioned laws. And yet why is lesbianism constituted as psychosis? From what cultural perspective is lesbianism constructed as a site of fusion, self-loss, and psychosis?

By projecting the lesbian as "other" to culture, and characterizing lesbian speech as the psychotic "whirl-of-words", Kristeva constructs lesbian sexuality as intrinsically unintelligible. This tactical dismissal and reduction of lesbian experience performed in the name of the law positions Kristeva within the orbit of paternal-heterosexual privilege. The paternal law which protects her from this radical incoherence is precisely the mechanism that produces the construct of lesbianism as a site of irrationality. Significantly, this description of lesbian experience is effected from the outside, and tells us more about the fantasies that a fearful heterosexual culture produces to defend against its own homosexual possibilities than about lesbian experience itself.

In claiming that lesbianism designates a loss of self, Kristeva appears to be delivering a psychoanalytic truth about the repression necessary for individuation. The fear of such a 'regression' to homosexuality is, then, a fear of losing cultural sanction and privilege altogether. Although Kristeva claims that this loss designates a place *prior* to culture, there is no reason not to understand it as a new or unacknowledged cultural form. In other words, Kristeva prefers to explain lesbian experience as a regressive libidinal state prior to acculturation itself rather than to take up the challenge that lesbianism offers to her restricted view of paternally sanctioned cultural laws. Is the fear encoded in the construction of the lesbian as psychotic the result of a developmentally necessitated repression, or is it, rather, the fear of losing cultural legitimacy and, hence, being cast—not outside or prior to culture—but outside cultural *legitimacy*, still within culture, but culturally "out-lawed"?

Kristeva describes both the maternal body and lesbian experience from a position of sanctioned heterosexuality that fails to acknowledge its own fear of losing that sanction. Her reification of the paternal law not only repudiates female homosexuality, but denies the varied meanings and possibilities of motherhood as a cultural practice. But *cultural* subversion is not really Kristeva's concern, for subversion, when it appears, emerges from beneath the surface of culture only inevitably to return there. Although the semiotic is a possibility of language that escapes the paternal law, it remains inevitably within or, indeed, beneath the territory of that law. Hence, poetic language and the pleasures of maternity constitute local displacements of the paternal law, temporary subversions which finally submit to that against which they initially rebel. By relegating the source of subversion to a site outside of culture itself, Kristeva appears to foreclose the possibility of subversion as an effective or realizable cultural practice. Pleasure beyond the paternal law can only be imagined together with its inevitable impossibility.

Kristeva's theory of thwarted subversion is premised on her problematic view of the relation between drives, language and the law. Her postulation of a subversive multiplicity of drives raises a number of epistemological and political questions. In the first place, if these drives are only manifest in language or cultural forms already determined as symbolic, then how is it that we can verify their pre-symbolic ontological status? Kristeva argues that poetic language gives us access to these drives in their fundamental multiplicity, but this answer is not fully satisfactory. Since poetic language is said to depend upon the prior existence of these multiplicitous drives, we cannot, then, in circular fashion, justify the postulated existence of these drives through recourse to poetic language. If drives must first be repressed for language to exist, and if we can only attribute meaning to that which is representable in language, then to attribute meaning to drives prior to their emergence into language is impossible. Similarly, to attribute a causality to drives which facilitates their transformation into language and by which language itself is to be explained cannot reasonably be done within the confines of language itself. In other words, we know these drives as 'causes' only in and through their effects and, as such, we have no reason for not identifying drives with their effects. It follows that either (a) drives and their representations are coextensive or (b) representations preexist the drives themselves.

This last alternative is, I would argue, an important one to consider, for how do we know that the instinctual object of Kristeva's discourse is not a construction of the discourse itself? And what grounds do we have for positing this object, this multiplicitous field, as prior to signification? If poetic language must participate in the symbolic in order to be culturally communicable, and if Kristeva's own theoretical texts are emblematic of the symbolic, then where are we to find a convincing 'outside' to this domain? Her postulation of a pre-discursive corporeal multiplicity becomes all the more problematic when we discover that maternal drives are considered part of a "biological destiny" and are themselves manifestations of "a non-symbolic, non-paternal causality" (1980, 239). This presymbolic nonpaternal causality is, for Kristeva, a semiotic, *maternal* causality or, more specifically, a teleological conception of maternal instincts:

> Material compulsion, spasm of a memory belonging to the species that either binds together or splits apart to perpetuate itself, series of markers with no other significance than the eternal return of the life-death biological cycle. How can we verbalize this prelinguistic, unrepresentable memory? Heraclitus' flux, Epicurus' atoms, the whirling dust of cabalic, Arab and Indian mystics, and the stippled drawings of psychedelics— all seem better metaphors than the theory of Being, the logos, and its laws. (1980, 239)

Here, the repressed maternal body is not only the locus of multiple drives, but also the bearer of a biological teleology, one which, it seems, makes itself evident in the early stages of Western philosophy, in non-Western religious beliefs and practices, in aesthetic representations produced by psychotic or near-psychotic states, and even in avant-garde artistic practices. But why are we to assume that these various cultural expressions manifest the self-same principle of maternal heterogeneity? Kristeva simply subordinates each of these cultural moments to the same principle. Consequently, the semiotic represents any cultural effort to displace the Logos (which, curiously, she *contrasts* with Heraclitus' flux), where the Logos represents the univocal signifier, the law of identity. Her opposition between the semiotic and the symbolic reduces here to a metaphysical quarrel between the principle of multiplicity that escapes the charge of non-contradiction and a principle of identity based on the suppression of that multiplicity. Oddly, that very principle of multiplicity that Kristeva everywhere defends operates in much the same way as a principle of identity. Note the way in which all manner of things 'primitive' and 'oriental' are summarily subordinated to the principle of the maternal body. Surely, her description not only warrants the charge of orientalism, but raises the very significant question whether, ironically, multiplicity has become a univocal signifier.

Her ascription of a teleological aim to maternal drives prior to their constitution in language or culture raises a number of questions about Kristeva's political program. Although she clearly sees subversive and disruptive potential in those semiotic expressions that challenge the hegemony of the paternal law, it is less clear in what precisely this subversion consists. If the law is understood to rest on a constructed ground, beneath which lurks the repressed maternal terrain, what concrete cultural options emerge within the terms of culture as a consequence of this revelation? Ostensibly, the multiplicity associated with the maternal libidinal economy has the force to disperse the univocity of the paternal signifier, and seemingly to create the possibility of other cultural expressions no longer tightly constrained by the law of non-contradiction. But is this disruptive activity the opening of a field of significations, or is it the manifestation of a biological archaism which operates according to a natural and "prepaternal" causality? If Kristeva believed that the former were the case (and she does not), then she would be interested in a displacement of the paternal law in favor of a proliferating field of cultural possibilities. But instead she prescribes a return to a principle of maternal heterogeneity which proves to be a closed concept, indeed, a heterogeneity confined by a teleology both unilinear and univocal.

Kristeva understands the desire to give birth as a species-desire, part of a collective and archaic female libidinal drive that constitutes an ever recurring metaphysical principle. Here Kristeva reifies maternity and then promotes this reification as the disruptive potential of the semiotic. As a result, the paternal law, understood as the ground of univocal signification, is displaced by an equally univocal signifier, the principle of the maternal body which remains self-identical in its teleology regardless of its "multiplicitous" manifestations.

Insofar as Kristeva conceptualizes this maternal instinct as having an ontological status prior to the paternal law, she fails to consider the way in which that law might well be the *cause* of the very desire it is said to *repress*. Rather than the manifestation of a prepaternal causality, these desires might attest to maternity as a social practice required and recapitulated by the exigencies of kinship. Kristeva accepts Levi-Strauss' analysis of the exchange of women as prerequisite for the consolidation of kinship bonds. She understands this exchange, however, as the cultural moment in which the maternal body is repressed rather than as a mechanism for the compulsory cultural construction of the female body as a maternal body. Indeed, we might understand the exchange of women as imposing a compulsory obligation on women's bodies to reproduce. According to Gayle Rubin's reading of Levi-Strauss, kinship effects a "sculpting of . . . sexuality" such that the desire to give birth is the result of social practices which require and produce such desires in order to effect their reproductive ends (Rubin 1975, 182).

What grounds, then, does Kristeva have for imputing a maternal teleology to the female body prior to its emergence into culture? To pose the question in this way is already to question the distinction between the symbolic and the semiotic on which her conception of the maternal body rests. The maternal body in its originary signification is considered by Kristeva to be prior to signification itself; hence, it becomes impossible within her framework to consider the maternal itself as a signification, open to cultural variability. Her argument makes clear that maternal drives constitute those primary processes that language invariably represses or sublimates. But perhaps her argument could be recast within an even more encompassing framework: what cultural configuration of language, indeed, of *discourse*, generates the trope of a pre-discursive libidinal multiplicity, and for what purposes?

By restricting the paternal law to a prohibitive or repressive function, Kristeva fails to understand the paternal mechanisms by which affectivity itself is generated. The law that is said to repress the semiotic may well be the governing principle of the semiotic itself, with the result that what passes as "maternal instinct" may well be a culturally constructed desire which is interpreted through a naturalistic vocabulary. And if that desire is constructed according to a law of kinship which requires the heterosexual production and reproduction of desire, then the vocabulary of naturalistic affect effectively renders that "paternal law" invisible. What Kristeva refers to as a "pre-paternal causality" would then appear as a *paternal* causality under the guise of a natural or distinctively maternal causality.

Significantly, the figuration of the maternal body and the teleology of its instincts as a self-identical and insistent metaphysical principle—an archaism of a collective, sex-specific biological constitution—bases itself on a univocal conception of the female sex. And this sex, conceived as both origin and causality, poses as a principle of pure generativity. Indeed, for Kristeva, it is equated with *poesis* itself, the activity of making that in Plato's *Symposium* is held to be an act of birth and poetic conception at once.[2] But is female generativity truly an uncaused cause, and does it begin the narrative that takes all of humanity under the force of the incest taboo and into language?

Does the prepaternal causality whereof Kristeva speaks signify a primary female economy of pleasure and meaning? Can we reverse the very order of this
causality and understand this semiotic economy as a production of a prior discourse?

In the final chapter of Foucault's first volume of *The History of Sexuality*, he
cautions against using the category of sex as a "fictitious unity . . . [and]
causal principle", and argues that the fictitious category of sex facilitates a reversal of causal relations such that "sex" is understood to cause the structure
and meaning of desire:

> . . . the notion of 'sex' made it possible to group together, in
> an artificial unity, anatomical elements, biological functions,
> conducts, sensations, and pleasures, and it enabled one to
> make use of this fictitious unity as a causal principle, an omni-
> present meaning: sex was thus able to function as a unique
> signifier and as a universal signified. (1980, 154).

For Foucault, the body is not 'sexed' in any significant sense prior to its determination within a discourse through which it becomes invested with an 'idea'
of natural or essential sex. As an instrument and effect of power, the body
only gains meaning within discourse in the context of power relations. Sexuality is an historically specific organization of power, discourse, bodies, and
affectivity. As such, sexuality is understood by Foucault to produce 'sex' as an
artificial concept which effectively extends and disguises the power relations
responsible for its genesis.

Foucault's framework suggests a way to solve some of the epistemological
and political difficulties that follow from Kristeva's view of the female body.
We can understand Kristeva's assertion of a "prepaternal causality" as fundamentally inverted. Whereas Kristeva posits a maternal body prior to discourse
which exerts its own causal force in the structure of drives, I would argue that
the discursive production of the maternal body as pre-discursive is a tactic in
the self-amplification and concealment of those specific power relations by
which the trope of the maternal body is produced. Then the maternal body
would no longer be understood as the hidden ground of all signification, the
tacit cause of all culture. It would be understood, rather, as an effect or consequence of a system of sexuality in which the female body is required to assume
maternity as the essence of its self and the law of its desire.

From within Foucault's framework, we are compelled to redescribe the maternal libidinal economy as a product of an historically specific organization
of sexuality. Moreover, the discourse of sexuality, itself suffused by power relations, becomes the true ground of the trope of the pre-discursive maternal
body. Kristeva's formulation suffers a thoroughgoing reversal: the symbolic
and the semiotic are no longer interpreted as those dimensions of language
which follow upon the repression or manifestation of the maternal libidinal

economy. This very economy is understood instead as a reification that both extends and conceals the institution of motherhood as compulsory for women. Indeed, when the desires that maintain the institution of motherhood are transvaluated as prepaternal and precultural drives, then the institution gains a permanent legitimation in the invariant structures of the female body. Indeed, the clearly paternal law that sanctions and requires the female body to be characterized primarily in terms of its reproductive function is inscribed on that body as the law of its natural necessity. And Kristeva, safeguarding that law of a biologically necessitated maternity as a subversive operation that preexists the paternal law itself, aids in the systematic production of its invisibility and, consequently, the illusion of its inevitability.

In conclusion, because Kristeva restricts herself to an exclusively *prohibitive* conception of the paternal law, she is unable to account for the ways in which the paternal law *generates* certain desires in the form of natural drives. The female body that she seeks to express is itself a construct produced by the very law it is supposed to undermine. In no way do these criticisms of Kristeva's conception of the paternal law necessarily invalidate her general position that culture or the symbolic is predicated upon a repudiation of women's bodies. I want to suggest, however, that any theory that asserts that signification is predicated upon the denial or repression of a female principle ought to consider whether that femaleness is really external to the cultural norms by which it is repressed. In other words, on my reading, the repression of the feminine does not require that the agency of repression and the object of repression be ontologically distinct. Indeed, repression may be understood to produce the object that it comes to deny. That production may well be an elaboration of the agency of repression itself. As Foucault made clear, this culturally contradictory enterprise of repression is prohibitive and generative at once, and makes the problematic of 'liberation' especially acute. The female body that is freed from the shackles of the paternal law may well prove to be yet another incarnation of that law, posing as subversive but operating in the service of that law's self-amplification and proliferation. In order to avoid the emancipation of the oppressor in the name of the oppressed, it is necessary to take into account the full complexity and subtlety of the law and to cure ourselves of the illusion of a true body beyond the law. If subversion is possible, it will be a subversion from within the terms of the law, through the possibilities that emerge when the law turns against itself and spawns unexpected permutations of itself. The culturally constructed body will then be liberated, not to its 'natural' past nor to its original pleasures, but to an open future of cultural possibilities.

NOTES

1. For an extremely interesting analysis of reproductive metaphors as descriptive of the process of poetic creativity, see Wendy Owen, 1985.

2. See Plato's *Symposium*, 209a: of the "procreancy . . . of the spirit", he writes that it is the specific capacity of the poet. Hence, poetic creations are understood as sublimated reproductive desire.

REFERENCES

Foucault, Michel. 1980. *The history of sexuality.* Vol. I. An introduction. Trans. Robert Hurley. New York: Vintage.

Kristeva, Julia. 1984. *Revolution in poetic language.* Trans. Margaret Walker. New York: Columbia University Press.

———. 1980. *Desire in language, a semiotic approach to literature and art.* Trans. Thomas Gorz, Alice Jardine, Leon S. Roudiez. New York: Columbia University Press.

Owen, Wendy. 1985. A riddle in nine syllables: Female creativity in the poetry of Sylvia Plath. Ph.D. diss., Department of English. Yale University.

Rubin, Gayle. 1975. The traffic in women: Notes on the "Political Economy" of sex. In Rayna R. Reiter, ed., *Toward an anthropology of women.* New York: Monthly Review Press.

The Uses and Abuses of French
Discourse Theories for
Feminist Politics

NANCY FRASER

I identify two distinct models of discourse that have been developed in recent French thought: 1) a structuralist model that treats language as a symbolic system or code and that is derived from Saussure, presupposed in Lacan, and abstractly negated in deconstruction; and 2) a pragmatic model that treats languages as sets of multiple and historically specific institutionalized social practices and that is associated with Mikhail Bakhtin, Michel Foucault, and Pierre Bourdieu. I argue that the second, pragmatic model is the more useful for feminist politics. On this basis, I then examine some features of the thought of Jacques Lacan and Julia Kristeva. I argue that to the degree that each writer relies on the structuralist model, his or her thought is not useful for feminist politics.

This essay grows out of an experience of severe puzzlement.[1] For several years now I have been watching with growing incomprehension as increasing numbers of feminist scholars have been trying to use or adapt the theory of Jacques Lacan for feminist purposes. I myself have felt a deep disaffinity with Lacan, a disaffinity as much intellectual as political. So while many of my fellow feminists have been using Lacanian ideas to theorize the discursive construction of subjectivity in film and literature, I have been relying on alternative models of language to develop a feminist social theory. Until now, I have explained neither to myself nor to my colleagues why it is that I have looked to the discourse models of writers like Foucault, Bourdieu, Bakhtin, Habermas, and Gramsci instead to those of Lacan, Kristeva, Saussure, and Derrida.[2] In this essay, I want to begin to provide such an explanation. I will try to explain why I think feminists should have no truck with Lacan and why we should have only the most minimal truck with Julia Kristeva. I will also try to identify some places where I think we can find more satisfactory alternatives.

I. What Do Feminists Want in a Discourse Theory?

Let me begin by posing two questions: What might a theory of discourse contribute to feminism? and What, therefore, do feminists want in a discourse theory? I suggest that a theory of discourse can help us understand at least four things, all of which are interrelated. First, it can help us understand how people's social identities are fashioned and altered over time. Second, it can help us understand how, under conditions of inequality, social groups in the sense of collective agents are formed and unformed. Third, a theory of discourse can illuminate how the cultural hegemony of dominant groups in society is secured and contested. Fourth and finally, it can shed light on the prospects for emancipatory social change and political practice. Let me elaborate.

First, consider the uses of a theory of discourse for understanding social identities. The basic idea here is that people's social identities are complexes of meanings, networks of interpretation. To have a social identity, to be a woman or a man, for example, just *is* to live and to act under a set of descriptions. These descriptions, of course, are not simply secreted by people's bodies; nor are they exuded by people's psyches. Rather, they are drawn from the fund of interpretive possibilities available to agents in specific societies.[3] It follows that in order to understand anyone's feminine or masculine gender identity, it does not suffice to study biology or psychology. Instead, one must study the historically specific social practices through which cultural descriptions of gender are produced and circulated.

Moreover, social identities are exceedingly complex. They are knit from a plurality of different descriptions arising from a plurality of different signifying practices. Thus, no one is simply a woman; one is rather, for example, a white, Jewish, middle-class woman, a philosopher, a lesbian, a socialist, and a mother.[4] Moreover, since everyone acts in a plurality of social contexts, the different descriptions comprising any individual's social identity fade in and out of focus. Thus, one is not always a woman in the same degree; in some contexts, one's womanhood figures centrally in the set of descriptions under which one acts; in others, it is peripheral or latent.[5] Finally, it is not the case that people's social identities are constructed once and for all and definitively fixed. Rather, they alter over time, shifting with shifts in agents' practices and affiliations. Thus, even the *way* in which one is a woman will shift, as it does, to take a dramatic example, when one becomes a feminist. In short, social identities are discursively constructed in historically specific social contexts; they are complex and plural; and they shift over time. One use of a theory of discourse for feminist politics, then, is in understanding social identities in their full sociocultural complexity, thus in demystifying static, single variable, essentialist views of gender identity.

A second use of a theory of discourse for feminist politics is in understanding the formation of social groups. How does it happen, under conditions of inequality, that people come together, arrange themselves under the banner of *collective* identities, and constitute themselves as collective social agents? How do class formation and, by analogy, gender formation occur?

Clearly, group formation involves shifts in people's social identities and therefore also in their relation to discourse. One thing that happens here is that preexisting strands of identities acquire a new sort of salience and centrality. These strands, previously submerged among many others, are reinscribed as the nubs of new self-definitions and affiliations.[6] For example, in the current wave of feminist ferment, many of us who had previously been "women" in some taken-for-granted way have now become "women" in the very different sense of a discursively self-constituted political collectivity. In the process, we have remade entire regions of social discourse. We have invented new terms for describing social reality, for example, "sexism," "sexual harassment," "marital, date, and acquaintance rape," "labor force sex-segregation," "the double shift," and "wife-battery." We have also invented new language games such as consciousness-raising and new, institutionalized public spheres such as the Society for Women in Philosophy.[7] The point is that the formation of social groups proceeds by struggles over social discourse. Thus, a theory of discourse is useful here, both for understanding social groups and for coming to grips with the closely related issue of sociocultural hegemony.

"Hegemony" is the Italian Marxist Antonio Gramsci's term for the discursive face of power. It is the power to establish the "common sense" or "doxa" of a society, the fund of self-evident descriptions of social reality that normally go without saying.[8] This includes the power to establish authoritative definitions of social situations and social needs, the power to define the universe of legitimate disagreement, and the power to shape the political agenda. Hegemony, then, expresses the advantaged position of dominant social groups with respect to discourse. It is a concept that allows us to recast the issues of social identity and social groups in the light of societal inequality. How do pervasive axes of dominance and subordination affect the production and circulation of social meanings? How does stratification along lines of gender, race, and class affect the discursive construction of social identities and the formation of social groups?

The notion of hegemony points to the intersection of power, inequality, and discourse. However, it does not entail that the ensemble of descriptions that circulate in society comprise a monolithic and seamless web, nor that dominant groups exercise an absolute, top-down control of meaning. On the contrary, "hegemony" designates a process wherein cultural authority is negotiated and contested. It presupposes that societies contain a plurality of discourses and discursive sites, a plurality of positions and perspectives from which to speak. Of course, not all of these have equal authority. Yet conflict and contestation are part of the story. Thus, one use of a theory of discourse for feminist politics is to shed light on the processes by which the sociocultural hegemony of dominant groups is achieved and contested. What are the processes by which definitions and interpretations inimical to women's interests acquire cultural authority? What are the prospects for mobilizing counterhegemonic feminist definitions and interpretations to create broad oppositional groups and alliances?

I trust that the link between these questions and emancipatory political practice is obvious. A theory of discourse that lets us examine identities, groups, and hegemony in the ways I have been describing would be a great aid to feminist practice. It would valorize the empowering dimensions of discursive struggles without leading to "culturalist" retreats from political engagement.[9] In addition, the right kind of theory would counter the disabling assumption that women are just passive victims of male dominance. That assumption overtotalizes male dominance, treating men as the only social agents and rendering inconceivable our own existence as feminist theorists and activists. In contrast, the sort of theory I have been proposing would help us understand how, even under conditions of subordination, women participate in the making of culture.

II. JACQUES LACAN AND THE LIMITS OF STRUCTURALISM

In light of the foregoing, what sort of theory of discourse will be useful for feminist politics? What sort of theory can best meet our needs to understand identities, groups, hegemony, and emancipatory practice?

In recent years, two general models for theorizing language have emerged in France. The first of these is the structuralist model, which studies language as a symbolic system or code. This model is derived from Saussure, presupposed in Lacan, and abstractly negated but not entirely superseded in deconstruction and in related forms of French women's writing. The second model, by contrast, I shall call the pragmatic model; it studies language at the level of discourses, as historically specific social practices of communication. This model is operative in the work of Mikhail Bakhtin, Michel Foucault, Pierre Bourdieu, and in some but not all dimensions of the work of Julia Kristeva and Luce Irigaray. In this section, I shall argue that the first, structuralist model is not very useful for feminist politics.

Let me begin by noting that there are good prima facie reasons for feminists to be suspicious of the structuralist model. This model constructs its object of study by abstracting from exactly what we need to focus on, namely, the social practice and social context of communication. Indeed, the abstraction from practice and context are among the founding gestures of Saussurean linguistics. Saussure began by splitting signification into *langue*, the symbolic system or code, and *parole*, speakers' uses of language in communicative practice or speech. He then made the first of these, langue, the proper object of the new science of linguistics, and relegated the second, parole, to the status of a devalued remainder.[10] At the same time, Saussure insisted that the study of langue be synchronic rather than diachronic; he thereby posited his object of study as static and atemporal, abstracting it from historical change. Finally, the founder of structuralist linguistics posited that langue was indeed a single system; he made its unity and systematicity consist in the putative fact that every signifier, every material, signifying element of the code, derives its meaning positionally by way of its difference from all of the others.

Together, these founding operations render the structuralist approach of doubtful utility for feminist politics.[11] Because it abstracts from parole, the structuralist model brackets questions of practice, agency, and the speaking subject. Thus, it cannot shed light on social identity and group formation. Moreover, because this approach brackets the diachronic, it will not tell us anything about shifts in identities and affiliations over time. Similarly, because it abstracts from the social context of communication, the model brackets issues of power and inequality. Thus, it cannot illuminate the processes by which cultural hegemony is secured and contested. Finally, because the model theorizes the fund of available linguistic meanings as a single symbolic system, it lends itself to a monolithic view of signification that denies tensions and contradictions among social meanings. In short, by reducing discourse to a "symbolic system," the structuralist model evacuates social agency, social conflict, and social practice.[12]

Let me now try to illustrate these problems by means of a brief discussion of the work of Jacques Lacan. Or rather, let me illustrate these problems by reconstructing, and criticizing, an ideal-typical reading of Lacan that I believe is widespread among English-speaking feminists. In so doing, I shall bracket the question of the fidelity of this reading, which could be faulted for exaggerating the centrality of phallo-centrism to Lacan's view of the symbolic order and for overemphasizing the influence of Saussure at the expense of other, countervailing influences, such as Hegel.[13] For my purposes, this ideal-typical Saussurean reading of Lacan is useful precisely because it evinces with unusual clarity difficulties which beset many "poststructuralist" theorists whose abstract attempts to break free of structuralism only render them all the more bound to it.

At first sight, this ideal-typical reading of Lacan seems to have some advantages for feminist theorists. By conjoining the Freudian problematic of the construction of gendered subjectivity to the Saussurean model of structural linguistics, it seems to provide each with its needed corrective. The introduction of the Freudian problematic promises to supply the speaking subject that is missing in Saussure and thereby to reopen the excluded questions about identity, speech, and social practice. Conversely, the use of the Saussurean model promises to remedy some of Freud's deficiencies. By insisting that gender identity is *discursively* constructed, Lacan appears to eliminate lingering vestiges of biologism in Freud, to treat gender as sociocultural all the way down, and to render it in principle more open to change.

However, these apparent advantages vanish upon closer inspection. Instead, it becomes clear that Lacan's theory is viciously circular. On the one hand, it purports to describe the process by which individuals acquire gendered subjectivity through their painful conscription as young children into a preexisting phallocentric symbolic order. Here the structure of the symbolic order determines the character of individual subjectivity. But on the other hand, and at the same time, the theory purports to show that the symbolic order must necessarily be phallocentric since the attainment of subjectivity requires submission to "the Father's Law." Here, then, the nature of individual subjectivity, as dictated by an autonomous psychology, determines the character of the symbolic order.

One result of this circularity is an ironclad determinism. As Dorothy Leland (1991) has noted, the theory casts the developments it describes as necessary, invariant, and unalterable. Phallocentrism, woman's disadvantaged place in the symbolic order, the encoding of cultural authority as masculine, the impossibility of describing a nonphallic sexuality, in short, any number of trappings of male dominance now appear as invariable features of the human condition. Women's subordination, then, is inscribed as the inevitable destiny of civilization.

I can spot several spurious steps in this reasoning, some of which have their roots in the presupposition of the structuralist model. First, to the degree Lacan has succeeded in eliminating biologism—and that is dubious for reasons I cannot take up here[14]—he has replaced it with psychologism, the untenable view that autonomous psychological imperatives given independently of culture and history can dictate the way they are interpreted and acted on within culture and history. Lacan falls prey to psychologism when he claims that the phallocentricity of the symbolic order is required by the demands of an enculturation process that is itself independent of culture.[15]

If one half of Lacan's circular argument is vitiated by psychologism, then the other half is vitiated by what I should like to call "symbolicism." By symbolicism, I mean, first, the homogenizing reification of diverse signifying practices into a monolithic and all-pervasive "symbolic order," and, second, the endowing of that order with an exclusive and unlimited causal power to fix people's subjectivities once and for all. Symbolicism, then, is an operation whereby the structuralist abstraction *langue* is troped into a quasi-divinity, a normative "symbolic order" whose power to shape identities dwarfs to the point of extinction that of mere historical institutions and practices.

Actually, as Deborah Cameron has noted, Lacan equivocates on the expression "the symbolic order."[16] Sometimes he uses this expression relatively narrowly to refer to Saussurean *langue*, the structure of language as a system of signs. In this narrow usage, Lacan would be committed to the implausible view that the sign system itself determines individuals' subjectivities independently of the social context and social practice of its uses. At other times, by contrast, Lacan uses the expression "the symbolic order" far more broadly to refer to an amalgam that includes not only linguistic structures, but also cultural traditions and kinship structures, the latter mistakenly equated with social structure in general.[17] Here he conflates the ahistorical structural abstraction *langue* with variable historical phenomena like family forms and childrearing practices; cultural representations of love and authority in art, literature, and philosophy; the gender division of labor; forms of political organization and of other institutional sources of power and status. The result is a notion of "the symbolic order" that essentializes and homogenizes contingent historical practices and traditions, erasing tensions, contradictions, and possibilities for change. It is a notion, moreover, that is so broad that the claim that *it* determines the structure of subjectivity is an empty tautology.[18]

The combination of psychologism and symbolism in Lacan results in a theory that is of little use for feminist politics. To be sure, this theory offers an account of the discursive construction of social identity. However, it is not an account that can make sense of the complexity and multiplicity of social identities, the ways they are woven from a plurality of discursive strands. Granted, Lacan stresses that the apparent unity and simplicity of ego identity are imaginary, that the subject is irreparably split by both language and drives. But this insistence on fracture does not lead to an appreciation of the diversity of the sociocultural discursive practices from which identities are woven. It leads, rather, to a unitary view of the human condition as inherently tragic.

In fact, Lacan differentiates identities only in binary terms, along the single axis of having or lacking the phallus. Now, as Luce Irigaray has shown, this phallic conception of sexual difference is not an adequate basis for understanding femininity[19]—nor, I would add, masculinity. Still less, then, is it able to shed light on other dimensions of social identities, including ethnicity, color, and social class. Nor could the theory be emended to incorporate these manifestly historical phenomena, given its postulation of an ahistorical, tension-free "symbolic order" equated with kinship.[20]

Moreover, Lacan's account of identity construction cannot account for identity shifts over time. It is committed to the psychoanalytic proposition that gender identity (the only kind of identity it considers) is basically fixed once and for all with the resolution of the Oedipus complex. Lacan equates this resolution with the child's entry into a fixed, monolithic, and all-powerful symbolic order. Thus, if anything, he actually increases the degree of identity fixity found in classical Freudian theory. It is true, as Jacqueline Rose points out, that the theory stresses that gender identity is always precarious, that its apparent unity and stability are always threatened by repressed libidinal drives.[21] But this emphasis on precariousness is not an opening onto genuine historical thinking about shifts in people's social identities. On the contrary, it is an insistence on a permanent, ahistorical condition, since on Lacan's view the only alternative to fixed gender identity is psychosis.

If the Lacanian model cannot provide an account of social identity that is useful for feminist politics, then it is unlikely to help us understand group formation. For Lacan, affiliation falls under the rubric of the imaginary. To affiliate with others, then, to align oneself with others in a social movement, would be to fall prey to the illusions of the imaginary ego. It would be to deny loss and lack, to seek an impossible unification and fulfillment. Thus, from a Lacanian perspective, collective movements would by definition be vehicles of delusion; they could not even in principle be emancipatory.[22]

Moreover, insofar as group formation depends on linguistic innovation, it is untheorizable from a Lacanian perspective. Since Lacan posits a fixed, monolithic symbolic system and a speaker who is wholly subjected to it, it is inconceivable how there could ever be any linguistic innovation. Speaking subjects could only ever reproduce the existing symbolic order; they could not possibly alter it.

It follows that one cannot even pose the question of cultural hegemony. There can be no question about how the cultural authority of dominant groups in society is established and contested, no question of unequal negotiations between different social groups occupying different discursive positions. On the contrary, on the Lacanian view there is simply "the symbolic order," a single universe of discourse that is so systematic, so all-pervasive, so monolithic that one cannot even conceive of such things as alternative perspectives, multiple discursive sites, struggles over social meanings, contests between hegemonic and counterhegemonic definitions of social situations, conflicts of interpretation of social needs. One cannot even conceive, really, of a plurality of different speakers.

With the way blocked to a political understanding of identities, groups, and cultural hegemony, the way is also blocked to an understanding of political practice. For one thing, there is no conceivable agent of such practice. None of the three moments that comprise the Lacanian view of the person can qualify as a political agent. The speaking subject is simply a grammatical "I" wholly subjected to the symbolic order; it can only and forever reproduce that order. The Lacanian ego is an imaginary projection, deluded about its own stability and self-possession, hooked on an impossible desire for unity and self-completion; it therefore can only and forever tilt at windmills. Finally, there is the ambiguous Lacanian unconscious, sometimes an ensemble of repressed libidinal drives, sometimes the face of language as Other, but never anything that could count as a social agent.

This discussion shows, I think, that there are many things wrong with Lacan. I have focused here on conceptual as opposed to empirical issues, and I have not directly addressed the question, is Lacan's theory true? With respect to *that* question, I will note only that Lacan himself was remarkably un-concerned with empirical confirmation and that recent research on the de-velopment of subjectivity in infants and young children does not support his views. It now appears that even at the earliest stages children are not passive, blank slates on which symbolic structures are inscribed but, rather, active participants in the interactions that construct their experience.[23]

Be that as it may, in focusing here on Lacan's conceptual shortcomings, I have stressed those deficiencies that have their roots in the presupposition of the structuralist conception of language. Lacan seemed to want to get beyond structuralism by introducing the concept of the speaking subject. This in turn seemed to hold out the promise of a way of theorizing discursive practice. However, as I hope I have shown, these promises have remained unfulfilled. The speaking subject introduced by Lacan is not the agent of discursive prac-tice. It is simply an effect of the symbolic order conjoined to some repressed libidinal drives. Thus, the introduction of the speaking subject has not suc-ceeded in dereifying linguistic structure. On the contrary, a reified concep-tion of language as system has colonized the speaking subject.

III. JULIA KRISTEVA BETWEEN STRUCTURALISM AND PRAGMATICS

So far, I have been arguing that the structural model of language is not es-pecially useful for feminist politics. Now I want to suggest that the pragmatic model is more promising. Indeed, there are good prima facie reasons for feminists to prefer a pragmatic approach to the study of language. Unlike the structuralist approach, the pragmatic view studies language as social practice in social context. This model takes discourses, not structures, as its object. Discourses are historically specific, socially situated, signifying practices. They are the communicative frames in which speakers interact by exchang-ing speech acts. Yet discourses are themselves set within social institutions and action contexts. Thus, the concept of a discourse links the study of lan-guage to the study of society.

The pragmatic model offers several potential advantages for feminist poli-tics. First, it treats discourses as contingent, positing that they arise, alter, and disappear over time. Thus, the model lends itself to historical contex-tualization, and it allows us to thematize change. Second, the pragmatic ap-proach understands signification as action rather than as representation. It is concerned with how people "do things with words." Thus, the model allows us to see speaking subjects not simply as effects of structures and systems, but rather as socially situated agents. Third, the pragmatic model treats dis-courses in the plural. It starts from the assumption that there are a plurality of different discourses in society, therefore a plurality of communicative sites from which to speak. Because it posits that individuals assume different dis-cursive positions as they move from one discursive frame to another, this

model lends itself to a theorization of social identities as nonmonolithic.
Next, the pragmatic approach rejects the assumption that the totality of social meanings in circulation constitutes a single, coherent, self-reproducing
"symbolic system." Instead, it allows for conflicts among social schemas of interpretation and among the agents who deploy them. Finally, because it links
the study of discourses to the study of society, the pragmatic approach allows
us to focus on power and inequality. In short, the pragmatic approach has
many of the features we need in order to understand the complexity of social
identities, the formation of social groups, the securing and contesting of cultural hegemony, and the possibility and actuality of political practice.

Let me illustrate the uses of the pragmatic model for feminist politics by
considering the ambiguous case of Julia Kristeva. Kristeva's case is instructive
in that she began her career as a critic of structuralism and a proponent of a
pragmatic alternative. However, having fallen under Lacan's sway along the
way, she has not managed to maintain a consistently pragmatic orientation.
Instead, she has ended up producing a strange, hybrid theory, one that oscil-
lates between structuralism and pragmatics. In what follows, I shall argue that
the politically fruitful aspects of Kristeva's thought are linked to its pragmatic
dimensions, while the political impasses she arrives at derive from structuralist lapses.

Kristeva's intention to break with structuralism is most clearly and suc-
cinctly announced in a brilliant 1973 paper called "The System and the
Speaking Subject."[24] Here she argues that, because it conceives language as a
symbolic system, structuralist semiotics is necessarily incapable of understanding oppositional practice and change. To remedy these lacunae, she
proposes a new approach oriented to "signifying practices." These she defines
as norm-governed, but not necessarily all-powerfully constraining, and as situated in "historically determined relations of production." As a complement
to this concept of signifying practices, Kristeva also proposes a new concept
of the "speaking subject." This subject is socially and historically situated, to
be sure, but it is not wholly subjected to the reigning social and discursive
conventions. It is a subject, rather, who is capable of innovative practice.

In a few bold strokes, then, Kristeva rejects the exclusion of context, practice, agency, and innovation; and she proposes a new model of discursive
pragmatics. Her general idea is that speakers act in socially situated, norm-
governed signifying practices. In so doing, they sometimes transgress the established norms in force. Transgressive practice gives rise to discursive inno-
vations and these in turn may lead to actual change. Innovative practice may
subsequently be normalized in the form of new or modified discursive norms,
thereby "renovating" signifying practices.[25]

The uses of this sort of approach for feminist politics should by now be apparent. Yet there are also some warning signs of possible problems. First,
there is Kristeva's antinomian bent, her tendency, at least in this early quasi-

Maoist phase of her career, to valorize transgression and innovation per se irrespective of content.[26] The flip side of this attitude is a penchant for inflecting norm-conforming practice as negative *tout court*, irrespective of the content of the norms. Obviously, this attitude is not particularly helpful for feminist politics, since such politics requires ethical distinctions between oppressive and emancipatory social norms.

A second potential problem here is Kristeva's aestheticizing bent, her association of valorized transgression with "poetic practice." Kristeva tends to treat avant-garde aesthetic production as the privileged site of innovation. By contrast, communicative practice in everyday life appears as conformism *simpliciter*. This tendency to enclave or regionalize innovative practice is not useful for feminist politics. We need to recognize and assess the emancipatory potential of oppositional practice *wherever* it appears—in bedrooms, on shopfloors, in the caucuses of the American Philosophical Association.

The third and most serious problem that I want to discuss is Kristeva's additive approach to theorizing. By this I mean her penchant for remedying theoretical problems by simply *adding* to deficient theories instead of by scrapping or overhauling them. This, I submit, is how she ends up handling certain features of structuralism; rather than eliminating certain structuralist notions altogether, she simply adds other, antistructuralist notions along side of them.

Kristeva's additive, dualistic style of theorizing is apparent in the way she analyzes and classifies signifying practices. She takes such practices to consist in varying proportions of two basic ingredients. One of these is "the symbolic," a linguistic register keyed to the transmission of propositional content via the observance of grammatical and syntactical rules. The other is "the semiotic," a register keyed to the expression of libidinal drives via intonation and rhythm and not bound by linguistic rules. The symbolic, then, is the axis of discursive practice that helps reproduce the social order by imposing linguistic conventions on anarchic desires. The semiotic, in contrast, expresses a material, bodily source of revolutionary negativity, the power to break through convention and initiate change. According to Kristeva, all signifying practices contain some measure of each of these two registers of language, but with the signal exception of poetic practice, the symbolic register is always the dominant one.

In her later work, Kristeva provides a psychoanalytically grounded gender subtext to her distinction between the symbolic and the semiotic. Following Lacan, she associates the symbolic with the paternal, and she describes it as a monolithically phallocentric, rule-bound order to which subjects submit as the price of sociality when they resolve the Oedipal complex by accepting the Father's Law. But then Kristeva breaks with Lacan in insisting on the underlying persistence of a feminine, maternal element in all signifying practice. She associates the semiotic with the pre-Oedipal and the maternal, and she valorizes it as a point of resistance to paternally coded cultural authority, a sort of oppositional feminine beachhead within discursive practice.

Now, this way of analyzing and classifying signifying practices may seem at first sight to have some potential utility for feminist politics. It seems to contest the Lacanian presumption that language is monolithically phallocentric and to identify a locus of feminist opposition to the dominance of masculine power. However, on closer inspection, this appearance of political usefulness turns out to be largely illusory. In fact, Kristeva's analysis of signifying practices betrays her best pragmatic intentions. The decomposition of such practices into symbolic and semiotic constituents does not lead beyond structuralism. The "symbolic," after all, is a repetition of Lacan's reified, phallocentric symbolic order. And while the "semiotic" is a force that momentarily disrupts that symbolic order, it does not constitute an alternative to it. On the contrary, as Judith Butler has shown, the contest between the two modes of signification is stacked in favor of the symbolic: the semiotic is by definition transitory and subordinate, always doomed in advance to reabsorption by the symbolic order.[27] And, moreover, more fundamentally problematic, I think, is the fact that the semiotic is defined parasitically over against the symbolic as the latter's mirror image and abstract negation. Simply adding the two together, then, cannot and does not lead to pragmatics. Rather, it yields an amalgam of structure and antistructure. Moreover, this amalgam is, in Hegel's phrase, a "bad infinity," since it leaves us oscillating ceaselessly between a structuralist moment and an antistructuralist moment without ever getting to anything else.

Thus, by resorting to an additive mode of theorizing, Kristeva surrenders her promising pragmatic notion of signifying practice to a quasi-Lacanian neostructuralism. In the process, she ends up reproducing some of Lacan's most unfortunate errors. She, too, often lapses into symbolicism, treating the symbolic order as an all-powerful causal mechanism and conflating linguistic structure, kinship structure, and social structure in general.[28] On the other hand, Kristeva sometimes does better than Lacan in appreciating the historical specificity and complexity of particular cultural traditions; much of her later work analyzes cultural representations of gender in such traditions. Even here, however, she often lapses into psychologism; for example, she mars her potentially very interesting studies of cultural representations of femininity and maternity in Christian theology and in Italian Renaissance painting by falling back on reductive schemes of interpretation that treat the historical material as reflexes of autonomous, ahistorical, psychological imperatives like "castration anxiety" and "feminine paranoia."[29]

All told, then, Kristeva's theory of discourse surrenders many of the advantages of pragmatics for feminist politics. In the end, she loses the pragmatic stress on the contingency and historicity of discursive practices, their openness to possible change. Instead, she lapses into a quasi-structuralist emphasis on the recuperating power of a reified symbolic order and thereby surrenders the possibility of explaining change. Likewise, her theory loses the pragmatic stress on the plurality of discursive practices. Instead, it lapses into a quasi-structuralist homogenizing and binarizing orientation, one that distinguishes practices along the sole axis of proportion of semiotic to symbolic, feminine to masculine, and thereby surrenders the potential to understand complex identities. Next, Kristeva loses the pragmatic stress on social context. Instead, she lapses into a quasi-structuralist conflation of "symbolic order" with social context and thereby surrenders the capacity to link discursive dominance to societal inequality. Finally, her theory loses the pragmatic stress on interaction and social conflict. Instead, as Andrea Nye has shown, it focuses almost exclusively on *intra*subjective tensions and thereby surrenders its ability to understand *inter*subjective phenomena, including affiliation, on the one hand, and struggle, on the other.

This last point can be brought home by considering Kristeva's account of the speaking subject. Far from being useful for feminist politics, her view replicates many of the disabling features of Lacan's. Her subject, like his, is split into two halves, neither of which is a potential political agent. The subject of the symbolic is an oversocialized conformist, thoroughly subjected to symbolic conventions and norms. To be sure, its conformism is put "on trial" by the rebellious, desiring ensemble of body-based drives associated with the semiotic. But, as before, the mere addition of an antistructuralist force does not lead beyond structuralism. The semiotic "subject" cannot itself be an agent of feminist political practice for several reasons. First, it is located beneath, rather than within, culture and society; so it is unclear how its practice could be *political* practice.[31] Second, it is defined exclusively in terms of the transgression of social norms; thus, it cannot engage in the reconstructive moment of feminist politics, a moment essential to social transformation. Finally, it is defined in terms of the shattering of social identity, and so it cannot figure in the reconstruction of the new, politically constituted, *collective* identities and solidarities that are essential to feminist politics.

By definition, then, neither half of Kristeva's split subject can be a feminist political agent. Nor, I submit, can the two halves be joined together. They tend rather simply to cancel one another out, one forever shattering the identitarian pretensions of the other, the second forever recuperating the first and reconstituting itself as before. The upshot is a paralyzing oscillation between identity and nonidentity without any determinate practical issue. Here, then, is another instance of a "bad infinity," an amalgam of structuralism and its abstract negation.

If there are no individual agents of emancipatory practice in Kristeva's universe, then there are no such collective agents either. This can be seen by examining one last instance of her additive pattern of thinking, namely, her treatment of the feminist movement itself. This topic is most directly addressed in an essay called "Women's Time' for which Kristeva is best known in feminist circles.[32] Here, she identifies three "generations" of feminist

movements: first, an egalitarian, reform oriented, humanist feminism, aiming to secure women's full participation in the public sphere, a feminism best
personified perhaps by Simone de Beauvoir; second, a culturally oriented
gynocentric feminism, aiming to foster the expression of a non-male-defined
feminine sexual and symbolic specificity, a feminism represented by the pro-
ponents of *écriture féminine* and *parler femme*; and finally, Kristeva's own, self-
proclaimed brand of feminism—in my view, actually postfeminism—a radically nominalist, anti-essentialist approach that stresses that "women" do not
exist and that collective identities are dangerous fictions.[33]

Now, I want to argue that, despite the explicitly tripartite character of this
categorization, there is a deeper logic in Kristeva's thinking about feminism
that conforms to her additive, dualistic pattern. For one thing, the first, egalitarian humanist moment of feminism drops out of the picture, since Kristeva
falsely—and astoundingly—assumes its programme has already been
achieved. Thus, there are really only two "generations" of feminism she is
concerned with. Next, despite her explicit criticisms of gynocentrism, there
is a strand of her thought that implicitly partakes of it—I mean Kristeva's
quasi-biologistic, essentializing identification of women's femininity with maternity. Maternity, for her, is the way that women, as opposed to men, touch
base with the pre-Oedipal, semiotic residue. (Men do it by writing avant-
garde poetry; women do it by having babies.) Here, Kristeva dehistoricizes
and psychologizes motherhood, conflating conception, pregnancy, birthing,
nursing, and childrearing, abstracting all of them from sociopolitical context,
and erecting her own essentialist stereotype of femininity. But then she reverses herself and recoils from her construct, insisting that "women" do not
exist, that feminine identity is fictitious, and that feminist movements therefore tend toward the religious and the proto-totalitarian. The overall pattern
of Kristeva's thinking about feminism, then, is additive and dualistic: she
ends up alternating essentialist gynocentric moments with anti-essentialist
nominalistic moments, moments that consolidate an ahistorical, undifferentiated, maternal feminine gender identity with moments that repudiate
women's identities altogether.

With respect to feminism, then, Kristeva leaves us oscillating between a
regressive version of gynocentric-maternalist essentialism, on the one hand,
and a postfeminist antiessentialism, on the other. Neither of these is useful
for feminist politics. In Denise Riley's terms, the first *overfeminizes* women by
defining us maternally. The second, by contrast, *underfeminizes* us by insisting
that "women" do not exist and by dismissing the feminist movement as a
proto-totalitarian fiction.[34] Simply putting the two together, moreover, does
not overcome the limits of either. On the contrary, it constitutes another
"bad infinity" and thus another proof of the uselessness for feminist politics of
an approach that merely conjoins an abstract negation of structuralism to a
structuralist model left otherwise intact.

IV. Conclusion

I hope the foregoing has provided a reasonably vivid and persuasive illustration of my most general point, namely, the superior utility for feminist politics of pragmatic over structuralist approaches to the study of language. Instead of reiterating the advantages of pragmatic theories, I shall close with one specific example of their uses for feminist politics.

As I argued, pragmatic theories insist on the social context and social practice of communication, and they study a plurality of historically changing discursive sites and practices. As a result, these theories offer us the possibility of thinking of social identities as complex, changing, and discursively constructed. This in turn seems to me our best hope for avoiding some of Kristeva's difficulties. Complex, shifting, discursively constructed social identities provide an alternative to reified, essentialist conceptions of gender identity, on the one hand, and to simple negations and dispersals of identity, on the other. They thus permit us to navigate safely between the twin shoals of essentialism and nominalism, between reifying women's social identities under stereotypes of femininity, on the one hand, and dissolving them into sheer nullity and oblivion, on the other.[35] I am claiming, therefore, that with the help of a pragmatic theory of discourse we can accept the critique of essentialism without becoming postfeminists. This seems to me to be an invaluable help. For it will not be time to speak of postfeminism until we can legitimately speak of postpatriarchy.[36]

Notes

1. I am grateful for helpful comments and suggestions from Jonathan Arac, David Levin, Paul Mattick, Jr., John McCumber, Diana T. Meyers, and Eli Zaretsky.

2. I group these writers together not because all are Lacanians—clearly only Kristeva and Lacan himself are—but rather because, disclaimers notwithstanding, all continue the structuralist reduction of discourse to symbolic system. I shall develop this point later in this essay.

3. Thus, the fund of interpretive possibilities available to me, a late-twentieth-century American, overlaps very little with that available to the thirteenth-century Chinese woman I may want to imagine as my sister. And yet in both cases, hers and mine, the interpretive possibilities are established in the medium of social discourse. It is in the medium of discourse that each of us encounters an interpretation of what it is to be a person, as well as a menu of possible descriptions specifying the particular sort of person each is to be.

4. See Elizabeth V. Spelman (1988).

5. See Denise Riley (1988).

6. See Jane Jenson (1989).

7. See Nancy Fraser (1989) and Denise Riley (1988).

8. Antonio Gramsci (1972).

9. For the critique of "cultural feminism" as a retreat from political struggle, see Alice Echols (1983).

10. For a brilliant critique of this move, see Pierre Bourdieu (1977). Similar objections are found in Julia Kristeva's "The System and the Speaking Subject," in Kristeva (1986), to be discussed below, and in the Soviet Marxist critique of Russian formalism from which Kristeva's views derive.

11. I leave it to linguists to decide whether it is useful for other purposes.

12. These criticisms pertain to what may be called "global" structuralisms, that is, approaches that treat the whole of language as a single symbolic system. They are not intended to rule out the potential utility of approaches that analyze structural relations in limited, socially situated, culturally and historically specific sublanguages or discourses. On the contrary, it is possible that approaches of this latter sort can be usefully articulated with the pragmatic model discussed below.

13. For the tensions between the Hegelian and Saussurean dimensions of Lacan's thought, see Peter Dews (1987).

14. Lacan's claim to have overcome biologism rests on his insistence that the phallus is not the penis. However, many feminist critics have shown that he fails to prevent the collapse of the symbolic signifier into the organ. The clearest indication of this failure is his claim, in "The Meaning of the Phallus," that the phallus becomes the master signifier because of its "turgidity," which suggests "the transmission of vital flow" in copulation. See Jacques Lacan (1982).

15. A version of this argument is made by Dorothy Leland (1991).

16. See Deborah Cameron (1985).

17. For an account of the declining significance of kinship as a social structural component of modern capitalist societies, see Linda J. Nicholson (1986).

18. In fact, the main function of this broad usage seems to be ideological. For it is only by collapsing into a single category what is supposedly ahistorical and necessary and what is historical and contingent that Lacan can endow his claim about the inevitability of phallocentrism with a deceptive appearance of plausibility.

19. See "The Blind Spot in an Old Dream of Symmetry" in Luce Irigaray (1985). Here Irigaray shows how the use of a phallic standard to conceptualize sexual difference casts woman negatively as "lack."

20. For a brilliant critical discussion of this issue as it emerges in relation to the version of feminist psychoanalysis developed in the United States by Nancy Chodorow, see Elizabeth V. Spelman (1988).

21. See Jacqueline Rose (1982).

22. Even Lacanian feminists have been known on occasion to engage in this sort of movement-baiting. It seems to me that, in her introductory chapter to The Daughter's Seduction, Jane Gallop comes perilously close to dismissing the politics of a feminist movement informed by ethical commitments as "imaginary." See Jane Gallop (1982).

23. See, for example, Beatrice Beebe and Frank Lachman (1988). I am grateful to Paul Mattick, Jr., for alerting me to this work.

24. See note 10, above.

25. "Renovation" and "renewal" are standard English translations of Kristeva's term, "renouvellement." Yet they lack some of the force of the French. Perhaps this explains why readers have not always noticed the change-making aspect of her account of transgression, why they have instead tended to treat it as pure negation with no positive consequences. For an example of this interpretation, see Judith Butler (1991).

26. This tendency fades in her later writings, where it is replaced by an equally undiscriminating, even shrill, neoconservative emphasis on the "totalitarian" dangers lurking in every attempt at uncontrolled innovation.

27. See Judith Butler (1991).

28. For an example, see Julia Kristeva (1982).

29. See Kristeva, "Stabat Mater" in Julia Kristeva (1986) and "Motherhood according to Giovanni Bellini" in Julia Kristeva (1980).

30. For a brilliant critical discussion of Kristeva's philosophy of language, one to which the present account is much indebted, see Andrea Nye (1987).

31. Judith Butler (1991) makes this point.

32. Reprinted in Kristeva (1986).

33. I take the terms "humanist feminism" and "gynocentric feminism" from Iris Young (1985). I take the term "nominalist feminism" from Linda Alcoff (1988).

34. For the terms "underfeminization" and "overfeminization," see Denise Riley (1988). For a useful discussion of Kristeva's neoliberal equation of collective liberation movements with "totalitarianism," see Ann Rosalind Jones (1984).

35. This point builds on work that Linda Nicholson and I did jointly and that she is continuing. See Nancy Fraser and Linda Nicholson (1988).

36. I borrow this line from Toril Moi (1987).

BIBLIOGRAPHY

Alcoff, Linda. 1988. Cultural feminism versus poststructuralism: The identity crisis in feminist theory. *Signs: Journal of women in culture and society* 13(3): 405-36.

Beebe, Beatrice, and Frank Lachman. 1988. Mother-infant mutual influence and precursors of psychic structure. In *Frontiers in self psychology, Progress in self psychology* 3, ed. Arnold Goldberg. Hillsdale, NJ: The Analytic Press.

Bourdieu, Pierre. 1977. *Outline of a theory of practice.* Cambridge: Cambridge University Press.

Butler, Judith. 1991. The body politics of Julia Kristeva. In this volume, 162-176.

Cameron, Deborah. 1985. *Feminism and linguistic theory.* New York: St. Martin's Press.

Dews, Peter. 1987. *Logics of disintegration: Post-structuralist thought and the claims of critical theory.* London: Verso.

Echols, Alice. 1983. The new feminism of yin and yang. In *Powers of desire: The politics of sexuality,* ed. Ann Snitow, Christine Stansell, and Sharon Thompson. New York: Monthly Review Press.

Fraser, Nancy. 1989. Struggle over needs: Outline of a socialist-feminist critical theory of late-capitalist political culture. In Fraser, *Unruly practices: power, discourse, and gender in contemporary social theory.* Minneapolis: University of Minnesota Press.

Fraser, Nancy, and Linda Nicholson. 1988. Social criticism without philosophy: An encounter between feminism and postmodernism. *Theory, Culture & Society* 5(2-3): 373-94.

Gallop, Jane. 1982. *The daughter's seduction: Feminism and psychoanalysis.* Ithaca, NY: Cornell University Press.

Gramsci, Antonio. 1972. *Selections from the Prison Notebooks of Antonio Gramsci.* Ed. and trans. Quinton Hoare and Geoffrey Nowell Smith. New York: International Publishers.

Irigaray, Luce. 1985. *Speculum of the other woman.* Trans. Gillian C. Gill. Ithaca: Cornell University Press.

Jenson, Jane. 1989. Paradigms and political discourse: Labour and social policy in the U.S.A. and France before 1914. Working Paper Series, Center for European Studies, Harvard University.

Jones, Ann Rosalind. 1984. Julia Kristeva on femininity: The limits of a semiotic politics. *Feminist Review* 18: 56-73.

194 Nancy Fraser

Kristeva, Julia. 1980. *Desire in language: A semiotic approach to art and literature.* Ed. Leon S. Roudiez, trans. Alice Jardine, Thomas Gora, and Leon Roudiez. New York: Columbia University Press.

———. 1982. *Powers of horror: An essay on abjection.* Trans. Leon S. Roudiez. New York: Columbia University Press.

———. 1986. *The Kristeva reader.* Ed. Toril Moi. New York: Columbia University Press.

Lacan, Jacques. 1982. The meaning of the phallus. In *Feminine sexuality: Jacques Lacan and the école freudienne.* Ed. Juliet Mitchell and Jacqueline Rose. New York: W. W. Norton.

Leland, Dorothy. 1991. Lacanian psychoanalysis and French feminism: Toward an adequate political psychology. In this volume, 113-135.

Moi, Toril. 1987. Lecture at conference on Convergence in crisis: Narratives of the history of theory. Duke University (September 24-27).

Nicholson, Linda J. 1986. *Gender and history: The limits of social theory in the age of the family.* New York: Columbia University Press.

Nye, Andrea. 1987. Woman clothed with the sun. *Signs: Journal of women in culture and society* 12(4): 664-86.

Riley, Denise. 1988. *"Am I that name?" Feminism and the category of "women" in history.* Minneapolis: University of Minnesota Press.

Rose, Jacqueline. 1982. Introduction—II. In *Feminine sexuality: Jacques Lacan and the école freudienne.* Ed. Juliet Mitchell and Jacqueline Rose. New York: W. W. Norton.

Spelman, Elizabeth V. 1988. *Inessential woman.* Boston: Beacon Press.

Young, Iris. 1985. Humanism, gynocentrism and feminist politics. *Hypatia* 3, published as a special issue of *Women's Studies International Forum* 8(3): 173-83.

Contributors

SANDRA LEE BARTKY is a professor of philosophy and women's studies at the University of Illinois at Chicago. She is the author of *Femininity and Domination: Studies in the Phenomenology of Oppression* (Routledge, 1990).

JUDITH BUTLER is Associate Professor of Humanities at Johns Hopkins University. She is the author of *Gender Trouble: Feminism and the Subversion of Identity* (Routledge, 1990).

MARA DUKATS is pursuing doctoral work in comparative literature at Northwestern University. She is writing a dissertation entitled "L'oeuvre d'Edouard Glissant et l'identité culturelle antillaise." She is interested in issues dealing with the social and literary constructions of gender and identity.

NANCY FRASER teaches philosophy and women's studies at Northwestern University. She is the author of *Unruly Practies: Power, Discourse, and Gender in Contemporary Social Theory* (University of Minnesota Press and Polity Press, 1989). She is currently at work on a new book, *Keywords of the Welfare State*, which she will coauthor with Linda Gordon.

DIANA J. FUSS is assistant professor of English at Princeton University. She is the author of *Essentially Speaking: Feminism, Nature and Difference* (Routledge, 1989) and the editor of *Inside/Out: Lesbian Theories, Gay Theories* (Routledge, 1991).

NANCY J. HOLLAND is associate professor of philosophy at Hamline University in St. Paul, Minnesota. She received her Ph.D. from the University of California at Berkeley. She has published several articles on contemporary French philosophy and her forthcoming book, *Is Women's Philosophy Possible?* (Rowman and Littlefield), compares the usefulness of Anglo-American and continental philosophy for doing feminist theory.

LUCE IRIGARAY holds doctorates in literature, linguistics, and philosophy. She is trained as a psychoanalyst. She is a director of research at the Centre Nationale de la Recherche Scientifique in Paris. Her work centers on arts and language. She has written numerous works, of which two are translated into English: *Speculum of the Other Woman* and *This Sex Which Is Not One*. Another, "The Ethics of Sexual Difference," is under translation. Her articles have appeared in *Signs*, *Paragraph*, and a collection on Levinas edited by Richard A. Cohen.

SARAH KOFMAN teaches philosophy at Paris I (Sorbonne). She has written eighteen books, of which the following deal specifically with questions pertaining to feminism: *L'Enigme de la femme* (1980), translated as *The*

Enigma of Woman (Cornell University Press, 1985); *Le respect des femmes* (Galilée, 1982); *Aberrations: le devenir-femme d'Auguste Comte* (Flammarion, 1978); "Ça cloche" in *Lectures de Derrida* (Galilée, 1984); "Baubô, perversion théologique et fétichisme" in *Nietsche et la scène philosophique* (Galilée, 1986). Kofman's first book, *L'Enfance de l'Art*, was recently translated as *The Childhood of Art* (Columbia University Press, 1988). Her last two books are *Paroles suffoquées* (Galilée, 1987), a reflection on concentration camps, and *Conversions, le marchand de Venise sous le sine de Saturne* (Galilée, 1988).

ELEANOR H. KUYKENDALL, who holds a Ph.D. from Columbia University, is chair of the philosophy department and coordinator of the linguistics program, SUNY College at New Paltz. From 1979 to 1981 she was director of the Paris philosophy program, SUNY New Paltz, in affiliation with l'Université de Paris I (Sorbonne).

DOROTHY LELAND teaches philosophy at Purdue University, where she is director of Purdue's doctoral program in philosophy and English. In addition to her research in contemporary French philosophy, she also writes on classical phenomenology. Her book, *Phenomenology and the Problem of Intentionality* (Hackett), is forthcoming.

DIANA T. MEYERS is a professor of philosophy and women's studies at the University of Connecticut, Storrs. She is the author of *Inalienable Rights: A Defense* and *Self, Society, and Personal Choice* (both Columbia University Press), and she has coedited a number of collections, including *Women and Moral Theory* (Rowman and Littlefield) and *Kindred Matters: Rethinking the Philosophy of the Family* (forthcoming, Cornell University Press). She is currently working on a book about the political philosophy of psychoanalytic feminism.

ANDREA NYE teaches philosophy and feminist theory at the University of Wisconsin-Whitewater. Her most recent published papers explore the intersections of feminism and philosophy of language, with special emphasis on poststructuralism. She is the author of *Feminist Theory and the Philosophies of Man* (Croom Helm, 1988) and *Words of Power: A Feminist Reading of the History of Logic* (Routledge, 1990).

MARGARET A. SIMONS, a professor of philosophy at Southern Illinois University at Edwardsville, served as editor of *Hyptia* from 1984 to 1990. She is currently working on a book on Beauvoir and feminist philosophy.

Index